THOMAS

30p

LIVING BIOGRAPHIES OF
Religious Leaders

LIVING BIOGRAPHIES OF
Religious Leaders

By HENRY THOMAS AND
DANA LEE THOMAS

W. H. ALLEN
LONDON
1959

Publ Mar 70   5/-

920

922

Contents

INTRODUCTION . . . . *vii*

MOSES 3

ISAIAH *17*

ZOROASTER 29

BUDDHA *41*

CONFUCIUS 57

JOHN THE BAPTIST 71

JESUS *81*

SAINT PAUL *91*

MOHAMMED *105*

FRANCIS OF ASSISI *125*

JOHN HUSS *137*

[*v*]

CONTENTS

LUTHER 153

LOYOLA 169

CALVIN 185

GEORGE FOX 201

SWEDENBORG 217

WESLEY 237

BRIGHAM YOUNG 253

MARY BAKER EDDY 269

GANDHI 285

Introduction

SEVERAL YEARS AGO H. G. Wells spoke of the need for a universal Bible—a book that would emphasize the essential unity of all religions. This need is as great today as it ever was in the past. We are too prone to quarrel about the differences between Judaism, Christianity, Mohammedanism, Buddhism, Hinduism, Confucianism, and Shintoism. But we forget that in these, as well as in all the other great religions, the differences are minor and unimportant. The important major fact is that all the religions embody a single truth. This truth—a Trinity harmonized into a Unity—proclaims the Fatherhood of God, the Brotherhood of Man, and the divine miracle of Love.

We shall see this essential truth embodied in the stories of the great religious leaders. These leaders, arising in different countries and at different times, have observed the selfsame truth from their different points of vantage. And thus their message may assume a divergent color and costume in the various Bibles of the world. But, stripped of their outer vestment, all the Bibles reveal an identical soul within.

This is the greatest lesson that a study of religion can teach us. The unity of humankind. As the Hindus expressed the idea,

"All individual souls are parts of One Universal Soul, just as the separate head, trunk, hands, and feet are parts of one connected body." St. Paul repeated this idea in almost identical words. "We are all parts of one another," he declared. And then he went on: "When one man suffers, all suffer"—just as when one finger suffers, the whole body suffers. And the Talmud, using somewhat different language but conveying the selfsame thought, asserted: "As the soul fills the body, so God fills the world. One divine self is in all human selves. If, therefore, you hurt another, you hurt not only yourself but God."

And this identical formula in all the great religions provides us with a universal law—the Golden Rule. This Golden rule of reciprocal kindness, like the Golden Truth of unity between the human and the divine, is the ethical basis for the teaching of all the great religious leaders. "Whatever ye would that men should do to you, do ye even so to them." This moral foundation for human conduct is emphasized in the Scriptures of all the great religions. Sometimes the idea assumes a negative form—"Whatever ye would *not* that men should do to you, do ye *not* so to them." At other times the idea is expressed from a somewhat different angle: "Love thy neighbor as thyself." But the substance of the thought is always the same.

Fatherhood, Brotherhood, Love—this, as you will see when you read the following biographies, is the philosophy that fuses all the colors of the various religions into a single all-pervasive and all-embracing light.

H. T.
D. L. T.

MOSES

Important Events in Life of Moses

Born in Egypt.

In his early manhood, Moses killed an Egyptian slave driver.

Escaped into wilderness.

Married daughter of Midianite priest.

"Beheld God face to face" in burning bush at Mount Horeb.

Returned to Egypt, at the age of 80, to deliver the Hebrew slaves.

Led his people out of Egypt.

Gave his people the Ten Commandments.

Learned from the Lord that he could not enter the Promised Land.

Died at Pisgah, at the age of 120.

Moses

Circa 1500 B.C.

THERE are those who deny the existence of Moses, just as there are those who deny the existence of Homer, of Shakespeare, of Jesus. Unable to explain the *great* men of the world, the *little* men of the world try to explain them away. But Mark Twain with his logical humor has disposed of all these cynics who doubt the reality of Moses. "If the Ten Commandments were not written by Moses," observes Mark Twain, "then they were written by another fellow of the same name." And Heine, with equal humor and with even greater logic, remarks that if Moses was not created by God, then the writers of the *Old Testament* did well to remind God of His oversight by creating Moses themselves. For the early Hebrews needed an extraordinary type of prophet to weld them into a living nation under the leadership of God. And the one prophet who succeeded in doing this was Moses, either as a man of flesh and blood who existed in Egypt, or as a fictitious national hero who to this day exists in the hearts of his people. A facetious lecturer once remarked that Moses was the greatest historical character who *never* lived. Whereupon a member of the audience corrected him. "What you really *meant*

to say, sir, is that Moses was the greatest *fictional* character who *forever* lives."

There is no scientific proof as to the actual historicity of Moses. Yet the *living personality* of Moses has inspired a veritable library of creative thought. And it is this personality—one of the enduring influences in human progress—that we shall here try to re-create.

II

THE picture of Moses as we have it today is the resultant composite of the Biblical stories and the Rabbinical legends. According to these stories and legends he was a child of Jewish parentage adopted by Pharaoh's daughter and brought up as an Egyptian prince. He was educated—we are told—for the priesthood and very likely became familiar, at an early age, with the teachings of Akhenaton, the wise Egyptian king who had introduced monotheism and who had been regarded as a madman for his trouble.

As he grew older, Moses was commissioned to lead an army against the Ethiopians. His expedition was successful, but his heart was not in the war. He was more interested in education. He entered the theological seminary at Heliopolis (the City of the Sun), shaved his face, took an active part in the college athletics, and was well on his way to a respectable career as an Egyptian nobleman during his lifetime and a glorious pickling into an honored and dignified mummy after his death.

But Moses was a rebel and a Jew. He took to slumming among the lower classes. At times he was to be seen talking to the Jewish workingmen who fashioned the bricks for the buildings of the city. He found, to his surprise, that these aliens were an interesting if uncouth lot. Like their Egyptian masters, they too had a proud history with its great men and its glorious moments. They told him about their Father Abraham, who had left the Chaldean city of Ur in search of freedom and who had found it in a new land between the desert and the sea. The beautiful land of Canaan, "flowing with milk and honey" and blessed with the presence of God. For a time Abraham and his followers dwelt there and multiplied their flocks and their fields and became rich. But the Jews were ever a restless nation. It seemed to be their preordained destiny, they told Moses, to wander over the earth from one land to another. And now at last, here they were in the country of the Pharaohs, reduced to slavery but still proud of the great pioneers of their race.

These men and their history fascinated Moses. He came to see them more and more often. His own aristocratic associates were at first amused at his peculiar conduct, and then they began to disapprove of it. Pharaoh warned him to stay away from these "uncultured and alien Semitics."

But Moses paid no attention to these warnings.

Once, as he was watching some of his Jewish friends at their labor, he saw an Egyptian gang-boss unmercifully whipping a member of the gang. In a fit of passion at the sight of this cruelty, Moses struck the Egyptian and killed him.

The killing of an Egyptian overseer in defense of a Jewish slave was a serious matter. Moses was obliged to flee into the desert to save his own life.

III

THE EGYPTIAN PRINCE is now a shepherd in the wild steppes that border on the desert. A new chapter in his education has begun. He has given up the dusty parchment scrolls of the university, with their crude stories about the shadows of the dead. In their place he has learned to read the scroll of the heavens at night, with its flaming syllables of living stars. He has cast out of his mind the ridiculous animal and bird and reptile divinities of the Egyptians, and he has undertaken to discover a new and more dignified kind of God. He finds Him in the wilderness, riding in the sandstorm. He hears His voice in the thunder.

In the early morning, when the rays of the sun have touched the shrubbery of the desert into sudden flame, he beholds Him face to face in the burning bush.

Moses has met his new God in the desert. A terrible God of the wilderness. An Arabian God. A God who leaps over the mountains, gallops across the wastelands, and reclines in tents of colorful splendor. A God who watches over His people while they sleep, leads them into battle, smites their enemies without mercy, changes His mind like the wind, is quick to avenge an insult, and is not above telling a falsehood when it serves His purpose to do so. Yet He is a God who will brook no injustice, who is generous to the alien, gentle to the fatherless and merciful to the poor. A God, in short, who possesses all the faults and the virtues of the Arabian Bedouin. It is as if Moses had looked into a mirror and recognized God in his own image. Indeed, the portrait of Jehovah as painted by Moses is the picture of Moses himself, magnified to superhuman proportions. The great religious leader, like the great artist, incorporates his *own* character into the character of his sitter.

IV

For a number of years Moses lived in the desert. He liked its spacious solitude. It gave his thoughts a chance to expand. His mystical nature found nourishing food in the vast stillness of the sand and the sky. He married the daughter of a well-to-do Bedouin chief and settled down to a life of quiet contemplation.

But once more his restlessness stirred him into action. He couldn't forget the slaves he had left behind him in Egypt. He often talked about them to his Bedouin friends. He told them about the present degradation and the glorious history of those Jewish laborers in the Egyptian brick kilns. And as the Bedouins listened to Moses, they sympathized with their proud and unfortunate kinsmen. For they too, like the Jews, were descended from that selfsame rebel chieftain, Father Abraham, whose courage had blazed a trail across the wilderness to a new home for his tribe.

Little by little the thought came to Moses that perhaps the Jews could be induced to escape from Egypt and find freedom in the desert. And later on, perhaps, he might even lead them back into Canaan, the ancient land of their fathers. To restore the Jews to their homeland, to unite them into a free nation, and to give them a religion and a God—what a glorious dream it was that Moses dreamed as he sat watching his flocks on the hillsides at Sinai!

In the meantime, the old Pharaoh had died and a new king had ascended the Egyptian throne. News of this change had come to Moses through the caravans that passed by his tent on their way from Egypt to the Orient. The time was ripe for him to act.

And so we find him once more in Egypt, going everywhere among the slaves and urging them to revolt. He told them to lay down their tools and to stop hauling stones and baking bricks for their oppressors.

Moses, the Egyptian prince and Arabian shepherd, had now become a Jewish labor leader. He was the organizer of the first Bricklayers' Union in history.

V

WHEN Moses petitioned Pharaoh to set free his Jewish slaves, the Egyptian monarch paid no attention to him. "By what authority," demanded Pharaoh, "do you come to me with such an extraordinary request?"

"By the authority of my God."

"And who," inquired Pharaoh, "is your God? How long has he reigned? What cities has he conquered? What dynasties has he overthrown?"

And Moses—the legends of the Rabbis inform us—replied: "Before the world, God was. After the world, He shall be. When He goeth in mercy, compassion is His girdle and love is His crown. But when He goeth in justice, fire is His arrow and flame is His spear; the clouds are His buckler, the lightning His sword."

But Pharaoh hardened his heart against God and His people. "There is but one supreme power in heaven and on earth. And this supreme power is myself." And to prove his power before God, Pharaoh ordered that every man should redouble his daily output of bricks. "In the evening, if a brick lacked, a child was torn from a mother to replace it. And the men who were building houses and cities were compelled, in place of the missing bricks, to bury their children alive in the walls."

And then, to enlighten Pharaoh and to rescue His children, Jehovah visited upon Egypt the ten plagues . . .

Such is the story of the Bible and of the Talmudic legends. The more scientific of the commentators, however, give us a more realistic version of the story. According to these commentators, the slaves in Egypt, as Pharaoh saw them, were a sickly race of rebels. Huddled together in their unsanitary quarters in the province of Goshen, they were a source of danger to their Egyptian masters. Many an epidemic in Egypt could be traced to the slum-tenements of Goshen. And Moses took good care to point out the apparent responsibility of the Jewish slaves for the "ten plagues" that had infested the land of the Pharaohs. So that, when the slaves departed from Egypt under the leadership of Moses, Pharaoh was none too loath to see them go.

As soon as they were gone, however, Pharaoh changed his mind. He felt that they were a far greater asset than liability to the material progress of his nation. And so he gathered an army and pursued them, only to be defeated on the shores of the Red Sea. (In the picturesque language of the Bible, the Egyptians were *swallowed up* in the sea.)

And then Moses sang a song of rejoicing over the death of his Egyptian foe. But God—the Rabbis tell us—rebuked him. "How can you sing when my children die? Henceforth, because you have looked with exultation rather than with sorrow upon the sufferings of your enemies, your future shall be written in a sorrowful strain."

And this—the legends explain—is why the music of the children of Moses has always been so sad.

VI

WHEN Moses took the Jews out of Egypt, he found himself the leader of an uncultured, contentious and disunited tribe. But his genius welded it into a powerful unit. It took Moses quite a number of years to perform this miracle. Before he could make an organic nation out of the disorganized rabble of his followers, he must first breathe a living soul into them. He must give them a new code of morals and a new standard of law. Born leader that he was, he knew that he could best do this by overwhelming their simple minds with an impressive ceremony amidst awe-inspiring natural scenery. He selected Mount Sinai for the purpose. With its five granite peaks rising above the clouds, its roaring avalanches of white sand, and its crags that seemed to re-echo with the laughter and the shouted commandments of God, it was a fitting pulpit upon which heaven and earth might be brought together into closer communion.

Here, then, Moses delivered his half-savage, half-sublime code of ethics which has guided and misguided humanity down to the present day. In spite of its occasional cruelty and its frequent lapses into childish inconsistencies, it is one of the first attempts in history to put humane thoughts into the human heart. His injunction to exact an eye for an eye is no more than what we should expect of a man who was just emerging from the jungle of primitive savagery. But his commandment to be friendly to the poor and compassionate toward the stranger is almost more than what we are accustomed to expect of the so-called civilized men of today. It is still fashionable to deride the unfortunate and to despise the foreigner. One of the legends dealing with the life of Moses depicts God as shedding tears when He delivers His Gospel at Mount Sinai. "Why dost thou weep?" inquires Moses, astonished to see this divine sadness on so joyous an occasion. And God replies: "Thou, O Moses, canst only see that I am giving my Gospel to mankind. But I, my child, can see what mankind will do with this Gospel." God—continues the legend—presented to each of His children, together with the Gospel, two guiding angels: one to give wisdom to his head, and the other to bring peace to his heart. "But thus far, the foolish children of the earth have learned neither wisdom nor peace."

VII

THE BIBLE as we have it today—we are told—is not the original Bible that God presented to Moses on Mount Sinai. That original Bible (the first version of the Ten Commandments) Moses destroyed in his anger when he saw his people worshiping at the feet of the Golden Calf. Pure religion was beyond the comprehension of the selfish human mind. Moses was compelled to revise his teaching and to bring it down from the heights of Sinai to the level of human understanding. "The first Bible was written on high, upon the sapphire of heaven; the second was written below, upon the granite of the earth ... . The first Bible spoke the language of God; the second speaks only the language of man."

Yet the Biblical code of Moses, adapted as it was to the imperfections of the human heart in that early period of its history, represented a solid foundation for the later and more enlightened teaching of the prophets. This Mosaic foundation for the religion of the prophets was designed to temper justice with mercy. "I, your Lord Eternal, am not only a God of Vengeance, but a God of Compassion." Moses envisioned pity as an integral part of piety. "Thou shalt restore his pledge to the poor man at sunset, that he may sleep in his garment." He enjoined kindness toward the toilers and the servants. "If a man strike his servant, he must give him his freedom as a recompense for the injury." And he recommended the emancipation of every slave at the end of six years of servitude. "In the seventh year thou shalt let thy slave go free, and with gifts. For thou wast a slave in the land of Egypt, and the Lord thy God redeemed thee."

Above all, Moses tried to mitigate human selfishness with the balsam of charity. "When thou gatherest the harvest of thy land, thou shalt not wholly reap the corners of thy field, neither shalt thou gather the gleaning of thy harvest. Thou shalt leave them for the poor, and for the stranger, for the widow and the orphan. For the Lord thy God upholdeth the orphan and the widow, and loveth the stranger . . . Thou, too, wast a stranger in the Land of Egypt."

The entire teaching of Moses may be summarized in a single precept—a formula which served for its day as an earlier version of the Master's Golden Rule. *Thou shalt love thy neighbor as thyself.*

VIII

AGAIN AND AGAIN—we are told—the life of Moses was in danger. "For the race he tried to save was wroth against its saviour." Moses was no prophet to the people of his own generation. While his vision was fixed upon the Promised Land, their eyes kept turning back to the fleshpots of Egypt. They preferred the degraded security of their bondage to the dignified uncertainty of their struggle for freedom. They were not willing—Moses complained that they were not *worthy*—to be free. And so they began to plot against the man who would liberate them. At first they were content with mere vilification. They criticized his every thought and act. If he rose early, they said: "He gets up with the sun to obtain the best manna for himself." If he rose late, they taunted: "He is sick abed with eating of too much manna." If, in his humility, he stayed by himself, they complained that he was too puffed up to associate with his fellows. But if, in his desire for companionship, he went among the people, they jeered: "Look how he crawls in our midst in search of our applause."

And then they went on from vilification to accusation. They charged him with stirring up class against class, lowborn against highborn, poor against rich. And they threatened to overthrow him. "We desire a leader no longer!" they cried. "For you, our leader, have betrayed us. You have stolen from us the joys of Egypt, the sure bread. You have lied to us with your Land of Promise that we shall never see, a dream that exists only in your mind!"

And they threatened to kill him unless he took them back to Egypt.

But Moses faced his accusers. He answered their threats with patience, and "their stones with the bread of forgiveness." The Lord, he said, would pardon them. "For your cries are the cries of anger and of pain; and what a man utters in his anger and his pain, to that utterance the Lord gives no ear."

Yet in his moments of bitter solitude, Moses could find no forgiveness in his own heart. "They are not deserving of the Promised Land, neither this generation nor the generation of their children. For how can you bring the light to them that have no eyes to see?"

And God—the story continues—observed the secret thoughts of Moses and was displeased.

IX

At last the old generation had died in the wilderness and the new generation was ready to enter into the Promised Land. But this land was not for Moses. "The time has come," said the Eternal, "when you must depart from life."

But Moses pleaded with the Eternal. "Let me first lead my people into Canaan, and then I shall be ready to go."

And the Eternal answered, "No."

"If I cannot come into Canaan as the leader," begged Moses, "then let me come in as the least among the followers."

And again the Eternal answered, "No."

"If I cannot enter it alive, let me enter it dead. Let my bones rest in the Promised Land."

Once more the Eternal shook His head. "You cannot enter it for your sins."

When Moses heard this, he was amazed. "Have I then sinned against God?"

"No, but you have sinned against man. You have doubted his instinctive hunger for the light . . . Man is cowardly, bestial, envious, lustful, lying, faithless, murderous and perverse. Yet what are you yourself if not a man? And if *you* have understood my teaching, why do you doubt that your *fellowmen* shall some day understand it?"

"But they are so slow to learn!"

"They have all eternity for their learning. Men must be patient; and I, the God of Mercy, shall be patient along with them."

And when Moses heard these words—concludes the story of the Rabbis—he resigned himself to his death. For he knew then that the Land of Promise is not Canaan, but the entire World— the everlasting school of justice, of mercy, and of love.

"And the Eternal laid Moses down gently and gathered up the soul from the Prophet's lips. And Moses died in the kiss of God."

*　　*　　*

Such is the idealized and somewhat sentimental picture of Moses as depicted in the Bible and in the Talmudic legends.

Examined under the light of modern realism, Moses stands out more prosaically but none the less heroically as a man who performed one of the miracles of history. He took into the desert the hopeless remnant of a dying race. He brought out of the desert a united nation that refuses to die.

ISAIAH

Important Events in Life of Isaiah

Born in Jerusalem.

Married about 740 B.C.

Entered upon career of prophecy, 739 B.C.

Had two sons—Shear-Jashub (born in 738) and Maher-shalal-hash-baz (born in 734).

Advised King Ahaz and King Hezekiah during national crises, 735–701 B.C.

Died a martyr's death, exact date unknown.

Isaiah

Circa 750 B.C.

JUDEA was in a panic. Uzziah the Great, the wisest ruler of Palestine since the days of King Solomon, had just died. The little country, caught between the upper and the nether mill-stones of the Assyrian and the Egyptian military powers, was on the verge of destruction. The new ruler, King Ahaz, was assailed by two opposing factions in Jerusalem. The one urged him to side with Egypt; the other, with Assyria. The king, unable to make up his mind as to which of the two aggressive nations he should accept as his protector, was one day brooding along the banks of the Upper Pool when he was confronted by Isaiah, a young nobleman of Jerusalem.

Isaiah, holding his little son by the hand, had been waiting for the king. At the death of Uzziah he had received the divine call to serve his people. "I heard the voice of the Lord saying: 'Whom shall I send?' And I said: 'Here am I; send me.' "

And so here he was, waiting to give his counsel to King Ahaz. In reply to the king's nervous apprehensions, Isaiah advised him to "keep calm, and be confident." He warned him to place his reliance upon neither of the two aggressors. "Lean not upon

those spears for thy salvation. For they shall pierce thy hand."
The king thanked Isaiah for his advice—and decided to dis-
regard it. He would place his trust in the Assyrian power. But he
said nothing of his decision to Isaiah. Instead, he stroked the
head of the prophet's little son. "What is your name, my child?"
"Shear-Jashub, Your Majesty."
The king turned to Isaiah. "Did I get it right? *Shear-Jashub—
a remnant shall return.* A strange name to give to a child."
"This name," said Isaiah, "is the keynote of my prophetic
faith. God will punish Judea for its sins. He will lay low the
mighty and destroy their houses and lead them captive under a
foreign yoke. And Jerusalem, bereft of her children, shall sit
mourning upon the ground . . . But God will not utterly abandon His people. In the end of days a remnant shall return . . .
This is my faith, and my child's name is the symbol thereof."

II

THE prophets of Palestine were a strange phenomenon in ancient
history—bold and uncouth radicals who spoke out of turn, defied
the rich, scandalized the priests and espoused the cause of the
lowly. An unsocial lot, they came from every walk of society—
lumberjacks, peasants, workers, businessmen and, as in the case
of Isaiah, members of the aristocratic class. Rough and ragged
outlaws—these self-appointed interpreters of the Lord—men who
rarely washed, who often concealed themselves like wild animals
in the mountains, eating roots and honey and even grass and
flowers at times, and who went about proclaiming the imminent
damnation of their fellowmen. They not only expressed the
strangest ideas, but they had a most disconcerting way of expressing them. One of the prophets, for example, defiled his bread
before he ate it, as a sign that God would defile His nation.
Another, with disheveled hair and flaming eyes, rushed into the
Temple carrying an earthen jug in his hand. He commanded

the worshipers to stop their service and to follow him out of the Temple. Then, lifting the jug up like a standard in the air, he left the sacred court and made his way to the public dumping ground on the outskirts of the city. A big crowd had gathered by this time. When the prophet arrived at the pile of refuse, he smashed the jug and threw the fragments in among the rest of the garbage. "Even so," he cried, "will I break this people and this city!"

Such were the bizarre methods employed by the prophets in their effort to arouse the public attention. Isaiah himself on one occasion walked naked through the streets of Jerusalem in order to demonstrate that the city would be stripped naked for her sins. All in all, the prophets were an object of ridicule to most men—particularly to those who belonged to the "better classes."

But the more serious among their contemporaries saw another side to these prophets. They noticed that "the eager ambassadors of God" were consumed with a passion for justice. They possessed a courage that was superb. They were not afraid to stalk into the very palace of the king and to denounce him to his face for his tyranny. Moreover, they set themselves against the empty cere-monies of the Temple worship. "I hate, I despise your prayers and your feasts, and I will not smell the savor of your festivals . . . Banish from me the noise of your psalms . . . But let justice roll on as a flood of waters, and righteousness as an unfail-ing stream."

The saving grace of righteousness and the destructive blight of injustice—this was the burden of their prophetic speech. The prophets were the moral prognosticators of the ancient world. They believed that they had discovered a vital historical law which enabled them to foretell future events. "The wages of sin, whether in the individual or in the mass, is death." The prophets maintained that they could rightly foresee the future because they had rightly interpreted the past. "What has been, will be. For there is nothing new under the sun." The prophets recognized, and tried to make everybody else recognize, the inflexible law of cause and effect—in the moral as well as in the physical sphere of human existence. "Just as surely as the rivers flow downward to the sea, just so surely will injustice flow downward to destruction."

This was the spirit that moved Isaiah to guide his nation through the critical days of the Assyrian War.

III

THE ASSYRIANS, like the modern Germans, wanted to rule the world. They were the most spectacular, the most ambitious, and the most warlike nation in ancient history. Heavy-bearded, long-nosed and thick-lipped, they swept down from Nineveh in their newly-invented war-chariots and terrorized the entire human race. War with them was not, as with many other nations in those lean and hungry days, a grim necessity. It was a fine art—or rather, an *unrefined* art. The Assyrian kings were especially pleased to order their likenesses modeled in the "gentle posture" of tearing out the tongues and gouging out the eyes of their prisoners. With their perfect military machine they hoped to overwhelm the world and to rule over it "for a thousand years."

And now one of the most ferocious of their military aggressors, King Sennacherib, was on the march against the "nations of the west." One by one he invited these helpless nations to clasp his hand in friendship; and one by one, when they accepted his proffered help, he crushed them with his crimson fist. Finally he moved on toward Judea, and as usual tried to seduce his victim to give up without a fight. He assured the new king of Judea—Ahaz had died and Hezekiah had ascended the throne—that he meant no harm to the Jews. He merely wanted them to be his friendly allies, he said. And, in token of their friendliness, he "requested" of them to send him a little "tribute"—amounting to the greater proportion of Judea's wealth. In return for this friendly act, Sennacherib promised Hezekiah, he would refrain from marching against Judea.

Isaiah cautioned his king against this trafficking with the Assyrian aggressor. But Hezekiah disregarded the prophet's warning, and paid the tribute to Sennacherib.

The Assyrian leader accepted the money, thanked Hezekiah most effusively—and then invaded Judea.

This was the moment for Isaiah to step forth in all his greatness. In earlier days, when the danger of external aggression was remote, he had castigated his city and his king. "How is the faithful city become a harlot! She that was full of justice . . . is now a nest of murderers . . . Thy princes are rebellious, and companions of thieves. Everyone loveth bribes, and followeth after rewards. They judge not the fatherless, neither doth the cause of the widow come unto them." And for these injustices, Isaiah had warned them, the Lord would chastise them with the lash of a foreign foe. The aggressor from an alien land would be but an instrument in the hand of an avenging God. "I do send him (the king of Assyria) as the rod of mine anger . . . against my people . . . I do send him against an ungodly nation . . . to take the spoil, and to take the prey, and to tread them down like the mire in the streets." But now that the aggressor is actually at hand, the angry tone of Isaiah changes into one of gentleness and encouragement and hope. Sennacherib, he assures his people, shall not conquer them. His very aggressiveness shall prove to be his undoing. This insolent warrior believes that he is the master of the world. As a matter of fact, he is not even the master of his own will. What he vainly regards as *his* will is but the will of God that drives him blindly on to his doom. "By the strength of *my* hand"—exulteth the foolish king—"have I cut off the nations, and by *my* wisdom have I robbed them of their treasures." But the Lord only laughs at the folly of the arrogant king. "Should the axe boast itself against him that heweth therewith?" King Sennacherib is but an axe wielded at the pleasure of the

Lord. "He shall rust before he strikes against the city of God."

While Isaiah was speaking these words, Sennacherib kept marching ruthlessly against Judea. He captured forty-six cities, put all the male inhabitants to the sword, and carried off two hundred thousand women and children into slavery.

Finally he arrived at the gates of Jerusalem. Exulting in his anticipated triumph, he commanded King Hezekiah to surrender. "I have locked you up," he boasted, "like a bird in his cage in the midst of your royal city." It would be useless, he declared, for Hezekiah to rely upon the protection of the Lord. "I, King Sennacherib, am the Lord. At my command the mountains tremble. And at my nod the nations live and die . . . By the strength of my hand have I conquered the world, and by the wisdom of my mind . . . have I removed the boundaries of the people, and robbed their treasures out of their nests. As one gathers eggs that are forsaken, have I gathered all the earth. And there are none that moved the wing, or that opened the mouth or chirped." Let Hezekiah, therefore, be wise and submit to the more-than-human might of Sennacherib, the conqueror of the world.

In answer to these boasts, Isaiah urged his people to maintain a defiant silence. Better to die in freedom than to live in slavery. But God, he confidently declared, would not allow His people to be enslaved. The very aggressiveness of Sennacherib would bring about his doom. "His breath is a fire which shall devour him." In accordance with the inflexible moral law by which nations live and die, the savagery of the aggressor is certain like a boomerang to rebound upon himself. "Woe to thee that spoilest, and thou wast not spoiled; and dealest treacherously, and they dealt not treacherously with thee! When thou hast ceased to spoil, thou shalt be spoiled; and when thou art weary with dealing treacherously, they shall deal treacherously with thee." Today our despoiler sits on high like a God. Tomorrow he will be plucked down from his lofty throne, together with the rest of the rubbish, to be "swept away with the besom of destruction."

For Sennacherib is a beast, and like a beast he will be treated at the hands of the Lord. "I will put my hook in thy nose, and my bridle in thy lips, and I will turn thee back by the way by which thou camest." Sennacherib has come determined to destroy Judea. But, declared Isaiah with the confidence born of supreme fanaticism—or of superior wisdom—"the destroyer shall be destroyed."

IV

ISAIAH'S PROPHECY was fulfilled. Sennacherib never captured Jerusalem. This we know, not only on the authority of the Bible but on the evidence of an Assyrian record discovered in the ruins of Nineveh about a hundred years ago. The story as told in this Assyrian record was written in the first person by Sennacherib himself. Boisterously he recounts his triumphal march of conquest through the countries of western Asia. One by one he enumerates the cities he has captured, the spoils he has acquired, the kings he has subdued. "All these cities I besieged, I submitted to my yoke, I carried off their wealth . . . Their commanders I put to death; on stakes I impaled their corpses . . ." And then he goes on to describe his advance against Jerusalem—and there his story abruptly ends.

Just what happened to Sennacherib at the siege of Jerusalem has not been exactly ascertained to this day. In accordance with the Biblical account, "the angel of the Lord went forth, and smote in the camp of the Assyrians a hundred and fourscore and five thousand; and when men arose early in the morning, behold, they were all dead corpses." This story is beautifully paraphrased in one of Byron's *Hebrew Melodies:*

> *The Assyrian came down like the wolf on the fold,*
> *And his cohorts were gleaming in purple and gold;*
> *And the sheen of their spears was like stars on the sea,*
> *When the blue wave rolls nightly on deep Galilee.*

Like the leaves of the forest when Summer is green,
That host with their banners at sunset were seen:
Like the leaves of the forest when Autumn hath blown,
That host on the morrow lay wither'd and strown.

For the Angel of Death spread his wings on the blast,
And breathed in the face of the foe as he pass'd;
And the eyes of the sleepers wax'd deadly and chill,
And their hearts but once heaved, and for ever grew still!

·   ·   ·   ·   ·

And the widows of Ashur are loud in their wail,
And the idols are broke in the temple of Baal;
And the might of the Gentile, unsmote by the sword,
Hath melted like snow in the glance of the Lord.

The Greek historian, Herodotus, gives us a different version of the story. Basing his evidence upon Egyptian records, he ascribes Sennacherib's defeat to the fact that "a horde of field mice gnawed away the strings of the bows of his soldiers."

Perhaps the truth lies somewhere between the Biblical account and the story of Herodotus. The defeat of Sennacherib's army was due possibly to a pestilence resulting from the unsanitary conditions of his greedy march for conquest—a pestilence brought on by the inexorable law of nature and depicted in the poetical language of Isaiah as the smiting of the angel of the Lord. And this pestilence may possibly have been, as the story of Herodotus hinted, the bubonic plague—an epidemic communicated to the Assyrian army by the rats that infested the Arabian bogs.

Whatever may have been the cause of the Assyrian defeat, this at least we know: King Sennacherib returned in disgrace to Nineveh. "And it came to pass"—Isaiah informs us—"that Adrammelech and Sarezer his sons smote him with the sword."

Thus ended the career of one of the most ruthless conquerors of the ancient world. "Those whom the Lord would destroy, He first makes mad with a lust for war."

V

AND now that God has "sifted the nations in the sieve of destruction"—Isaiah prophesies—He will take the remnant and bring it back under His fatherly protection. For in this remnant, not alone of the Jews but of *all* the nations of the world, "lieth the hope of the future." Purged of their iniquity in the furnace of suffering—declares this first internationalist in the history of mankind—they will reorganize their society upon the firm rock of righteousness under the leadership of God. Mankind shall "cease to do evil, learn to do well, seek justice and relieve the oppressed." And in that day—declares the Lord—"I will cause the arrogancy of the proud to cease, and I will lay low the haughtiness of the tyrants."

And then, as he becomes more and more impassioned with the fervor of his vision, Isaiah goes on to picture the golden age that will be ushered into the world at the coming of the Messiah, God's messenger of good will among men. "And the wolf shall dwell with the lamb, and the leopard shall lie down with the kid, and the calf and the lion's whelp and the fatling together. And a little child shall lead them . . . For the earth shall be full of the knowledge of the Lord, as the waters cover the sea." In that day the aggressive nations, too, shall lose their aggressiveness through the destruction of their dictators and through the dispensation of equal justice to all the peoples of the earth. "All the nations shall be unto Me for a blessing; for all of them are My children, the work of My hands." And so "I prophesy unto you that are of a fearful heart"—declares Isaiah—"be strong, fear not; for mine eyes have seen the glory of the coming of the Lord."

And then Isaiah rises to the topmost peak of his prophecy—of all prophecy—in the first recorded utterance of humanity's eternal hope: "And it shall come to pass in the end of days, that the mountain of the Lord's house shall be established as the top of the mountains . . . and all the nations shall flow into it and

say, 'Come ye, and let us go up to the mountain of the Lord . . .
and He will teach us of His ways, and we will walk in His paths.'
. . . And He shall judge between the nations, and shall decide
for many peoples; and they shall beat their swords into plow-
shares, and their spears into pruning-hooks; nation shall not lift
up sword against nation, neither shall they learn any more war."

VI

THIS is the precious vision that Isaiah, son of Amoz, left to his
generation. And how did his generation repay him? As most of
the generations repay most of their prophets. "They cut him
asunder," the chroniclers tell us, "with a saw."

The world, observes the Apostle in his *Letters to the Hebrews*,
is not worthy of its prophets. "But God allows them to undergo
all their sufferings because He thinks of the generations that are
to follow, and He wants them to have a better place to live in."

ZOROASTER

Important Events in Life of Zoroaster

Born of noble ancestry.
At 30, beheld divine vision.
Went to court of King Vish-
    taspa.
Imprisoned for his unorthodox
    beliefs.

Freed, converted King Vish-
    taspa.
Established new creed.
Slain by invaders of his coun-
    try, while officiating in
    temple.

Zoroaster

Circa 650 B.C.

THIS, according to the Persian gospel, is the story of the birth and the life and the death of Zoroaster, the Protector of mankind:

Ever since the creation of the first man, there has been an everlasting struggle between Ahura Mazda, the Lord of Light, and Ahriman, the Prince of Darkness. "I, Ahura Mazda, have not rested at my ease because of my desire to provide protection for those whom I have created; and in like manner he, Ahriman, has not rested because of his desire to bring destruction upon those whom I have created."

God, in his eternal effort to *protect* mankind, has taught them the arts of peace—thrift, friendship, love, the domestication of the cattle and the cultivation of the land. But the Devil, in his eternal effort to *destroy* mankind, has taught them the arts of war—waste, enmity, hatred, the plunder of one another's cattle and the devastation of one another's land.

"And in the course of this struggle between Ahura Mazda and Ahriman there came a time when the world was in a sad plight." The bandits of the hills were assailing the inhabitants of the plains. "All the evil spirits of Ahriman had rushed together in

violence, determined to put an end to the peaceful life of man."
The human race was bowed with grief. Even the animals were
sad at the prospect of being violently torn away from their masters. And so they called upon Gosurvan, the soul of the sacred
bull, to intercede in their behalf before the throne of God. "And
Gosurvan cried unto God, as much as a thousand men when they
sustain a cry, thus—'With whom hast thou left the guardianship
of thy creatures, when ruin hath broken upon the earth, and
vegetation is withered, and water is despoiled and men are slain?'
"And God spoke to Gosurvan, saying, 'I will produce him who
will bring salvation to the creatures of the earth.' "
And this is why Zoroaster was born.

II

AT THE BIRTH OF ZOROASTER—his Persian name was Zarathustra
—all nature rejoiced. The very trees and the rivers and the mountains sang a song of triumph at the victory of God over the Devil.
A divine light illuminated the world, and a loud burst of laughter rang upon the lips of the child as he came into the light.

But the evil spirits set immediately to work in order to bring
about the saviour's death. One of them tried to twist off the
infant's head as he lay in his cradle. But the murderer's hand
was withered as he stretched it forth toward the divine child.
Another of the evil spirits threw the child into the path of a herd
of stampeded cattle. But one of the oxen, guided by the hand
of Ahura Mazda, stood guard over Zoroaster and saved him from
being trampled to death. Still another of Ahriman's evil spirits
imprisoned the child in a den of wolves. But the wolves refused
to harm even a hair of Zoroaster's head. On the contrary, they
went out and fetched a sheep to suckle the divine child.

And thus Zoroaster escaped the machinations of the Devil and
at the age of seven was put under the care of a wise and learned
man who taught him the ways of God. The evil spirits, however,

were not as yet through with him. They tried to destroy his body with poisoned herbs and his mind with poisoned lies. But he thwarted them with the help of his tutor—according to some of the ancient writers this tutor of Zoroaster was the Hebrew prophet, Jeremiah—and at the age of fifteen he completed his education and was ready to assume the "sacred girdle of religion."

During the next fifteen years he refined his character in the "sacred waters of compassion." He helped the aged; he healed the sick; he fed the hungry; he lightened the loads of the beasts of burden; he wandered among his fellows to comfort them in their hours of distress. He perfected himself as a master in the practical art of interdependent living.

And then, at thirty, he was ready to enter upon his profession as the teacher of a new religion. For he had seen a vision upon the Mountain of Sabalan. Here, in a natural cave which he had fitted out with a representation of the heavenly bodies, a lonely spot in which he had spent many an hour of meditation, he had beheld Ahura Mazda face to face.

Or, to be more exact, he had beheld the *seven faces* of Ahura Mazda. For Zoroaster, though he conceives of God as a single divine being, attributes to Him a sevenfold personality. Ahura Mazda represents Eternal Light, Omniscient Wisdom, Righteousness, Power, Piety, Benevolence, and Eternal Life.

And then, having revealed himself to Zoroaster, the "sevenfold glorious" Ahura Mazda ushered the prophet into heaven and taught him the distinction between "the Truth and the Lie." And the prophet, having taken the lesson to his heart, returned to teach it to his fellowmen.

At this juncture the spirits of evil—the guardians of the Lie—began once more to assail Zoroaster. "From the land of the North —the region of frost and discomfort and death—rushed Ahriman at the head of his legion of fiends. 'Let us kill him, the all-too-righteous Zarathustra. For if he lives, evil dies. And without evil we, too, die.'

[31]

"But Zarathustra, girding himself with the breastplate of right-eousness and holding before him the saber of truth, warded off the attack of the demons.

"And the demons, seeing that their evil assault had failed, resorted to an arsenal of new weapons—the poisoned arrows of flattery and the disarming seductions of (illicit) love." Disguising himself in the form of Spendarmat, "the beautiful goddess of secrets and sins," Ahriman tempted the prophet with the pleas-ures of the flesh. But again Zoroaster drove off the fiend and returned to the "business of the Lord."

And for ten years he went about the world, proclaiming the Lord's business to a race of men whose ears the demons had "sealed against the truth." Everywhere he was met with jeers and stones—the current wages paid for that most precious com-modity, the bread of life. At last he succeeded in getting one convert—his cousin Metyoma. Together they wandered and suf-fered, and out of their sufferings they fashioned the "golden syl-lables" of the *Avesta*—the Persian Gospel of Truth.

III

THE *Avesta*—better known to the Occidental world as the *Zend-Avesta*—is a book of theology, of ethics, and of philosophy. It deals with the nature of God, the duty of man, and the destiny of life. We have today but a fraction of the original version—a book whose composition, we are told, covered no less than twelve thousand cowhides. This original version was destroyed when Alexander, in his reckless march of conquest, set fire to the city of Persepolis. Enough of the fragments have been preserved, however, to give us a fairly accurate picture of Zoroaster's ideas about God, man, and destiny.

The Zoroastrian God, Ahura Mazda, is closely akin to the Mosaic God, Jehovah. Zoroaster, like Moses, visualized God in his own image. Ahura Mazda is a divine Husbandman of the

Persian plateau just as Jehovah is a divine Bedouin of the Arabian desert. He is the all-knowing, all-powerful, and all-pitying Creator of the universe, Father of the human race, and Provider of sustenance for all living things. "His body is the light and the sovereign glory; the sun and the moon are his eyes; his raiment is the solid vault of the firmament." He it was who made the heavens to give light and the earth to produce life. He "determined the paths of the suns and the stars . . . sustained the earth and the firmament from falling . . . sustained the waters and the plants . . . harnessed swiftness with the winds and the clouds" . . . provided man with the desire to plant and the seed with the power to grow. Ahura Mazda, in short, is the sum total of all the natural forces that make for harmony. As for the forces of disharmony, these—maintained Zoroaster—emanate from the Devil. "It was Ahriman who created the darkness and all the ugly and venomous creatures thereof." These evil forces, with all their obnoxious brood of serpents, locusts, whirlwinds, floods, diseases, ants, rats, adders, vultures and vermin, are engaged in eternal warfare against the powers of goodness, justice, forbearance, piety, compassion and peace.

But in spite of all their temporary triumphs, the forces of evil shall not prevail against the omniscience and the omnipotence of God. For God has foreseen the struggle and has prepared for it through the creation of the one unconquerable weapon against evil—the righteous man.

Before he could create the righteous man, Ahura Mazda had to conduct many an experiment with his human clay. First of all he fashioned Mashya and Mashyói (the Adam and Eve of the Persian scripture) and he placed them in an earthly Paradise. "And God spoke to them, saying: 'You are man and woman, the ancestors of the world, and you are created to worship justice. Perform devotedly the duty of the law, think good thoughts, speak good words, do good deeds, and worship no demons.' "

And for a time Mashya and Mashyói "devotedly performed

their duties, and worshiped the Truth, and were mated, and brought forth seven pairs of offspring, male and female . . . and from every one of them, in fifty years, children were born, and they themselves died in a hundred years."

But the new children of the human race had forgotten the worship of the Truth and had fallen under the spell of Ahriman, the father of lies. And God had sent upon them a flood of melting snows. And in this flood all men had perished save a faithful few. Out of these faithful few, declared Ahura Mazda, the Truth shall be born again. These shall become the seed of the righteous man.

And who is the righteous man? He who shall establish the life of his fellowmen upon the three-cornered foundation of *Good Thoughts, Good Words,* and *Good Deeds.*

First of all, it is necessary for mankind to *think* justice. We must "sharpen our minds upon the whetstone of experience." We must learn to sympathize with other people's sorrows, and to rejoice in other people's joys. We must abolish ignorance with the light of reason. "Ignorance it is which ruins most people." For ignorance is "the cause of mutual injuries among men." The foolish man is unaware of the fact that in hurting his neighbors he is only hurting himself. The wise man, on the other hand, knows that a kindness done to another, "whether from near or from afar," will be repaid in kind. And so, to seek the proper relationship between yourself and your fellowmen—that is, to think justice—is the first requisite of the Zoroastrian religion.

The second requisite is to *speak* justice. "He who speaks an unjust word may deceive his fellowman, but he cannot deceive God." It is necessary to be honest not only in thought, but in speech. The Zoroastrian religion, in other words, is not a *negative* but a *positive* path to salvation. To save ourselves, we must teach others to be saved. "Our duty," declares the *Avesta,* "is to teach friendliness to the enemy, righteousness to the wicked, and wisdom to the ignorant." Above all, we must hate falsehood. "He who utters a falsehood is of all men the most to be despised." For he wounds not only the ear but the soul of his neighbor. Zoroaster is ready to forgive everybody but the liar. To forgive him who dispenses falsehoods is to be a dispenser of falsehoods yourself. "He is himself a liar who is good to a liar . . . For he helps to water the seed of untruth which blossoms into the weed of injustice."

Next to the active lie, Zoroaster despises the passive withholding of the truth. To adhere to the principle of *Good Words,* declares the Persian prophet, you must not only speak *justice,* but you must also speak *against injustice.* You must raise your voice whenever you see a wrong to be righted, an injury to be avenged, a cruelty to be exposed. "He is most pleasing in the eyes of the Lord above who here below intercedeth for the poor and the oppressed." For man is not an isolated creature who can stand aloof from his fellowmen. He is a related brother in the united family of the human race. "God Himself standeth ever at thy door in the persons of thy brothers throughout the world."

And this leads us from *Good Thoughts* and *Good Words* to the third Zoroastrian principle—*Good Deeds.* Once you have learned to *think* justice and to *speak* justice, you are well on the way to *do* justice. And this is the final aim of the righteous man. Every follower of Zoroaster considers himself a soldier in a lifelong crusade for fair play. "I will, while I have power and strength, do good to my fellowmen." He holds himself ready, at all times, to "put down violence" and to "take a stand against cruelty." He is a sworn enemy to all the "despoilers of men." The greatest happiness of man—and this is a thought which Zoroaster repeats again and again—is to afflict the oppressor and to relieve the oppressed. "See to it, O man, that thou hast afflicted the Evil One, that thou hast caused prosperity and joy to flow from thee unto others, and that no pain or injury may issue from thee unto them." Well-doing, to Zoroaster, is not a duty but a joy; for it leads to well-being. "When men love and help one another to

[35]

the best of their power, they derive their greatest pleasure from loving their fellowmen." Zoroaster believes that goodness begets good will. "Partake not of food until thou hast fed the needy. For the day may come when thou wilt ask them to feed thee." But on the other hand, "if thou refuse bread to the hungry, that bread shall be a burning coal upon thy head." A man's greatest enemy is his own greed. "For greed begets hatred; and hatred begets violence; and violence begets death."

Such is the teaching of Zoroaster as regards man's relationship to his fellowmen. In one of the sublime passages of the *Avesta* he summarizes this relationship, as Confucius and Hillel and Jesus have summarized it, in the universal language of the Golden Rule: "Do not unto another whatever is not good for thyself." This, declares the Persian prophet, is the way of justice; and this is the final purpose of human life.

For life—maintains Zoroaster—does not end in death but goes on beyond the grave. When a righteous man dies, his good deeds appear before him in the shape of a beautiful young maiden "whose fragrance is like the combined fragrance of all the flowers on earth." And when an unrighteous man dies, his evil deeds appear before him in the guise of an ugly old hag "whose stench is like the combined stench of all the dunghills on earth." And the respective souls of these dead are conducted, each by his appropriate guide, to the Bridge of the Sifting. "And he who is of the righteous, passeth over this bridge on the ascent and goeth unto Heaven, the abode of light and the house of song . . . But he who is of the wicked, falleth from the end of the bridge head foremost unto Hell, an abyss of terror and darkness and tortures and tears." And the agents of his punishment in Hell are the demons born of his own sins—his evil thoughts, his evil words, his evil deeds.

And thus, observes Zoroaster, virtue brings about its own victory; and vice, its own defeat.

But in the end, vice itself shall be defeated. And sickness and suffering and death shall be no more. For, after the rewards and the punishments have been fulfilled, "the dead shall rise, life shall return to the bodies and they shall breathe again." And the Kingdom of Heaven shall be established on earth. "The world shall become a slopeless and iceless plain"—the Persians dreaded the mountains, out of which came the marauders who despoiled them of their cattle and the winds that robbed them of their health—"and life shall become righteous and painless and death-less, free from fear and from malice," free from injustice and discord and falsehood and folly and strife. "All creation shall become immortal, and the Lord of Light shall reign supreme!"

IV

WRAPPED in this vision of a better world, Zoroaster at last found refuge from his wanderings. King Vishtaspa accepted his teachings and welcomed him into his palace. Miracle of miracles, a prophet had attained honor within his own country! He married three times, brought up a sizable family, and acquired a reputation as a "maker of magic." His contemporaries were more interested in the external *signs* than they were in the internal *spirit* of his mission. They ignored him as a saviour and worshiped him as a clown. They related to one another how this "holy magician" could fly through the air, walk upon the waters, enter a house through a solid wall, summon the winds to confound his enemies, and bring the dead back to life. But they were blind to the one true miracle of his greatness—his ability to make gentle the hardened heart.

Even the king, we are told, refused to adopt the teachings of Zoroaster until Ahura Mazda had sent down to the royal palace three archangels in a fiery chariot. "If you accept this prophet," declared the leader of the archangels, "you shall be blessed with a long life and a reign of a hundred and fifty years. But if you reject him, you shall be consumed with the fire of the Lord."

And so it was "in the fear of the Lord's anger" that King Vishtaspa received the Creed. Whereupon the archangels "gave him to drink of the fountain of life" and invested him with the "robe of victory" over his foes.

Vishtaspa had good need of his robe of victory. For the "hordes of unbelievers" in the surrounding nations had leagued themselves under the banner of the Devil, in "an unholy crusade against the Faith." Eight resplendent hosts advanced against his kingdom, and eight inglorious mobs returned routed to their homes.

In these "Wars of the Religion" the Persian king won the victory but lost his prophet. Zoroaster, in company with eighty priests, was attending to his devotions at the Temple of the Sacred Fire when the invading army rushed into the city "and the world became darkened with rapine and murder . . . The soldiers, intoxicated with their (temporary) triumph, burned the *Avesta,* and destroyed the Temple, and slew the prophet together with his priests and put an end to their life of devotion . . . And the blood of these dying men extinguished the Sacred Fire of Zoroaster . . ."

But, at the very moment when Zoroaster breathed his last breath, a rainbow burst over the sky above the Temple. "What is the rainbow?" Zoroaster had once asked Ahura Mazda. And Ahura Mazda had replied: "The rainbow is the smile of the souls in heaven giving courage to the sorrowing souls upon earth."

BUDDHA

Important Events in Life of Buddha

Born 563 B.C.

Brought up in palace of father, King of the Sakyas.

Married beautiful cousin.

Royal pleasures interrupted by sights of suffering and death.

At 29, left palace in quest of truth.

At 35, "found truth" under a bo-tree (the Tree of Enlightenment).

Began to preach new religion at Benares.

Formed order of teaching friars.

Wandered over India to spread "knowledge of life."

Died at Kusinagara, at the age of 80.

Gautama Buddha

563 B.C.—483 B.C.

HIS ORIGINAL NAME was Siddhartha Sakya-muni Gautama—which, translated into English, means *Gautama who belongs to the Sakya tribe and who has reached the goal of perfection.* He was born of an ancient Indian prince five centuries before Jesus was born to a humble Judean carpenter. His father ruled the tribe of Sakya under the shadow of the Himalayas. His mother was one of the Rajah's two wives—both of them daughters of a neighboring king. When the princess felt that the time of her delivery was near, she set foot—as was the tribal custom—to her father's palace for the confinement. But her labor overtook her on the journey, and she gave birth to Gautama in a quiet grove of satinwood trees.

The boy grew up amidst the pleasures of the royal court at Kapila-vastu. For all the contact he had with the outer world of his people, he might have been a prisoner in a fortress of marble and gold. His life was all too happy and all too unreal in its dazzling splendor. He plucked every luscious fruit from the tree of life, reaching the ever higher branches as he grew taller and more ambitious. And then at nineteen he garnered the fairest prize—he married his beautiful cousin, Yasodhara. But the brilliance of his marriage was darkened by the shadow of disappointment. For his wife was childless. The young prince began to brood. And he made up his mind to examine these footsteps of sorrow that sullied the garden of his life. Why, he asked himself, is the gift of life even at its best like a counterfeit jewel given to us by a stingy god? Why must even the happiest existence be full of the flaws of unfulfilled hopes? Was life worth the living after all?

One day he went driving through the countryside with his charioteer, Channa. On the way he met an aged man bent and broken by the weight of his years. Gautama turned away in horror. And his charioteer whispered, "This, my prince, is the way of life." And before he could absorb the shock of this discovery, the prince came upon a beggar covered with the sores of a loathsome disease. "This, too, is the way of life," said Channa. Gautama drove on. And he chanced upon a naked corpse, swollen, discolored, and rotting in the sun. "This," said Channa, "is the *end* of life."

Back to the palace went the prince to meditate. Now that he had been brought face to face with the misery of man, he was determined to do something about it. He opened his heart to the wandering monks who begged at the doorstep of his palace. He listened to their discourse and asked them to tell him about the indignities and the deceptions of this world. And then he made up his mind to leave the palace and its pleasures and to become a lonely pilgrim in search of the truth.

As he was ready to commence his journey, word came to him that his wife had at long last given birth to a son. The people pressed around him in wild celebration. "Happy the father, happy the mother, happy the wife of such a son and husband," they sang. But the young prince thought to himself grimly, "This is another strong tie that I shall have to break." He attended the banquet prepared by his father, the Rajah, to celebrate the birth; and then, in the middle of the night, he tiptoed into the chamber of his wife. In the dim light of the lamp he bent over her sleeping face. She was breathing the fragrance of the flowers that encased the bed. One arm held the head of the little infant. He longed to embrace them, but refrained for fear that he might wake them. One last look—and then he tiptoed out of the room and ordered his charioteer to saddle two of his swiftest horses.

Through the black and silver stretches of the night he rode with Channa, and the voice of the Tempter pursued him. "Return and be a King, and I will make you the greatest monarch over the four continents. Only give up this mad enterprise."

But the young prince refused to listen to the voice. The promise that it held out to him was but the empty wind of the night. In the dawn he reached the bank of a river. He cut off his long, flowing hair, stripped himself of his princely robes and his jewelry, and gave them all, together with his horse and his sword, to his servant Channa, bidding him to return home and to tell his father and his wife about his new resolve. And then, having put on a peasant's smock, he set out to seek wisdom from the priestly sages who lived in the caverns of the hills.

II

BUT he found that he had nothing to learn from the teachers of the old religions. It was not for *their* wisdom that he had given up his wealth and his family to assume the raiments of a beggar. Like the Rajahs of India, these religious teachers were the masters of the people; and they held the souls of the masses in the bondage of superstition and witchcraft and ritual and ceremony. They were a race of conquerors who called themselves *Aryans* and who divided the people into social castes, ranging all the way from the arrogant Brahmans at the top to the "untouchable" Outcastes at the bottom. No, these Brahman priests knew nothing of the truth. For six years he had followed their advice to the letter of the law. The only way to salvation, they had proclaimed, was through living the life of an ascetic. He must do continual penance and mortify his flesh. Then only—they said—would he succeed in purifying himself of his sins. He had fasted and prayed and mortified his flesh, and his great endurance had won for him the admiration of many a weaker man. But through all this asceticism he had arrived no nearer to the truth. The way to his peace of mind lay not through the agony of his body. He began to eat and to lead a normal life again. And the superstitious men who had flocked to him as his disciples began to desert him now in their disappointment at his "apostasy." Once more he found himself alone.

And one night, as he sat under a bo-tree struggling with his doubt and his loneliness, a great peace descended upon him. And when he rose in the dawn, he was no longer Gautama the Skeptic but Buddha the Enlightened. For at last he had grasped the great mystery of human suffering, its causes and its cure.

III

AT THE OUTSET he felt a great spiritual pride in the gift of his revelation and a hesitation to preach to others. But the zeal of the prophet soon overwhelmed him. He set out for the city of Benares, where he preached his first sermon in a park of deer. Five laymen came to listen.

What he said sounded to them at first rather familiar—like the teachings of their own priests. But as they continued to listen they felt strange and terrified at something new. He told them that the true path to salvation lay in no outward realm, but within the spirit of each individual. Ceremonies and prayers and pious offerings were of no avail, he said. He would offer them "none of the rights, the charms, the various creeds, the priestly powers, or any of the gods in whom men so love to trust." He declared that unlike the Brahman priests, who speculated on "the future existence after death and on the past existence before birth," he was concerned only with men's conduct in their present existence. The philosopher who searches for the answer to the impractical questions of metaphysics is no wiser than the layman "who, being wounded by an arrow, seeks to discover facts about the person who discharged it, without trying to remove the missile."

In his effort to remove the arrow from his own wound, Buddha told them, he had sought after both extremes of passion—the voluptuary pleasures of the prince, and the self-mortifications of the hermit. And he had found that both the king and the hermit were wrong.

As rain breaks down upon an ill-thatched hut,
So passion breaks down upon the untrained mind.

And then, after his blind searchings into the extremes of passion—Buddha went on—he had discovered the Middle Path "which opens the eyes and bestows understanding, which leads to peace of mind, to the higher wisdom, to full enlightenment." It is the control of a man over the emotions which bind him forever to the "endless turning of the cycle of life, the pains of birth, the misery of death, like a slave upon a wheel that never stops."

And then Buddha in an age of semi-savagery proclaimed his golden rule of conduct which two thousand years of civilization are still trying to achieve. The Middle Path is an "Eightfold Way of right views, high aims, kindly speech, upright conduct, a harmless livelihood, perseverance in well-doing, intellectual activity, and profound meditation . . . Only through this Eightfold Way of righteousness can the individual deliver himself from the craving of his passions." This was the substance of his early teaching.

The fame and legend of the Buddha began to spread through all India. Many stories were told about his wisdom and his sympathy. And these stories became interwoven into a great Buddhist gospel.

Once—it was related—a beautiful young woman saw her baby child grow sick and waste away. When the little form became lifeless, the mother went mad with sorrow. Clasping the dead child to her breast, she wandered from house to house, begging the people for medicine that would bring it back to life. And finally she came to the dwelling of a monk. "She does not understand," he murmured pityingly. And aloud he said to her, "My poor child, I myself have no medicine such as you ask for, but I know of one who has."

"Tell me who he is!" implored the mother.

"He is the Buddha. It is to him you must go."

Eagerly she sought out Gautama. And the "Enlightened One" declared: "Yes, I know of the proper medicine. It is the ordinary mustard seed." But as the young mother rejoiced at the injunction to procure so common a drug, he continued: "You must get it from some house where no son or husband or parent or slave has ever died."

The young woman set out on her errand. Wherever she came, the people were only too willing to give her the mustard seed. But when she asked, "Has this house been free from the death of a son or a husband or a parent or a slave?" they replied sadly: "Such a house is nowhere to be found. The dead are many; and the living, few." And then the young mother, deep in thought, went silently to a forest and buried her child. When she returned to Gautama, he asked, "Have you found the mustard seed?" And the mother replied: "No, my master, but I have found the medicine. I have buried my sorrow in the forest. And now I am ready to follow you in peace."

Gautama taught the joy, not of possession but of renunciation. This doctrine of renunciation, he said, lies at the very root of the secret of life. Our human existence represents the soul's journey from earth to heaven. But this journey, declared Gautama, is a successive migration of the soul through many bodies. At first, under the influence of the hermit priests, Buddha followed the popular conception about the transmigration of souls. That is, he taught that the individual soul is born over and over again, traveling from one body-prison to another, until finally, freed from the necessity of another imprisonment within a living body, it dissolves into *Nirvana,* or heavenly bliss. His own soul, he told his disciples, had once inhabited the body of a quail.

This crude conception about the transmigration of souls became refined into a more poetical idea as Buddha grew older. In his later philosophy he no longer represented the individual soul as undergoing a series of personal migrations. Instead, he began to teach his disciples that each living soul is like a torch whose flame is handed down in turn to another torch, and so on through the ages until at last it melts into the universal flame of immortal life. Or, to use the metaphor of the bells, each life is a note which is sounded in an open room and which causes similar instruments to vibrate with the same sound all the way down the corridors of time until at last the note is swallowed up in the universal harmony of heaven.

Stripped of its poetical imagery, this doctrine means merely that the consequences of every life are far-reaching and that every human being is an important part of all humanity.

As for personal immortality, Buddha did not believe in it, nor did he desire it. Each human soul, he thought, is but a fragment of the world-soul, and to crave for personal immortality is to indulge the part at the expense of the whole. All human misery, he told his disciples, is caused by our selfish ambitions both for this world and for the next.

But he who subordinates his little personal self to the larger self of humanity is ready at last to end his weary pilgrimage from life to life and to enter into the *Nirvana* of eternal rest.

Nirvana, according to Buddha's doctrine, is "the complete extinction of all bodily desire." *Nir* means *out,* and *va* means *to blow.* Heaven is "a blowing out of the flame of selfish passion"— the complete extinguishment of the individual soul of sorrow and strife, the final release from the tempestuous sea of existence. "Existence is the ocean; the breaking of its waves are the many births of man; the foam on the wave-crest is this perishable body; and the further shore is *Nirvana,* the haven of peace."

In order to arrive at this peace of Selflessness in its deepest sense, all men must rid their social and political and economic institutions of their selfish spirit. The caste system, which set off one Hindu from another by "unreason" of birth, must be abolished. Buddha taught that all men are born to an "equality of rights." Brave words, these, in the world's cold dawn! "A man is noble or ignoble through his conduct and not through his birth."

Like all the other great prophets, Buddha preserved whatever was good in the religion of his fathers while striking out against their religious institutions. But unlike most of the other prophets, he made no claim that God was speaking through him. He did not "bribe" his people to do good by promising them future rewards in heaven or by threatening them with punishments in hell. He refused to base his moral code upon supernatural sanctions of any kind. Man must rid himself of his egotistical quest for a blissful life after death. Speculation as to whether the saint will find a reward in Paradise is "the jungle, the desert, the puppet show." All good men must be above the petty egocentricity of such a dispute. Buddha gives his people an adult and noble counsel. Do good for its own sake; for the good of your spiritual peace; for the purpose of becoming a Siddhartha, a man "whose will has accomplished its aim."

Buddha's is a doctrine of renunciation, and of tolerance. He does not assume the infallible truth of his own religion. Nor does he believe that any other religion has the right to such an assumption. Religious dogma, he declares, leads only to discord and hatred, and never to wisdom and peace. The surest path to salvation, he says, is through the mutual respect of all men, all races, all creeds. He bids his followers to use no weapon for con-

[*48*]

version save the gentle weapon of a persuasive tongue. "If I cannot convince you, I must never convict you."

Buddha was not interested in the theology of his religion. He was interested only in its ethics. "I know nothing about the mystery of God, but I know something about the misery of man."

And he made it his business to relieve this misery to the best of his human ability. He devised a system of "piety and pity" based upon the moral triangle of moderation, patience, and love.

By his own action he showed the wisdom of moderation. He had been born into a life of too great luxury, and he soon got tired of it. Then he tried a life of excessive mortification, and before long he grew weary of that, too. At last he chose a middle course and found true happiness in the sensible doctrine of "nothing too much." He taught self-control as against self-indulgence. He was equally opposed to the intoxication of lust, the intoxication of power, and the intoxication of conquest. All three alike lead to madness in the end. It is the sign of a diseased soul to be over-ambitious, to crave for mastery over the weak and for conquest in war. For conquest is the father of death, and of hatred which is worse than death.

How, then, are we to overcome this thirst for conquest in the human heart? By the paradox of patience, said Buddha. By forgiving the conqueror. By treating him as a sick child. By repaying hatred with kindliness. For it is only in this way that you can get a world of savage and quarrelsome children to grow up into civilized and peaceful men and women. Buddha taught his people the heroism of suffering without inflicting pain, and the courage of dying without killing. Above all, he taught them patience— the quiet patience of the East—and forbearance. "Never shed a drop of blood for the glory of God."

For Buddha taught, not the glory of God but the power of love. It was his purpose "to flush the world with love." He gave up a throne to live among the disinherited. And he enjoined his followers to do likewise—to give up the throne of their arrogance and to mingle humbly among their fellowmen. Every novice who entered his brotherhood of monks—the Order of the Yellow Robe —was obliged to assume the life of a "wanderer upon the face of the earth." He took a vow to emancipate his mind completely from "the things of time and sense." He devoted himself to but a single aim—happiness through peace. Free from prejudice and superstition, simple, faithful, and gentle, he lived in such a way as to bring no harm to any living thing—for the belief in reincarnation inspires in every Buddhist a feeling of blood relationship not only with every human being but with every form of life.

> As the bee—injuring not
> The flower, its color, or scent—
> Flies away, taking the nectar;
> So let the wise man dwell upon the earth.

Devoted to this principle of coöperative brotherhood, the Buddhist monk wore his yellow robe, carried a "begging bowl," an axe for chopping firewood, a razor and a water dipper. He needed nothing more for his protection. For he was encased in the invisible armor of his Siddhartha—the knighthood of hateless chivalry. "Go into the lands, and preach my gospel. Tell them that the poor and the lowly, the rich and the high, are all one, and that all castes unite in this religion as do the rivers in the sea."

IV

ONCE, in the midst of his wanderings, Gautama turned his steps toward Kapilavastu, the city ruled by his father, the home of his birth. His brothers and his uncles came to meet him in a grove of the ancient capital. And when they saw "the condition of poverty and humility into which the prince had fallen," they turned their faces from him and walked home in grief. Gautama took his begging bowl and made his way among the people for alms. His father the Rajah, having learned that his son was begging in the streets, went out to meet him. "Why do you put us to shame?" he demanded.

"Maharajah," replied Gautama, "this is the custom of our holy order."

"But we are descended from an illustrious race of warriors—men who give and take but who never beg."

The son looked indulgently at his father. "You and your family may claim descent from the kings; my descent is from the prophets. And they have always lived on alms." And then, with a burst of his ancestral pride, Gautama went on: "I, too, have something to give. When a son has discovered a hidden treasure, it is his duty to present his father with the most precious of the jewels." And Gautama preached to him the cardinal principles of his doctrine.

The Rajah made no reply. But taking his son's begging bowl, he led Gautama home where the members of the family and the servants of the household gathered to do him honor.

One member of the family, however, refused to come to him. This was Yasodhara, his wife. "If I am of any value in his eyes, he will come to me," she declared.

When Gautama noticed that she was not present, he went in search of her. He found her in the chamber where he had last looked upon her as she slept with their child in her arms. When she saw the recluse in his yellow robe, with his shaven head and his emaciated face, the memory of their former happy life over-whelmed her and she fell upon her knees and clutched his feet, sobbing.

And the Rajah, seeing her sorrow, spoke to Gautama: "My son, forgive her as she has forgiven you. Through all these years Yasodhara has continued to love you. She has refused all comforts of clothing and food, waiting patiently for her Lord's return. She has eaten but one meal a day and slept on the ground refusing the bridal bed."

[51]

And Gautama, hearing these words, lowered his eyes in silence.

Then Yasodhara rose and sought her son, Rahula. She dressed him in his best robes and told him that she was going to take him to his father.

"I know of no father but the Rajah," replied the boy. "Who else is my father?"

As Rahula was speaking, they entered the room where Gautama sat eating his bowl of rice. "This man is your father," said Yasodhara. "I have heard him tell of a great hidden treasure he has discovered. Go to him now and ask for your rights; say to him, 'I am your son, and shall be the head of the clan, and shall want my inheritance. Give it to me.'"

The boy made his way to Gautama. "Father, I am glad you have come to give me my inheritance."

Gautama was silent, deep in meditation. When he had finished his meal, he rose and walked to the grove on the outskirts of the city. Rahula followed him and once more asked for his inheritance. "Father, pray give me what is rightfully mine."

Finally they reached a bo-tree, where Gautama spoke to Rahula with a gentle smile. "You do well, my son, to ask for your rightful inheritance." And turning to his attendant, he said, "Give Rahula his begging bowl and admit him into our holy order of monks and bid him follow me."

V

THROUGHOUT the remaining years of his long life, Gautama wandered from town to town and pitched camp in the wooded outskirts, in the gardens, or by the bank of a river. And many were the disciples to whom he gave their "rightful" inheritance.

At length one day when he had passed eighty, he stopped at the hut of a blacksmith for his noonday meal. And then he returned to the grove and stretched himself out on a bed of leaves, deathly sick. His disciples gathered anxiously around him. And he raised his eyes to them. "Do not think that because your teacher is gone, the Word is ended."

But as he approached "the blessed silence of peace," Buddha would have been amazed to know what a new turn his Word was destined to take. For the religious teacher who disbelieved in God was to become the God of a new religion.

CONFUCIUS

Important Events in Life of Confucius

Born at Lu (modern Shantung), 551 B.C.

At 3, lost father.

At 19, married.

At 20, became father.

At 22, opened "School of Wisdom."

At 33, exiled from Lu.

At 37, restored to Lu.

From 37 to 52, studied and taught.

Appointed chief magistrate of city of Chungtu.

Appointed Minister of Crime in province of Lu.

At 56, fell into royal disfavor.

Went into self-imposed exile.

Acquired 3000 disciples.

At 69, returned once more to Lu.

Compiled his teachings.

At 70, lost son.

At 71, lost favorite disciple.

Died 478 B.C.

Confucius

551 B.C.—478 B.C.

THE SAGE was the son of a soldier—an obscure little soldier who regarded himself as the least worthy of a long line of noble ancestors. Shu-liang Heh was a sad man when he had passed the age of seventy. His wife had given him nothing but daughters; and his concubine, a crippled and illegitimate son. It was a cardinal tenet of the Chinese faith that a father must leave behind him a legitimate son to pray for him after his death. Shu-liang Heh's spirit could not rest easy in the afterworld. And so, just before his preparation for the final journey he took to wife a girl of seventeen. Soon a new soul stirred within her. And a boy was born.

The ancient soldier marveled at the huge ears of the baby. It was a Chinese tradition that ears of this size denoted the characteristics of wisdom in the head. "He will grow up to be a sage," prophesied the joyful father. And he named him *Kung-fu-tse,* which means "the wise Mr. Kung."

And, indeed, Kung-fu-tse—or Confucius—turned out to be no ordinary child. And his burden in life was no ordinary burden. When he was three he lost his father; and when he reached adolescence he was obliged to support his young mother. At seventeen he applied for a civil service post and was appointed "custodian of the national grain supply." Apparently he gathered a respectable financial harvest. For when he reached nineteen he was able to afford the luxury of a wife. Moreover, he won the esteem of the highest officials in the state. On his wedding day he received from the duke a "most generous and practical present"—a pair of carp. And the young groom graciously returned the honor of the gift one year later when he named his son *Po-Yu,* "Fine Fish."

The "wise Mr. Kung" was successful in his official post. But he was not contented. For he was by nature a man of thought rather than of action. He wanted above all to be a teacher.

And the opportunity came through the channel of sorrow. For his mother had died and he had thus been freed from the burden of her dependency. For three years, in accordance with the Chinese custom, he withdrew to a hut near his mother's grave; and then, taking his wife and his little son by the hand, he started on his journey in quest of pupils. "I live now," he said laconically, "in the north, the south, the east and the west." But his fixed residence, he might have added, was in his thought.

II

IN THE sixth century before Christ, China was a land of many feudal princes who bowed blandly before their emperor and who stabbed one another during the pauses in the ceremony. It was a period in which the gangster minds of the nation had seized temporary control of affairs. But China had behind her a long period of history—thousands of years—in which the sages and not the savages had risen to the top of the state. And now that "the mad dogs of misrule" had been unleashed from their kennels, the wise men of China sought comfort in the recorded "manners and virtues" of the past. Among these explorers into the past history of China was Confucius, whose own ancestors had gathered wisdom over a period of a thousand years. And one day in his quest for wisdom he arrived at the court of Chou and sought out Lao-Tze, the renowned philosopher and curator of the royal library.

For several hours he discoursed with Lao-Tze and showed off his own scholarship. And the old philosopher listened to the younger man with a smile of amusement. Finally he spoke to Confucius. "The subjects and the people you talk about are dead . . . I have heard that a good merchant, though he has rich treasures hoarded in the ground, is no better situated than a pauper."

The young man returned from his visit sorely puzzled. "I can tell how birds fly, how fishes swim, how animals run through the forest. But in the presence of the dragon I am all adrift. I cannot tell how he mounts on the wind through the clouds and rises to the heavens. Today I have seen Lao-Tze, and I can only compare him to the dragon."

But gradually, as the abashed young teacher gathered his pupils and matured his thoughts, the meaning of Lao-Tze's words became somewhat clearer to him. His own native province of Lu had been plunged into a series of civil wars. His lifelong friend, the Duke of Kao, was compelled to flee across the border into the neighboring kingdom of Ch'i. And Confucius, realizing the fate of any of the duke's adherents who might fall into the hands of the enemy, selected a few of his aptest pupils and followed the duke into exile. As he passed through a mountain wilderness, he saw a woman kneeling in tears by a newly-made grave. Confucius asked her for the cause of her grief. "My husband's father," she replied, "was killed on this spot by a tiger, and my husband also. And now my son has met the same fate."

"Then why have you not moved to a civilized community?" asked the teacher.

"Here," said the woman, "there is no oppressive government."

When Confucius arrived at Ch'i, he presented himself before the prince, and offered his services with a view to abolishing "oppressive government." For now at last he fully understood the words of Lao-Tze. The currency of learning was meant to be taken from its hoarding place and to be circulated until it reached the coffers of humanity. In times of great social unrest, the scholar must turn statesman.

At first the ruler of Ch'i was glad to welcome a philosopher to his court. He was fond of discussing the problems of statecraft with Confucius, whose counsel both amazed and amused him. One day he asked Confucius for his definition of good government. "There is good government," replied Confucius, "when the ruler is ruler, and the minister is minister; when the father is father, and the son is son." The Prince of Ch'i nodded his assent. "I don't understand what you're saying, but it *sounds* good."

The philosopher impressed him. He would give Confucius a province to rule over. "I will make him minister of Lin-ch'iu," he told his politicians. But the politicians were thunderstruck. What? Entrust this philosopher with a town? They would sooner see China headed toward perdition! With much bowing and wringing of the hands the chief minister implored the prince to abandon his "fatal" idea. "These scholars, Sire, are unpractical, and cannot be understood by the people. They are haughty and conceited in their views. They are too dangerous." Whereupon the prince shrugged his shoulders and agreed that "to introduce philosophy into the counsels of the state might after all be far worse than revolution." And he let it be known to Confucius that perhaps his life at court was not very congenial to a man of the philosophic temperament.

The sage was wise enough to take the hint. He left the kingdom of Ch'i and returned to his native city where the political situation had once more become favorable to his friends. These friends had heard of his treatment at the court of Ch'i; and in a spirit of sheer rivalry, if not of generosity, they offered him the administration of the city of Chungtu. A cleansing tide of justice —one of those rare historic purgations—had just swept over the human heart. In the west, the philosopher-statesman Solon had bestowed a "blessed code of liberty" upon the enslaved people of Greece. In India, Prince Buddha the Enlightened had awakened his countrymen to the beauty of a new religion. In Babylon the prophet Ezekiel had arisen to denounce the idolatry of the ruling classes. And now in China "the wise Mr. Kung" was presented with a city in order that he might undertake an experiment in honest government. For a while it began to look as if the human family, withdrawn at last from its savage prowling in the wilderness, might be "getting on."

III

MUCH of the duty of the new minister at Chungtu would seem somewhat amusing to a modern American. Among other things, he had charge of "regulating the manners and the morals of the people." He prescribed the different kinds of food that the people of different ages were allowed to eat, the sort of costumes they must wear on private and on public occasions, the number of bows they must make on saluting one another. "The men must be careful to walk on the right side of the road, the women on the left." He stipulated the thickness of the wood in the coffins and the width and the depth of the graves. And he formulated the *law of renunciation*. "Anything dropped on the ground cannot be picked up again."

He was so successful in the "humane enforcement" of these laws that the prince appointed him Minister of Crime. "And crime stopped as if by magic . . . Dishonesty and dissoluteness hid their heads . . . Loyalty and good faith became the characteristics of the men; and chastity and docility, the ornaments of the women . . . Confucius was hailed as the idol of the people, and his name shone brightly in the songs of their mouths."

Finally the prince promoted him to the office of Prime Minister. But this promotion was the beginning of his downfall. For the princes of the neighboring provinces were becoming jealous of his success as a reformer. They feared the strength of a ruler who could win the hearts of his people. "With Confucius at the head of the government, Lu will soon become supreme among the states. Our subjects will leave our lands and flock to Lu."

And so the frightened rulers put their heads together and laid plans to separate the Prince of Lu from his minister. This prince, as they observed, was charmed with the philosophy of his minister. There was but a single way to break the spell—and that was, with another sort of charm. Accordingly they dispatched to their "exalted brother, the Prince of Lu," a present of eighty beautiful dancing girls. And the prince swallowed the bait. He received beauty into his palace and threw wisdom into the street. All state business had stopped. A full season had passed and still Confucius waited patiently for his master to regain his sanity. And then, with a philosopher's fortitude, he went once more into exile.

IV

FOR THIRTEEN YEARS he wandered from town to town with his faithful and oftentimes sad disciples. Once a strange old man accosted these disciples of Confucius. "My friends, why are you distressed at your master's ill fortune? The world has long been without the principles of truth and right. Heaven is using him as a bell to ring out God's message."

But if the ears of men were loath to hear, their mouths were eager to scold. It was only in the mountain fastnesses and the forests that Confucius found a friendly silence. Wherever he spoke to the people, he was hooted and stoned. When he reached the province of Wei, the prince inflicted a special indignity upon him. He took out his favorite courtesan for a drive and forced Confucius to ride in a carriage directly behind. And the populace shouted gleefully, "Behold Virtue trailing after Lust!" The ruler of another province gave orders to chop down the tree under which Confucius was preaching. "Let it fall upon him and crush out his meddlesome life." When he came to the province of Chiang, the keeper of the gate wouldn't let him pass. "Don't you know who he is?" said one of his disciples.

"All I know," replied the keeper, "is that he looks like a stray dog."

And, indeed, he looked bedraggled enough in those days. Bedraggled, and serenely happy. "Confucius," he wrote of himself, "is a man who in his eager pursuit of knowledge forgets his food, who in the joy of his attainment forgets his sorrows, and who does not perceive that old age is coming on."

So intent was he upon helping others that he had no time to bother about himself. On one occasion a hermit upbraided him for wandering through the city streets and begging audiences with people. "Had you better not follow those who flee the world entirely, without enduring its insults and blows?" And Confucius replied in hurt surprise: "I cannot mingle with birds and beasts; and if I may not associate with suffering mankind, with whom am I to associate?"

And so he associated with his fellowmen, and tried to mitigate their sufferings with the balm of his wisdom. Many of those with whom he conversed were impatient with the appearances of the world and were anxious to find its ultimate meaning. When they asked him what he knew about death, he replied with a gentle rebuke, "How can I understand death when I do not as yet understand life?" And he continued in the tone of a father speaking to his children: "Let us not trouble ourselves with supernatural things and beings, while we do not know how to serve men."

Confucius was realistic in his attitude toward life. He was no visionary philosopher. When a young disciple asked him whether evil should be repaid with good, he replied: "And with what then should good be repaid?" The sage Mr. Kung was a practical son of the Orient. "Repay evil neither with goodness nor with evil, but with justice."

He condensed his entire ethical philosophy into a single negative sentence which five centuries later was to be translated into the positive philosophy of the *Golden Rule*. "My one formula for human conduct," he said, "is Reciprocity. *What you would not have others do unto yourself, do not unto others.*"

He formulated no consecutive system of thought. Rather he regarded himself as an occasional sower of the living seeds of wisdom. "Should these seeds take root in the human heart, they may perhaps blossom into the flower of harmonious living."

For the kings, however, he had no seeds but nettles. He knew how to sting those who would hear him only to jeer him. "What are the three requisites of your perfect government?" a prince once asked him in a tone of facetious condescension.

"Food enough, troops enough, and a trusting people."

"And suppose you couldn't have all these factors," continued the prince, "what would you sacrifice?"

"Troops, first. And then, food. But I would never sacrifice trust. Without trust, a government cannot stand."

Another of the petty rulers asked him: "Does not the princely man value courage above all things?"

The sage answered: "He puts righteousness first. The man of high station who has courage without righteousness is a menace to the state; the common man who has courage without righteousness is nothing more than a brigand."

Confucius believed neither in heaven nor in hell, but he did believe tremendously in the potentialities of his fellowmen. "It is not easy to find a man who has studied wisdom for three years without becoming good." He dreamed of a day when a race of moral supermen would arise to govern his country. "If mankind would be governed justly for but a single century," he maintained, "all violence would disappear from the earth."

It was his overmastering passion to seek for the just government and for the "Superior Man" who might establish this sort of government as a model for all future time. "The Superior Man moves so as to make his actions in all generations a universal path; he behaves so as to make his conduct in all generations a universal law; he speaks so as to make his words in all generations a universal norm."

Above all things the Superior Man cherishes four principles: scholarship, good conduct, honesty, and faithfulness. Weaving his wisdom and his virtue into a pattern of action, he tries to follow the "ninefold way" of the good life. "In regard to the use of his eyes, he is anxious to see clearly. . . . In regard to his countenance, he is anxious that it should be benign. In regard to his demeanor, he is anxious that it should be respectful. In regard to his speech, he is anxious that it should be sincere. In regard to the conduct of his business, he is anxious that it should be honest. In regard to his doubts, he is anxious to question others. In regard to his temper, he thinks of the sufferings his anger may inflict. In regard to his ambition, he thinks of righteousness."

While the common man is exacting of others, the Superior Man is exacting of himself. He loves men for their virtues and he tries to understand their failings. "Love and wisdom are the heart and soul of the Superior Man." In the darkest hours of his wanderings Confucius declared: "It does not greatly concern me that men do not understand *me*. My great concern is in not understanding *them*."

The subtle wisdom of this advanced doctrine was above the heads of the tyros and the tyrants of the world. But the disciples who lived and suffered with the master through the weary cycle of the years understood the value of the man even though they did not always understand the value of his words. "It is not the principles that give breadth to the man; it is the man who gives breadth to the principles."

The disciples of Confucius found in their master not a philosopher, but a prophet. He never tried to dazzle them with his exclusive knowledge. He merely tried to enlighten them with his inclusive sympathy. "There are men," he observed, "who seek for some abstruse meaning in religion and philosophy, and who lead a singular life in order that they may leave a name to posterity. This is what I never do."

He was merely a "statesman in search of a state"—a man who realized that the character of the individual is the foundation of society, and that "everybody from the emperor down to the humblest citizen must consider the cultivation of the *person* as the root of everything, if China is to be saved from her devastating civil wars."

Would there ever be an end to this internal anarchy? "The organization of society must stem out from the discipline of the family"—a discipline based upon sincerity and mutual respect. The emperor must perform the role of the father. "He must be an affectionate guide." The people are his sons. They must be reverent and obedient. "When the wind blows, the grass must bend." All must frown upon dissension among the members of this family as nothing less than fratricide. For the filial piety of the people and the paternal solicitude of the ruler are ordained by the laws of heaven. And yet, if the father makes an unjust demand, the sons must be governed by their sense of duty— which is a higher morality than the loyalty of kinship. They must resist the injustice of their father. So too, if the emperor chooses his ministers unwisely or misuses his prerogatives as head of the family, the people must resist. "The right of rebellion is of divine origin."

And when shall this "family-state" be launched upon the way to prosperity and strength? "When its members have started to seek for the all-pervading harmony of mutual understanding."

The happy state, observes Confucius, endeavors to set itself up as an independent unit and to avoid, if possible, all foreign entanglements. It limits the luxury of its court and it tries to distribute its wealth among the people. It seeks to decrease punishment and to increase education. It teaches manners and music to all. "For music is akin to benevolence, and good music to righteousness." (Confucius himself was a competent flute-player.) The happy state—he continues—prepares for the day when the great principle of harmony shall dwell on earth among men. "Then the whole world shall become a republic . . . Men shall converse sincerely with one another and cultivate universal peace . . . And then they shall no longer regard as their parents only their parents, or treat as their children only their children . . . Every man shall have his rights, and every woman her individuality . . . Selfish schemings shall be repressed and shall find no way to rise again . . . Robbers, filchers and traitors shall no longer infest the earth . . . This is the state of what I call the Great Harmony."

When would the day of this great World-Republic dawn upon men? And the master, recalling the reason for his exile, took the flute from his mouth and smiled mournfully. "When I have met with a man who loves Virtue as he loves Beauty!"

V

IN HIS SIXTY-NINTH YEAR he returned at last to his native city of Lu. The cycle of his exile was complete. The prince had long since died from an excess of high living. And the people had not forgotten their old Prime Minister. Once more they flocked to him for counsel and comfort. But as the years remaining to him grew thin, he was anxious to retire from the world. He devoted himself to literary labors, collected the Chinese poetry of the past, undertook a reform of the music played at the public ceremonies, and edited a monumental history of his country. More and more resignedly he became preoccupied with the Approaching End.

The great mountain must crumble;
The strong beam must break;
And the wise man wither away like a plant.

His disciples made much ado about him when they finally laid him to rest. They compiled books of his sayings and fabricated miraculous tales of his doings. "He is the sun, the moon—glorious, unapproachable, supreme . . . The impossibility of equaling him is like the impossibility of scaling a ladder from the earth to the sky."

His fame after his death was as pronounced as his neglect during his lifetime. The emperors displayed his portrait in state, engraved his sayings in stone, erected temples in his name and ordered sacrifices to be offered up to him four times a year. Before many generations had passed, they designated him with the official title, *Most Divine*. But, in the frenzy of their worship, most of them had forgotten the sanity of his words. "All that I can be called is this—an insatiable student, an unwearied teacher —this, and nothing more."

JOHN THE BAPTIST

Important Events in Life of John the Baptist

Born in hill country of Judea, 5 B.C.

Lost parents in early childhood.

Rejected offer to become priest.

Wandered off into desert for meditation.

Adopted life of hermit.

Began, in 15th year of reign of King Tiberius, to preach the approaching Kingdom of Heaven.

Administered baptism to Jesus —"the Lamb of God."

Recognized Jesus as the Messiah.

Denounced marriage of Herod Antipas to Herodias.

Imprisoned by Herod in fortress of Machaerus.

Beheaded (30 A.D.) at instigation of Salome, daughter of Herodias.

John the Baptist

5 B.C.–28 A.D.

THERE CAME to be a man, sent from God, his name was John . . . He was not the light, but came that he might witness the light . . . And the priests and the Levites came to ask him, Who art thou? And he confessed . . . I am not the Christ . . . Behold in the midst of you standeth one . . . the latchet of whose shoe I am not worthy to unloose . . .

"On the morrow he seeth Jesus coming unto him, and saith, Behold, this is he . . . That he be manifested to Israel, for this cause came I . . ."

The story of John the Baptist is the drama of a man who, aware of his own greatness, is yet eager to step aside in order to make room for one greater than himself.

II

BORN in the province of Judah, he was the son of Zacharias, a priest, and of Elisabeth, the daughter of a priestly family and a distant cousin of Mary, mother of Jesus. "And both Zacharias and Elisabeth were righteous before God . . . and blameless."

But they were unhappy, for "Elisabeth was barren and both were now well stricken in years." But one day, as the old priest was burning incense in the Temple, the angel Gabriel appeared before him—we are told in the Gospel according to Luke—and said to him: "Thy wife shall bear thee a son, and thou shalt call his name Johanan (John)." This child of their old age, continued Gabriel, would be dedicated to the sacred task of turning the sons of Israel "unto the Lord their God." He would direct "the hearts of the fathers to their children, and the disobedient to walk in the wisdom of the just."

And when Elisabeth's time was fulfilled, her husband Zacharias was inspired to prophesy about his son: "Blessed be the Lord, the God of Israel. For he hath visited and wrought redemption for his people . . . Thou, my child, shalt be called . . . to give knowledge of salvation to his people . . . to shine upon them that sit in the darkness and the shadow of death . . . and to guide our feet into the way of peace."

Thus consecrated from his birth, the son of Zacharias "grew and waxed strong in spirit," spending much of his time in the loneliness of the desert, and waiting for the day when he could enter upon the business of his life.

This public entry upon his life's business was in the fifteenth year of the reign of the Emperor Tiberius (A.D. 28). We see him now as a preacher in the wilderness—a man with long hair, an untrimmed beard, a ringing voice and eyes that flash fire. He is dressed in a tunic of coarse camel's hair and feeds on locusts and wild honey. A reincarnated Elijah, rushing through the country like a whirlwind to cleanse the bodies and to purify the thoughts of his people. "Repent ye, for the Kingdom of Heaven is at hand!" And when the crowds asked him what it was that he expected them to do in order to prove their repentance, he replied: "Who hath two coats, let him impart to him that hath none; and who hath food, let him do likewise . . . Practice no extortion, accuse no man unjustly, and be content with your lot."

As a symbolical preliminary to repentance, he enjoined the physical purification of his converts in the waters of the Jordan. But a mere external washing was not enough. Indeed, he refused to baptize those who were unwilling to purge their hearts of their arrogance and their greed. "Ye offspring of vipers, who (was it that) warned you to flee from the wrath to come?" You cannot escape from your own evil thoughts. The prophet of salvation had no magic formula for the sinner save a complete turning away from his sin. A tree is judged by the soundness of its fruits. "Even now the axe lieth at the root of the trees; every tree that bringeth not forth good fruit is hewn down and cast into the fire."

Thus far John the Baptist was no different from many of his contemporary preachers in Palestine. A whole host of them—they belonged to a mystical fraternity of hermits called the Essenes—kept wandering over the countryside, urging their people to confess their sins, and proclaiming the early arrival of the Messiah, the Anointed One, who would rescue his nation from bleeding to death under the talons of the Roman Eagle. They were all of them Baptists (from the Greek verb *baptizein,* to immerse), for it was a mystical custom among the Essenes to "purify their souls by washing their bodies." But little by little the hermit John, son of Zacharias, began to stand out from among his fellow preachers along the Jordan. He had one quality which most of the others lacked: a superlative degree of courage.

III

IN HIS COURAGE, just as in his piety, John the Baptist seemed to be a counterpart of the earlier prophet, Elijah. And, like Elijah, he focused his courage upon the one spot where it could be most dramatically displayed—the royal palace. Elijah had hurled his denunciation into the very face of King Ahab. And John the

Baptist emulated his teacher by his public castigation of the Tetrarch Antipas.

The immediate reason for John's disapproval of Antipas was the tetrarch's marriage to Herodias. This marriage, declared John, was not only illegal, but immoral, since Antipas had taken Herodias away from his living half-brother, Herod. Moreover, Antipas had repudiated his own former wife in order to please the "ambition and the passion" of Herodias. "This sort of marriage," cried the outraged John, "is nothing short of incest!"

Antipas was furious at these words. But Herodias found a deep fascination in the man who had uttered them. A fascination and a hope. Here was a fighter who could lead his people to victory against the Romans—and her husband and herself to an undisputed throne over Israel. She summoned John to her castle at Machaerus. "You must rouse our people," she said. "Plant within their hearts the conviction that you are their Messiah, that you have come to liberate them from the Roman yoke."

"And to what end?"

"To the end that they may be ruled once again by a royal house of their own."

"A native tyrant to replace a foreign tyrant," mocked the prophet. "A home-made firebrand in exchange for one imported from abroad."

"And do you see no difference between the two?"

"They both consume with an equal flame," retorted John.

And then Herodias tried to point out what she regarded as an inconsistency in his teaching. "When you tell us to prepare for the Kingdom of Heaven, why then do you object to the restoration of the ancient House of Israel, the Anointed of the Lord?"

"In the Kingdom of Heaven that I preach, God rules and not man."

And thus their first interview came to an end and their words had failed to build a bridge of understanding between them. Herodias was unable to fathom his simple thoughts because of their very simplicity. Here was a man who had it within his power to become the guiding star of his people. All he needed to do was to proclaim himself as their Saviour, their Messiah. Thousands were waiting for his signal, ready to break out in revolt against the Romans. He could be another Maccabee, if he so desired. Yet he deliberately withheld the signal, prating foolishly—as it seemed to Herodias—about establishing a mythical Kingdom of Heaven instead of reëstablishing the Jewish kingdom on earth.

Yet for the present she induced her husband to release him. "Let him prate on as loudly as he likes and gather the people about him. As his power grows, I believe he will come to his senses. And then he will listen to our plan for the restoration of our kingdom."

And so Antipas dismissed the prophet—with a promise and a threat. "If you are willing to lead our forces against our Roman oppressors, you shall have the rank and the riches of our commander-in-chief. But if you persist in your silly prattle and especially in calling us unseemly names, we shall be compelled to put an end to your career."

A simple choice for John the Baptist. He persisted in preaching the Kingdom of Heaven and in denouncing his earthly king.

IV

IN THE MEANTIME another preacher had begun to proclaim the Kingdom of Heaven. A young carpenter from the village of Nazareth—Jesus, son of Joseph. This young man had come to John to be baptized. "There was something in that man's eyes . . . like the holy flame in the Temple . . ." John recalled the feeling of reverence with which he, the master, had performed the religious rite for that new disciple of his. "I have need to be baptized of thee," he had said to Jesus with a tender smile, "and thou comest to me?"

John had been thinking a great deal about this young carpenter who had come to him on the single occasion of the baptism. "Pity I can't see more of him." But both of them were so very busy, each in his own sphere. When John heard that the Galilean had begun to baptize and to preach like himself, he sent him, with the affectionate pride of a teacher, several members of his own audience to swell the audience of Jesus. "Go bring him willing ears. It will give him courage to go on."

But before long he received word that Jesus was attracting greater throngs than himself. And he was filled with a sad amazement and at the same time with a sudden hope. "Can it be that this young man of Nazareth is he whom I have been sent to proclaim?"

Little by little this thought grew upon him. As he kept preaching in the wilderness and denouncing the tetrarch and his wife, he knew that his own days were numbered. His work apparently was done, his mission fulfilled. He, John the Baptist, had been sent to pave the way for the Messiah. And now the way was ready and the Messiah was here. The Lord had sent him an unmistakable sign—his own *decreasing* power and the *increasing* power of Jesus. He was now convinced that he had made no mistake about Jesus from the very first. "It *is* he!"

And so he was neither surprised nor dejected when the guards of Antipas came to arrest him. "It is the end for me, but for him it is the beginning."

They took him once more to the fortress of Machaerus. And once more they offered him not only his freedom, but great honors and riches if only he would proclaim himself as the Redeemer and stir the people into a revolt against Rome.

John the Baptist shook his head. "The Redeemer is here in your midst. But I am not the Redeemer."

"You are not by any chance referring to this—what do you call him—this Jesus of Nazareth?"

"It is he," replied John.

Whereupon Antipas and Herodias exploded into laughter. "Jesus a Redeemer? A man who preaches forgiveness? And love? And turns the other cheek when he is struck? How ridiculous to expect *such* a man to lead you to victory!"

But John was obdurate. "He alone knows the way to the Kingdom."

Antipas and Herodias looked upon John with a disdainful smile. There was nothing to be done with this preacher. They were convinced that he was mad.

But his madness, they felt, was dangerous. It would be best for their own peace of mind to have him imprisoned in the cesspool under the fortress of Machaerus. Sealed up for life—a fate reserved for many another Essene preacher whose tongue "prattled too freely about the amusements of his betters."

They sent him down to the cesspool and might have speedily forgotten his existence were it not for another member of the royal household. Salome, the daughter of Herodias, was a proud and passionate and untamed young whelp of a princess who always had her way with the courtiers of the palace. When John the Baptist had been brought into the court, she had smiled upon him seductively. But the prophet had cut her to the quick with his scornful look. "Get thee gone, harlot!" Salome was determined to avenge her wounded pride.

Now it happened shortly after the imprisonment of the prophet that Antipas was celebrating his birthday at Machaerus. "And Salome, the daughter of Herodias, danced before the assembled guests and pleased Antipas. Whereupon he promised with an oath to give her whatever she should ask." And the princess made her request, and her eyes were aflame with a hatred begotten of unfulfilled love. "I ask for the head of John the Baptist."

V

"AND his head was brought on a platter, and given to the princess . . ."

Without knowing it, the guards had set down the platter with the head of the prophet facing toward the Mountain. And down from the Mountain came the voice of him whom John had foretold. "Blessed are they that have been persecuted for righteousness' sake, for of such is the Kingdom of God."

JESUS

Important Events in Life of Jesus

Born in reign of Herod, at Bethlehem, 4 B.C.

At 12, taken by Joseph and Mary to Jerusalem.

Baptized by John.

Commenced ministry after imprisonment of John.

Acquired fame as healer of men.

Adored as Bringer of Peace.

Selected twelve disciples.

Recognized by Peter as the Messiah.

Foretold his arrest and death.

Made preparations for journey to Jerusalem.

Arrived in Jerusalem, "lowly and riding upon an ass."

Aroused enmity of the powerful and the rich.

Partook of Last Supper with disciples. "One of you shall betray me."

Betrayed by kiss of Judas.

Crucified 29 A.D.

Jesus
4 B.C.–29 A.D.

A STRANGE YOUNG MAN appeared in Capernaum—a carpenter of Nazareth by the name of Jesus, son of Joseph. One day, it was reported, this young man was walking by the sea of Galilee when he saw two fishermen, Simon and Andrew, casting their nets. "Come with me," he said, "and I will make you fishers of men." And such was the power of his personality that they immediately left their work and followed him as his disciples.

Wherever he went among the villages of Galilee, he attracted throngs of people who listened to the music of his voice. At Capernaum, a Roman officer came to him and begged him to save his son, who was lying in his bed a helpless paralytic. And Jesus said, "Go to your son. Even as you believe, so be it." And at that very hour—reported the people of Capernaum—the boy was healed.

"This young man possesses divine powers," said the Galilean villagers to one another. "I with my own eyes," said a young boatman, "saw him perform one of his miracles. We were sailing over the Galilean sea. Suddenly a storm arose. We felt sure the boat would capsize. Jesus was asleep as if nothing was the matter.

We were so scared, we woke him up and begged him to save us. 'Don't be afraid,' he said, and then he spoke to the winds. And the winds listened to him and they became calm."

"What sort of a man is this," asked an amazed bystander, "that even the winds and the sea obey him?"

"Some say," whispered another bystander, "that he is the John the Baptist come to life again."

"That's what Herod Antipas believes," remarked a third.

"But I," declared the young boatman, "believe that he is greater than John the Baptist. For my part I am convinced that Jesus of Nazareth is the Messiah."

II

As a child of twelve he already displayed the character of an independent seeker for the truth. When his parents brought him to Jerusalem, he got into an argument with the reactionary rabbis in the Jewish Temple. His inquiring young mind insisted upon distilling the dogmas of tradition through the filter of his reason. "How is it that ye sought me?" he asked when his anxious elders had found him in the Temple. "Knew ye not that I must be engaged in asking questions about my Father?" Strange words from a young child. His elders were used to obeying, not asking. "They understood not," we read in the Gospel according to Luke, "the saying which he spake to them."

What Jesus did during the next eighteen years is not recorded. At the age of thirty, however, we find him leaving his native village and wandering away to the banks of the Jordan where he joins the followers of John the Baptist. John possessed more temper but less tenderness than Jesus. He was interested not so much in saving the repentant as in punishing the unrepentant. Pleasure to him was a sin, and prosperity a disgrace. To seek for happiness in this life was to deserve eternal damnation in the life to come.

This doctrine, austere as it was, at first attracted Jesus. He, too, like John, was a rebel. He, too, hated the conventions and the hypocrisies of the people about him. He was baptized in the Jordan, and became John's leading disciple.

John was arrested, and Jesus was left to himself. For a time he wandered in the wilderness, and tried to project his own thoughts against the silent background of the desert and the sky. Then he came back to his native village, eager to bring his new message to his people.

But he was greeted with stones and with jeers. The prophet had returned to his country and had found all the doors shut in his face. The beasts in the field had their lairs, but the lonely outcast of Nazareth had nowhere to lay his head.

And so he wandered off into the hills of Judea. He gathered about him a group of fishermen and laborers and other unfortunates whom Destiny had cast into the rubbish heap of despair. He brought them the hope of better things. He told them to lay down their burdens and to follow him into a new Kingdom. Together they would go from town to town, and from village to village, and establish everywhere the Kingdom of Heaven on earth.

They were a tempestuous fellowship of comrades. Once, when they were refused the hospitality of a certain village, they wanted to burn it to the ground. But Jesus dissuaded them. They took delight in flouting the moth-eaten traditions of society. If they were accused of "desecrating the Sabbath," they retorted that the Sabbath had been made for the people, and not the people for the Sabbath. They condemned all those who were unwilling to listen to them, calling them *whited sepulchers,* and they prayed to God to destroy them even as He had destroyed the inhabitants of Sodom and Gomorrah. They were the militant radicals of Galilee, and Jesus was their leader. He tried to restrain them if they went too far. But at times he found it difficult to control his indignation at the stupidity and the savagery of men.

[*83*]

Jesus loved children. Wherever he went, they flocked about him and asked him to play with them. We can see his sturdy and sun-tanned figure trudging along the dusty roads of the country, a child perched upon his shoulder, another clinging to his hand, and a whole troop of them trailing after him, all of them gesticulating and shouting and singing the Jewish folk songs of Palestine. The arrival of Jesus in a village was always a holiday for the children. He was the Pied Piper of Nazareth, and they were ready to follow him to the ends of the earth.

He centered all his hopes on his little playmates. Of such was the Kingdom of Heaven. "Whoso shall give to drink to one of these little ones a cup of cold water only . . . he shall in no wise lose his reward." The children understood him. To them there was nothing strange or impossible or fantastic in his fascinating stories about the new Kingdom. He was going to lead them himself into that beautiful land. There would never be any hatred or fighting in it, and never any unhappiness or sickness or death. "There the wisdom of God will be revealed unto babes." As they sat and listened to his stories, their eyes big with wonder and their faces flushed with the excitement of their fancies, he felt that it was these little ones, and not the grownups, who would help him to build a new heaven on earth.

For the grownups were spoiled and no longer fit for the adventure. Each of them was bent upon watching the mote in his neighbor's eye, forgetting the beam within his own eye. Reality had bitten too deeply into their hearts, and the craftiness of a savage world had made them blind to the comradeship of a more gentle world. When he spoke to his adult followers about the Kingdom, they completely misunderstood him. "When we come into your Kingdom," they asked him, "who of us shall sit on your right side, and who on your left?" They too, he saw, were nothing but children—poor, pitiable, irrational children, immature in everything save their grown-up capacity to do evil.

And as he looked upon them and listened to their foolish

words, he began to realize more and more that he was living in a world of children. And realizing this, he was no longer angry with them, but pitied them. This was the turning point of his life. "Come unto me, all ye that labor and are heavy laden, and I will give you rest." His character began to advance rapidly from human maturity to divine mercy. Jesus became a wandering ambassador of good will among men. The prophet who spoke the *Sermon on the Mount* was far removed from the agitator who once called upon God to slay his enemies. Pity them for their ignorance, and teach them that they may know. Bless them that curse you. Heal, like a kindly physician, those who suffer from an evil heart—even if, in the delirium of their sickness, they strike you down when you try to help them.

The *Sermon on the Mount* represents the noblest aspiration of man in his gentlest mood. "Blessed are they that hunger and thirst after righteousness, for they shall be filled." But righteousness alone is not enough. The bread of justice must be seasoned with the manna of mercy. "Blessed are the merciful, for they shall obtain mercy."

In thus releasing the living spirit of mercy from the dead letter of the law, Jesus said that he was but following in the footsteps of the earlier prophets. "Think not that I came to destroy . . . the prophets. I came not to destroy, but to fulfill."

Jesus was opposed to the priestly traditions of the Church—or as it was then called, the Synagogue. Instead, he advanced the prophetic vision of a heavenly Kingdom. Cleanse your temples and your souls. Ring out your old system of rituals. Ring in a new spirit of righteousness. Replace your conventions with convictions. The conviction of justice, of compassion, of lovingkindness, of peace. Away with your assumption of smug superiority to other races and nations. All of us are brothers in a world of sorrow, the interdependent children of our Father in Heaven. "Love yc one another." Cease to oppress one another in your scramble for the so-called "goods" of the earth. There is only one good on earth as in heaven—and that is, a gentle heart. Be gentle not only to your friends, but to your enemies. For what is an enemy but a man with a wounded soul? Soften the bitterness of his wound with the balm of sympathy. "Pray for them that persecute you." Jesus was an expert in the art of harmonious living. He knew that aggression is not only the *cause* but also the *result* of injustice. The tyrant is a man who has been deeply hurt. The oppressor regards himself as an avenger. He avenges injuries done either to himself or to those near to him. Like begets like. The *weed* of hatred can grow only out of the *seed* of hatred. How, asks Jesus, can you expect hatred to be abolished from the earth if you give a man "a stone when he asks for a loaf," or "a serpent when he asks for a fish"?

There is only one way, therefore, in which you can establish the Kingdom of Heaven on earth, concludes Jesus. And here he turns into a positive Golden Truth the negative Golden Rule of Zoroaster, of Confucius and of Hillel. These earlier prophets had said: "All things whatsoever you *would not* that men should do unto you, even so *do not* unto them." But Jesus said: "All things whatsoever you *would* that men should do unto you, *do* likewise unto them." Jesus was the prophet who translated passive justice into active love.

III

WHEN Jesus was arrested, most of his disciples ran away for fear that they too might be captured. Although his enemies clamored for his blood, Jesus—like Socrates—refused to defend himself. Peter drew his sword and tried to rescue him, but Jesus only smiled when he saw this. He had outgrown the silly quarrels of children, with their primitive weapons of iron and steel. He knew that a victory gained by the sword is only a prelude to another fight. "Put up your sword," he said to the astonished Peter. "For they that take the sword shall perish by the sword."

These words of Jesus, spoken in the presence of the Roman

soldiers, were prophetic. For the Romans, though they were then in the midst of their triumphant march of conquest, were marching steadily to their death. But they paid no attention to Jesus. Pilate passed sentence upon him and ordered him to be nailed, in accordance with the Roman custom, to a wooden cross.

Together with Jesus the Romans crucified two robbers, one on either side of him. In their agony the other two cursed, but Jesus forgave.

IV

JESUS was rejected by his townsmen, deserted by his friends, crucified by his enemies, and misinterpreted by many of his followers. He was a simple, unpretentious soul. "I am meek and lowly in heart." He despised pomposities and ceremonies and stuffy houses of prayer. His church was the open country; his altar, a rock by the wayside; his surplice, a rough and travel-torn tunic; and his choir, a host of Galilean workingmen singing the songs of their native land. Were he among us today, he would be aghast at the intolerances, the hatreds, the persecutions and the crimes that have been perpetrated in his name. Once more he would ask us to listen to his words of wisdom—words as tragically necessary today as they were nineteen hundred years ago. "Lay not up for yourselves treasures upon earth, where moth and rust consume, and where thieves dig through and steal. For where thy treasure is, there will thy heart be also." It is this lusting after the worthless material prizes—he would remind us—this exploiting of man for the profit of his fellowman, this cruel, competitive, life-and-death scramble after the perishable treasures of the earth, which have sent the nations reeling to their destruction in a series of world revolutions and wars. If only the world, having *heard* the words of Jesus, would begin to *heed* them! "Every one who heareth these words of mine, and doeth them, shall be likened to a wise man, who built his house upon the rock. And the rain descended, and the floods came, and the winds blew, and beat upon that house; and it fell not, for it was founded upon the rock. And every one who heareth these words of mine, and doeth them not, shall be likened to a foolish man, who built his house upon the sand. And the rain descended, and the floods came, and the winds blew, and smote upon that house; and it fell, and great was the fall thereof."

Too many men and too many nations have built their ethical and their political houses upon the shifting sands. "Hearken to my words, *and do them*." The greatest of Christ's teachings is yet to be fulfilled: the building of a temple of world peace upon a foundation of fair play. It is for this purpose that "the Lord appointed him" to work among the stubborn children of the human family. "Lo, my servant whom I have chosen; my beloved in whom my soul is well pleased. I will put my spirit upon him, and he shall declare judgment to the nations . . . *till he send forth justice unto victory, and in his name shall the nations hope.*"

From justice to hope; from hope to understanding; from understanding to peace.

SAINT PAUL

Important Events in Life of Saint Paul

Born at Tarus, 2 A.D.

Learned trade of tentmaking.

Sent to Jerusalem for rabbinical education.

Took leading part in persecution of Christians.

Started for Damascus to act against Christians in that city.

Beheld vision of Christ just before arrival in Damascus. "Saul, Saul, why persecutest thou me?"

Entered Damascus to proclaim Jesus as the Messiah.

Encountered persecution himself at Damascus.

Escaped to Arabia.

Meditated for 3 years.

Returned to Jerusalem. Guest at Peter's house.

Went on mission to Syria and Cilicia.

Started from Antioch, with Barnabas, to preach Christianity to Gentiles as well as to Jews.

Traveled, "on the Lord's business," through Asia Minor and Europe.

Narrowly escaped death on several occasions.

Arrested, sent to Roman governor, Felix, at Caesarea.

Appealed to Roman emperor.

Shipwrecked on way to Rome.

Arrived in Rome safely.

Died 67 A.D.

Saint Paul

2 A.D.–67 A.D.

HIS NAME WAS SAUL. But his parents affectionately called him Paul, the Little One—the Greek nickname for the "runt" of the family. Little Saul was not only the smallest but the brightest of the children in the family of the rich Galilean Pharisee—a member of the Jewish "Interpreters of the Law." Born in the city of Tarsus, the wool-trading center of the ancient world, the child was brought up with an understanding not only of the "will of the Lord," but of the ways of men. His education was strictly Jewish, with a leavening of Greek literature and of Greek philosophy. At fifteen, in accordance with the injunction of the Jewish teachers, he was sent to "study doctrine" at the Rabbinical College in Jerusalem. But before his matriculation at the college, he had learned the trade of cloth-weaving. This, too, was in accordance with the injunction of the Jewish teachers. "He who does not teach his son a trade teaches him robbery."

When he graduated from the college he was ready, like the rest of his classmates, to "employ his hands for his livelihood and his head for the free instruction of the law."

And he was a strict adherent of his Biblical law. He fasted

regularly, carried no bundles on the Sabbath, washed his hands and scoured his dishes—"the Pharisees," laughed their Sadducee rivals, "would scour the sun itself if they could"—and meticulously observed every one of the 248 prescriptions and 365 prohibitions of the Mosaic Code.

And he insisted that his neighbors must observe these prescriptions and prohibitions as rigidly as himself. He regarded it as part of his duty to hate those who offended God. He believed that the most grievous offenders against God were the "Jewish Christians," and he made it his business to take an active part in their persecution. "Many of the saints did I shut up in prison, and when they were put to death, I gave my voice against them." On one occasion he watched the stoning of a Christian by the name of Stephen. Far from feeling pity at this tragic spectacle, he was "fired with a zeal" to stone the entire sect out of existence. With this object in view, he set out on his mission of hatred to the city of Damascus.

On this journey something happened to Paul. Renan calls it "an attack of ophthalmia." Paul himself regarded it as "a vision of light." Whatever it was, whether we characterize it by a scientific or a supernatural name, it produced a miraculous transformation in his character. It transformed a man of hate into a man of love.

But let Paul himself tell us about this vision. "And it came to pass, as I made my journey and drew nigh to Damascus, about noon, suddenly a great light shone from the heaven round about me. And I fell unto the ground, and heard a voice saying to me, Saul, Saul, why persecutest thou me? And I answered, Who art thou, Lord? And he said unto me, I am Jesus of Nazareth . . . And they that were with me beheld indeed the light, but they heard not the voice of him that spake to me. And I said, What shall I do, Lord? And the Lord said, Arise, and go into Damascus; and there it shall be told thee of all things which are appointed for thee to do . . . And when I could not look up for the glory of that light, being led by the hand of those with me I came into Damascus . . ."

Paul had started for Damascus to persecute. He arrived there to bless.

II

THERE IS an old cynical proverb in the Orient. "Why do you hate me? Have I ever done you a kindness?" The moment that Paul ceased to persecute, he began to be persecuted. First of all, he tells us, "I suffered the loss of things." But before long he came near to suffering the loss of his life. The fanatics "took counsel to kill him . . . and watched the gates (of Damascus) by day and night." It was only through a clever ruse that he managed to escape—his friends lowered him over the city wall in a basket.

And then began a voluntary life of exile. He gave up his purse for a crown of thorns. Like the Apostles, he became a peddler of peace—an unprofitable commodity for which he was repaid with cuffs and with stones. Even the Apostles were at first inclined to distrust him. All they knew about him was that he had been one of their principal oppressors. They were skeptical about his conversion. "Perhaps he is a spy? Who knows?"

And so for a time, shunned both by the Jews and by the Gentiles, he remained a voice unheard. And a body wracked with torture. In the course of his wanderings he had contracted a "thorn in the flesh"—a chronic case of malaria, it seems—and throughout his missionary work he was unable to rid himself of his physical suffering. Again and again, in his despondency, he thought of laying down his burden for "braver and sturdier" shoulders. But always at such moments he remembered the words he had heard in his vision. He must stick to his dedicated business—to carry out, with patience and without complaint, "all things which are appointed for thee to do." And he resolved to go on.

In this resolution he found encouragement from two sources— the Apostle Peter, and the cloth merchant Barnabas.

Peter was the first of the Apostles to accept Paul into his heart and his home. "The man is no spy. He is a true disciple of the Lord." He invited Paul to spend a fortnight with him—a period in which the two friends exchanged many an idea about Jesus. And indulged perhaps in not a few arguments. For both of them were quick-tempered and disputatious—and lovable for all that. His contact with Peter inspired Paul with a belief in the simple goodness of the human heart.

So, too, did his contact with Barnabas. This encourager of men—*Barnabas* means the *son of consolation*—gave up, like Paul himself, a profitable career in order to preach the word. Or, rather, to embolden Paul to preach it. He himself was a man of action rather than of words. Jovial, fearless and unvexed, this fatherly old man with the strong beard and the hearty face was keeping "the brethren" supplied with money and with hope. He first met Paul at Tarsus, whither he had gone of his own accord "for to seek" him. He was captivated by the slender young man of the eloquent voice who jestingly referred to himself as a "rabbi without a congregation." He urged Paul to "seek" his congregation from land to land. "If our Jews will not listen to you, then go among the Gentiles."

Paul took to heart the advice of the older man. It was a daring and dazzling idea—this plan to take "the word" out of its tribal confines and to spread it among all the nations of the earth. "I will do as you say," he said to Barnabas.

And thus "the word of God grew."

III

TOGETHER the younger and the older man set out for Antioch (45 A.D.). Nestled between Mount Silvius and the Orontes River, this "Queen of the East" was a jewel-box of statues and palaces and cataracts and parks. The boulevard that ran for two miles across the center of the city was paved with "dazzling white marble—a fit thoroughfare for the footsteps of the gods." It was into this stronghold of the pagan gods that the exiled Jew came to create a new religion.

For it was in Antioch that Christianity was born. Prior to Paul's arrival in that city, the followers of Jesus had formed but another of the many Jewish sects. They revered the Jewish prophets, they obeyed the Jewish law—"I came not to destroy the law," Jesus had declared, "but to fulfill"—and they observed the Jewish holidays. They had no separate church, but like the rest of the Jews forgathered in the synagogues. The word *Christianity* had not as yet been invented. The disciples of the "Nazarene Prophet" merely called their revolutionary doctrine *The Way*.

This was the situation for a number of years after the death of Jesus, until one day "the disciples were named Christians in Antioch." The term *Christian* is the Greek translation for the Hebrew word *Messianist*—that is, a follower of The Anointed. But for a time even after they had received their new name, the Christians adhered to their old religion. "To be a Christian, you must first be a Jew."

And then came Paul of Tarsus and built a new temple to fit the new name. Christianity, he declared, is no longer a religion for the Jews alone, but for the Gentiles as well. (*Gentiles* is a Latin word which means *the nations of the world*.) And in order to make it easy for the non-Jewish nations, with their lax pagan practices, to adapt themselves to the new religion, he removed from it all the prescriptions and the prohibitions of the old orthodox Judaism. In their place he substituted just one requisite for salvation—faith in the divinity of Christ. "Therefore we conclude that a man is justified by faith without the deeds of the law."

It was a bold stroke of genius. For the human mind is ever on the search for the simple road to freedom. Christianity became popular among the Gentiles. Yet before long they discovered that their road was not so simple as they had anticipated. "The old gods are jealous when the new gods arrive." The pagan rulers of the world, especially the Roman Caesars, were incensed at these new "apostates from the ways of their fathers." They were determined to burn them out of the world upon the wooden cross. The roads of the Roman empire became lighted up with human torches. It was by the light of these torches that Paul made his way from city to city, intent upon the business of "Jesus, the Son of God." To his original principle of faith, he now found it necessary to add two more principles—hope and love. His wisdom had grown with his suffering. His temple of Christianity was now built upon three cornerstones. "And the greatest of these," he wrote (in his First Epistle to the Corinthians), "is love."

IV

PAUL was one of those rare individuals who translated passive love into active charity. He devoted his life not only to the preaching of the word but to the organizing of relief funds for the poor. Wherever he came among the Christians, he was doubly welcome. For he brought to them a double blessing— food for their body and manna for their soul.

But in the non-Christian communities it was another story. The pagan world, accustomed to its multiplicity of gods, couldn't make up its mind as to just how to receive him. One day, together with Barnabas, he arrived at Lystra—a village tucked away within the folds of Kara-Dagh, the Black Mountain. It was here, according to the Greek legend, that the two pagan gods, Jupiter and Mercury, had once paid an earthly visit to Philemon and Baucis. As Barnabas and Paul walked down the village street, the awe-struck inhabitants stared upon the two strangers —the one with the flowing white beard, and the other with the lithe and graceful figure. That evening, Paul preached to them the "glad tidings—how that the promise which was made unto the fathers, God has fulfilled." Again the inhabitants stared, and with even greater awe. The next morning, Paul was awakened by a loud singing and shouting. The people had come to his lodging with a garlanded bull prepared for the sacrifice.

"For whom is your sacrifice intended?"

"For you, and you," replied the spokesman of the people, as he pointed to Barnabas and to Paul. "For verily we believe that you two are Jupiter and Mercury come back to earth."

Paul explained to the people that he and Barnabas were not gods but men. "We have come amongst you to turn you away from the licentious pagan gods to the Christian God of love."

Having spoken these words, Paul returned to his lodging. But not to his rest. If this stranger was not a god, concluded the inhabitants of Lystra, then he must be a blasphemer. And so they dragged him out of his lodging "and stoned him in the street and carried him down the mountain into a field."

They left him for dead. But Paul was possessed of a supreme vitality. And a supreme courage. "As the disciples stood round about him," Saint Luke tells us, "he rose up and came back into the village."

And this time the people listened to him and understood him for what he was—a man who was ready "to lay down his life for the truth."

V

THE TRUTH, as Saint Paul envisioned it, embraces a threefold spiritual reality—the fatherhood of God, the sonhood of Jesus, and the brotherhood of man.

God, declared Paul, is the single God of the Jewish prophets, the Father of the human race. "To us there is one God, the Father, of whom are all things, and through whom are all things." Sixteen hundred years after the declaration of this Pauline creed, we find the same conception of the Godhead expressed in the philosophy of Spinoza. "I hold," writes this Jewish pantheist, "that God is the immanent . . . cause of all things. I say, All is God; all moves and lives in God. And this I maintain with the Apostle Paul."

Paul believed in God the Father, and in Jesus the Son. Jesus, maintained Paul, is not only the Son of God, but the Revealer of God to mankind. A revealer of God's mercy through his own suffering. Saint Paul, like the ancient Hebrews, believed in sacrifice—but of a different sort. Instead of man sacrificing himself for God (as in the story of Isaac), God sacrificed himself for man. In the Old Testament, man comes occasionally face to face with God. In the New Testament, God comes for a divine season face to face with man. And in thus bringing himself down to the level of mankind, Jesus brings mankind up to the level of God.

For only through Jesus, asserted Paul, can man know his relationship to God—and to his fellowman. "All men are brothers in the fatherhood of God." Paul was one of the first genuine democrats in the history of the world. He believed in the spiritual democracy of fraternal good will. All humanity is one family—nay, one organic unit of life. "For just as there are many parts united in our human bodies . . . so we form one body through union with Christ, and we are individually parts of one another." Therefore, urged Paul, "serve the Lord" by serving your fellows . . . "be unfailing in hospitality . . . live in harmony with one another . . . and peaceably with all mankind." In this injunction to the peaceful relationship of the human family, Saint Paul included not only the Christians but all men—Jews and Gentiles alike. "My heart's desire and supplication . . . is for them all, that they be saved . . . For (in the eyes of the Lord) there is no distinction between Jew and Gentile . . . he is the same Lord of all . . ."

Paul declared that all of us, believers and unbelievers alike, are the human brothers of the divine Son of God. Jesus sacrificed Himself for all mankind. And it was for the sake of all mankind that He revealed Himself after His crucifixion. His resurrection after His death was meant as a proof to the world that there is a resurrection after *every* death. There *is* no death.

The belief in immortality was one of the cardinal principles in the Pauline creed. At the beginning of his mission he had felt certain that nobody was going to die. The Kingdom of Heaven, he declared, was actually at hand. But as time went on and he saw his comrades burned and crucified and stoned, he stopped preaching an endless life this side of the grave and began to look forward to a life beyond. All men must die, but death is only a transition from one stage of life to another.

He explained this doctrine in his letters to his disciples. He began with an analogy between the human body and the seed of a plant. The seed must rot in the earth that the plant may grow above. "That which thou sowest is not quickened, unless it die. And that which thou sowest, thou sowest not the body which shall be, but bare grain . . ." Let us therefore not despair when we see the "bare grain" of the body lying lifeless on the ground. For man has not only a *natural* body but a *spiritual* body. The body of flesh and blood dies, but the body of the spirit flowers into immortal beauty. Every death means a resurrection to a more perfect life. The old life is "sown in corruption, and is raised in incorruption; it is sown in dishonor, it is raised in glory; it is sown in weakness, it is raised in power; it is sown in a body . . . (which) is of the earth, earthy; it is raised in a body . . . (which) is from heaven, heavenly . . ."

This, then, is the hope that Saint Paul holds out to every son of man in his immortal brotherhood to the Son of God. "O death, where is thy sting? O grave, where is thy victory?"

VI

AND thus armed with the armor of the spirit against the fear of death, Saint Paul went on with his mission. The common folk everywhere listened to him and were comforted. But the misleaders of men—those who had turned their religion into a career for personal profit—were afraid of him and persecuted him. For he repeatedly and relentlessly exposed their dishonest aims. His eloquent tongue could not only soothe but scorch. "Behold the truth, ye despisers, and wonder, and perish." He was not always able to control his hasty temper. Like Jeremiah and Jesus before him, he walked into the very Temple to denounce the priests to their faces. They arrested him and sent him for trial to Felix, the Roman governor of Judea—a man who, in the words of the ancient historian Tacitus, "exercised the authority of a king with the spirit of a slave."

Paul stood before Felix, not as a prisoner stands before his judge but as a master stands before his pupil. "Felix," writes Saint Luke, "was terrified" at the words of this bold Christian. He would have been pleased to hand him over to his soldiers for a flogging. But Paul knew his legal rights. "It is not lawful for you to flog a man who is a Roman citizen, and uncondemned."

And then he went on to explain to Felix that he was guilty of no crime save that of comforting his Christians and of collecting funds for their physical needs.

At the phrase "collecting funds" the governor pricked up his ears. This man might become a source of profit for himself. Perhaps he might be able to induce Paul to *buy* his freedom. At any rate he would try.

And so he put the Apostle into "light custody"—*liberam custodiam*. He allowed him the freedom to move around within the city (of Caesarea), to converse with his friends, and even to visit him at his castle. But he did not allow Paul to leave the city. In this way he hoped to keep this "collector of funds" within reach and to persuade him finally to open his purse. Again and again he invited Paul for a "friendly" chat. But all he could get him to speak about, Luke tells us, was "righteousness, temperance, and the judgment to come."

For two years the elderly Apostle remained confined within the city. And then a new ruler came to Judea—and a new hope to Paul. As a Roman citizen he had a right to appeal for a retrial before the Roman emperor. Felix had repeatedly denied him this appeal. But here was another chance with another man. Paul asked for an audience with the new governor, Festus, and once more presented his plea. *"Appello Caesarem*—I call upon Caesar to try me."

"Very well," said Festus, a far more liberal man than his predecessor, "to Caesar thou shalt go."

VII

IT WAS on his journey to Rome that the Apostle arrived at the climax of his tempestuous life. After the ship had "sailed slowly for many days"—the story is graphically told in the language of Saint Luke—"there came down a storm of wind." For many days they sailed under the lashing northeaster, "when neither sun nor stars shone upon us, and all hope that we should be saved was now taken away." Throughout this period of suspense, there was but a single cheering voice. "Fear not," said Paul, "our ship may sink but our lives shall be saved." He had foreseen this outcome, he said, in a divine vision.

And sure enough, they lost their ship but not their lives. In the supreme hour of their peril, when the seas had begun to break up the stern, the Apostle took command of the crew. He always made it his business to lead in a crisis. First of all he ordered the men to partake of food. For they had fasted a long time and they needed strength for the coming ordeal. And then, when they had refreshed themselves, he "commanded that they who could swim should cast themselves overboard, and get first to the land; and the rest, some on planks and others on bits of wreckage from the ship. And so it came to pass, that they all escaped safe to the land."

Then, finally, the calm after the storm. The higher court of

Rome acquitted him of all political charges and allowed him to live in peace. "And Paul dwelt two whole years in his own hired house"—again we are quoting Saint Luke—"and received all that came in unto him; preaching the Kingdom of God and teaching those things which concern the Lord Jesus Christ with all confidence, no man forbidding him." He wrote his letters of comfort to his disciples, and in return received from them all sorts of "gifts"—trifling tokens of affection, things of little cost but great value. "What is there more precious than the tender regard of friend for friend?"

There is no substantial evidence for the belief, entertained by some of his biographers, that Paul died a martyr's death. In one of his last letters (to the Philippians), he wrote that he was unmolested while he made converts "in the palace." It was in this business of "making converts" that he ended his days. And it was with a smile of contented relief that he finally laid down the burden. "I have fought the good fight, I have finished the course, I have kept the faith."

MOHAMMED

Important Events in Life of Mohammed

570—Born in Mecca, Arabia.
570—Lost father.
576—Lost mother.
595—Hired as caravan salesman by wealthy widow, Khadija.
595—Married Khadija.
610—Beheld vision of God.
613—Launched new religion.
619—Lost Khadija.
619—Lost leading disciple, Abu Bekr.
622—Fled from Mecca to Medina.
627—Won victory over Abu Sofian at Medina.
630—Marched against Mecca and conquered it.
632—June 7, died.

Mohammed

570–632

Religions generally grow in hot soil. God walks among the
primitive peoples in the Orient and touches their brow with the
fire of His presence so that they see the vision and bring it westward to Europe. But not infrequently, when the eastern message
reaches the colder regions of the west, it loses the tenderness of
poetry and becomes hardened into the dry dogma of sectarian-
ism. For the peoples of the west are the citizens of science and of
subtle disputation. They are clever only with their hands and
their heads. They have not as yet grown up to the wisdom of the
heart.

In the seventh century, when the world seemed dry, when
Judaism had lost the home of its birth and Christianity had
undergone a series of admixtures with Roman and with barbarian blood, a new fountain of pure faith welled suddenly out of
the Orient and gave drink to the thirst of half the world. But
God's ways are of powerful irony. For this new faith sprang from
the driest scrap of land among the acres of the divine—the desert
of Arabia.

II

ARABIA was a land of elemental contrasts. The blazing heat of the day pressed forward against the cooling dews of the night. The sand tides of the desert dashed against the island oases of fertility. And this contradictory plan of the tides was to be found not only in the external world of the Arabian landscape but in the internal world of the Arabian character. In olden times the Arab blood boiled to shed a neighbor's blood in a family feud, yet at the same time it yearned to defend the life of the stranger. The Arab heart was divided against itself—furious and impulsive, yet it was filled with poetry and song. The Arab head was cluttered with idols of stone—and enlightened with wisdom and humor. The food of the land included milk and honey to wash down the dry, sandpapery dates. The palm trees looked brittle and unreal, like the skeletons of prehistoric things; yet when you came near, they gave out their living breath in shade.

This was the paradoxical world into which Mohammed was born. His native city, Mecca, had an interesting history even before the birth of the Prophet. It was built around the sacred well of Zem-zem—the name is derived from the gurgling sound of the water—where Hagar, the wife of Abraham, was said to have stopped for rest from her wandering over the desert with her little son Ishmael. Near the well there is a holy black stone, a meteorite fallen from the sky—which the Arabians regarded as another sign that the spot was consecrated to the gods. Around this stone and near the well of Zem-zem the ancient Arabians had built a temple, which they called the Caaba. Here a host of pilgrims from all over the desert came to worship every year, until finally the flourishing town of Mecca grew up around the temple. The pilgrims held contests in poetry and offered up prayers and sacrifices to the black stone, the sacred well, and the wooden idols that represented the stars, or the "divine daughters" of heaven. The Caaba was guarded by a number of officers chosen out of a special clan, called the Koreish, who lived in the holy city of Mecca.

Mohammed was born into the Koreish clan, the appointed guardians of the Caaba. In the year of his birth, A.D. 570, an Abyssinian army invaded Mecca. This army was accompanied by an elephant—the first one ever seen in that part of Arabia. Hence the year 570 came to be known as "the year of the elephant."

According to some of the early writers, the invading army was miraculously destroyed. A flock of birds with stones in their beaks, they declared, swooped down upon the soldiers and dropped the stones on their heads. The more sophisticated writers of modern times, however, have ascribed the defeat of the invading army to an epidemic of smallpox.

Tradition relates other miracles attending the birth and infancy of Mohammed. His father, it was said, was prepared for the child's arrival by a draught from a sacred stream. The stream suddenly appeared in the region of Mount Ararat, and just as suddenly disappeared after the father had taken the drink. At the moment the child was born, idols in the temples of Arabia toppled to the ground, thrones were overturned, kings lost their power of speech, and sorcerers were deprived of their magic skill.

Mohammed himself, it must be noted, never acknowledged these or any other miracles attributed to his person or his mission. "There is only one miracle to which I bear witness," he said, "and that is the Koran, God's revelation to mankind."

His father died shortly before Mohammed was born, and his mother died when the boy was six. He was given into the custody of his grandfather, who was a hundred years old. Two years later the grandfather "went abroad to heaven," and Mohammed was transferred to the care of his uncle, Abu Taleb. This man, a successful caravan trader, taught Mohammed to fear the gods and to respect all mankind.

Mohammed had no book learning, but he became adept in the interpretation of the Book of Nature—the ways of the camel and the horse, the signs of a coming sandstorm, and the flaming syllables of the stars.

His uncle took him along on his trading journeys and tried to make a good businessman out of him. But Mohammed, a sensitive and poetic young dreamer, had a heart for other things. As he rode with the bearded tradesmen along the shores of Syria and Egypt, his eyes lit up at the spectacle of the sea waves taking up the task of the desert where the sand waves had left off—the selfsame restless commotion of the winds and the tides. He mingled among the world markets and observed the assorted members of the human family—people of different cheekbones and interests and colors and backgrounds and creeds. His horizon had become widened to the largeness and variety and diversified power of the world. It was evident that the eyeless idols at Mecca hadn't created *this* world. His people back home were not worshiping the true power of creation. Among the smells and the sounds and the sweat of life's endless caravan the vigor of a true God began to assert itself in Mohammed.

But mostly he enjoyed the quiet hot hours when he stayed away from his trips and watched the flocks on the hillsides. It was like playing with divine fire through the fingertips of your soul— this ability to stretch out on your back with your face and your heart and your senses reaching upward toward the sky.

At his uncle's recommendation, he became a caravan manager for Kadijah—a wealthy, brilliant, and beautiful widow of forty. Like Mohammed, she was deeply religious. She found it interesting to engage him in conversation. He was a man of little schooling but great depth of thought. As he talked, she liked to watch the mobility of his handsome features, which changed with every changing emotion. Now his face would glow with a happy idea, now it would be suffused with the peace of quiet meditation, and now suddenly it would flare up with a righteous anger. He was as restless as the wind. Tall, quick, graceful, a good rider as well as a good talker, he was a man after her own heart. A just, rigorous, practical, demanding leader of the Bedouins. Yet a thoughtful, melancholy, and gentle dreamer—a poet whose voice was like the music of the sacred well and whose moods were unfathomable, like the bottomless depths of its waters.

Kadijah fell in love with Mohammed and married him. There was a difference of fifteen years in their ages—Mohammed was twenty-five at the time. But it was an ageless union of two harmonious hearts.

Their marriage was supremely happy. Mohammed attended to Kadijah's business, and Kadijah ministered to Mohammed's comfort. Once a year, in the holy month of Ramadan, he retired, after the Arabian fashion, into a cave near his native city, and for thirty days and nights he meditated upon the meaning of life. Sitting at the mouth of the cavern and gazing at the expanse of the sand and the sky, he tried to find a solution to the three perplexing questions of the ages: "Who am I? What am I destined for? And what must I do in order to attain this destiny?" But the sky hung over the earth like a heavy tent, for Allah was not yet ready to draw aside the curtain and answer.

III

ONE DAY, however, when Mohammed was in his fortieth year, he returned from his meditations in the cave and told Kadijah that heaven had at last replied to his questions. Gabriel, the angel of Allah, had told him that the idols of the nation were nothing but pieces of wood and stone and that Allah alone was supreme— Allah Akbar. This God of Mohammed was not a new divinity but the Eloha of the Old Testament revealed to Mohammed in a new light.

He spoke of his vision to Kadijah and she replied: "I believe that whatever thou sayest is true."

He also spoke of his vision to his uncle, Abu Taleb, who advised him to keep his revolutionary thoughts to himself. But Mohammed retorted that "if the sun stood on his right hand and the moon on his left, ordering him to hold his peace, he could not obey." And, having said this, he burst into tears.

He kept on speaking about his revelation in spite of his uncle's warning. And a few listened—his young cousin, Ali, the son of Abu Taleb; a slave by the name of Zeid; Abu Bekr, a well-to-do merchant of Mecca; and a handful of others. But for a time the rest of the people laughed at him. To deny the power of the idols and to deprive them of their sacrifices was, in the eyes of the masses, the highest kind of blasphemy. They looked upon Mohammed as a harmless lunatic. Most of the leaders of the city avoided him, and the children ran after him and pelted him with stones.

But, in spite of all their ridicule, Mohammed insisted that Allah still spoke to him through His interpreter, Gabriel. In the silence of the night the Voice came to him, he said, and soothed him with songs of comfort and with words of wisdom. "By the brightness of the morn that rises, and by the darkness of the night that descends, thy God hath not forsaken thee, Mohammed. For know that there is a life beyond the grave, and it will be better for thee than thy present life; and thy Lord will give thee a rich reward. Did He not find thee an orphan, and did He not care for thee? Did He not find thee wandering in error, and hath He not guided thee to truth? Did He not find thee needy, and hath He not enriched thee? Wherefore oppress not the orphan, neither repulse the beggar, but declare the goodness of the Lord."

It was the old religion of Abraham, of Moses, and of Christ that Mohammed tried to introduce into Arabia under a new name. The new-old religion of charity, of compassion, of gentleness, and of love. And of hopeful resignation. It was the religion of *Islam*—the joy of submitting to the will and the wisdom of Allah, since His will is the ocean in which our human desires are but drops of water, and His wisdom is the sun which puts to shame the murky flickerings of our mortal thoughts. Let us glory in the sun's light and warmth and power to give life and beauty to the earth, but let us not dare to look into its face lest in our folly we go blind. Let us cheerfully and without question accept our destiny, whatever it may be, for it is a necessary thread in the weaving of Allah's plan. Allah knows best, and he who worships Allah and loves his fellow men *lives* best.

Mohammed himself was an ardent lover of his fellow men. His habits were simple. He lived on barley bread and water; and, in spite of his wealth, he waited upon himself. He refused to strike or even to upbraid anyone. When he was asked on a certain occasion why he did not curse his enemies, he replied, "I have not been sent to curse, but to be a mercy to mankind." He reproached himself for having been unkind to a beggar who had asked for alms. He preached the gospel of Allah the Compassionate.

And so he went among the people and proclaimed to them: "There is no God but Allah, and Mohammed is His prophet."

Little by little the religion made headway. His disciples gathered in Mohammed's house and greeted one another with the phrase, "Peace unto you"—the watchword of a new faith and a new hope. But as Mohammed gained more followers, he encountered greater opposition. It was now an open struggle between the old and the new.

For some time Mohammed tried to meet hatred with love. Religion, he declared, was to come quietly into the human heart. "Use no violence against anyone. For all the creatures of God are members of one family. And he is the most beloved of God who shows the greatest love to all of God's creatures."

The idol worshipers of Mecca, however, were moved neither

by the words nor by the acts of Mohammed. All they could see in him was a dangerous iconoclast—a breaker of their favorite images and their pet prejudices and traditions. They tortured some of his followers to death and sent others to a concentration camp—a narrow enclosure east of Mecca. At first they refrained from imprisoning Mohammed himself. His relationship to the aristocratic Koreish clan protected him from the fury of his enemies. But in the end, as he continued his denunciations against the "stupid worship of sticks and stones," his enemies became more emboldened. They began to threaten the liberty and even the life of Mohammed.

Just then deliverance came from an unexpected oasis in the desert—the city of Medina, some two hundred miles to the north of Mecca. In that city the people had been engaged in a religious controversy. The Hebrew believers had been trying to impress upon the Arabian idolaters the idea of One God and His Messiah. One day a number of Arabs from Medina who had made a pilgrimage to Mecca overheard Mohammed on a street corner. He was telling his followers about Allah Akbar and his prophet Mohammed. This talk seemed to re-echo the religious belief of the Hebrews. Perhaps this Mohammed was the very Messiah whose coming had been announced by the followers of Jehovah. They listened to Mohammed and, impressed by his message, invited him to come to Medina.

It was high time for Mohammed to depart from Mecca. His wife, Kadijah, and his uncle, Abu Taleb, were dead. Mohammed himself was now a hunted man. Forty of the leading people in Arabia, one from each tribe, had sworn to take his life. And thus in 622, the thirteenth year of his mission, he fled to Medina. Mohammed was fifty-two at the time.

The flight to Medina, known to history as the *Hegira,* marks the beginning of the Muslim era.

IV

THUS FAR Mohammed had tried to establish his new religion by peaceful means alone. "Better than fasting, alms, and prayers is the making of peace between man and man." But after the years of persecution against himself and his followers, he decided to meet force with force. Some of the historians believe that this was a mistake on his part. As they see it, his final reliance upon the sword disfigures an otherwise superb character. But even some devout Christians, like Thomas Carlyle, excuse his final resort to armed resistance. He was, in the words of Carlyle, "one man against a nation." In order to save himself and his disciples, and—what was even more important—in order to establish "his heaven-sent message, the deep cry of his heart," Mohammed "resolved to defend himself, like a man and Arab." And—let it be remembered—the Christians, too, have relied at times upon the sword. "Charlemagne's conversion of the Saxons," as Carlyle reminds us, "was not by preaching." The early Hebrews likewise proclaimed their new religion in Canaan at the point of the sword.

But whatever we may think about the moral justification for Mohammed's Jehad—or Holy War—we can have nothing but admiration for his spiritual message. "The best of all Jehads is the Holy War for the conquest of one's self."

It was after his flight to Mecca that Mohammed dictated his sublime message known to the world as the Koran (the Book-of-Things-to-be-Read). The Prophet's revelations, as included in the Koran, were transcribed by his followers just as they heard them from their Master. He revealed his inspiration to them bit by bit, and they jotted it down on whatever happened to be lying at hand—a scrap of parchment, a date leaf, the shoulder blade of a sheep, or a smooth white pebble. But these fragments, when collected, produced a miracle of beauty, just as the cells of a body are collected to produce a miracle of life.

Mohammed himself, however, did not pretend to perform miracles. "I am a public preacher," he said, "and not a magician." The world, as he saw it, contains but a single supreme work of magic—the creative plan of Allah.

And all this wonderful Creation is based upon a divine law—"that we must have compassion upon one another."

The word "compassion" lies at the very heart of Mohammed's teaching. Again and again we find in the Moslem tradition such sentiments as the following:

"Feed the hungry and visit the sick, and free the captive, if he be unjustly confined. Assist any person oppressed, whether Moslem or non-Moslem."

"When the bier of anyone—whether Jew, Christian, or Mohammedan—passes you, rise to your feet."

"The greatest enemies of God are those who without cause shed the blood of man."

"What actions are most excellent? To gladden the heart of a human being, to feed the hungry, to help the afflicted, to lighten the sorrow of the sorrowful, and to remove the wrongs of the injured."

One of the finest things in the teaching of Mohammed is his injunction for every man to set apart a certain percentage of his annual income as the property of the poor. Referring to this "social consciousness" of Mohammed, Bernard Shaw declared: "I believe that if a man like him were to assume the dictatorship of the modern world, he would succeed in bringing it much needed peace and tranquillity."

V

"IN HEAVEN," said Mohammed, "all grudges shall be taken away out of your hearts." There will be no quarrels in the life to come, since there is heaven enough for all.

In other words, there is no inequality in heaven, and there should be none on earth. The religion preached by Mohammed was a democratic faith. Every man, whether master or servant, was equal in the eyes of Allah. Mohammed insisted that there was to be no ecclesiastical hierarchy in the Moslem Church. Every man was his own priest and confessor when he knelt in prayer and received the light of Allah into his heart. When Mohammed returned in triumph to Mecca and the populace assembled for the first prayer under their new faith, he delegated a Negro slave to lead the worship. "For all Moslems are the children of Allah, and among them there is no distinction of race or color or tribe."

Mohammed was profoundly gentle to all those who came to him for advice. There is a story that an ugly old woman came forward daily after his preaching and threw herself at his feet, imploring him to reserve a place for her in heaven. One day, tired from his heavy burdens and somewhat annoyed at her continual prattle, he said: "There is no place in heaven for repulsive hags." But seeing the pain in her face, he broke into a compassionate smile. "For at the threshold of heaven, all repulsive old women are changed into beautiful young maidens."

And yet, he declared, heaven could not be had for the mere asking. He insisted upon a regulation of abstinence and prayer— a rigid social contract between God and man. Five times a day the Moslem must turn toward Mecca in holy prayer to Allah. He must pray wherever he happens to be at the moment. "Every spot for divine service is equally pure." This precise number of five daily prayers, declared Mohammed, "has been fixed by the solemn will of Allah." One night, said the Prophet, the archangel Gabriel had taken him out of his bed and transported him to heaven. But before he had reached the seventh heaven and the presence of Allah, asserted Mohammed, in another heaven he had visited Moses, who dwelt there "together with his Hebrews," and he had consulted him as to whether Allah would be appeased with fifty prayers a day. And Moses had answered, "I am an old prophet, grown honorably gray in the service of men. I know them only too well. They will never say fifty prayers." Whereupon Mohammed reported this declaration to Allah, and the Almighty reduced the required number of prayers to twenty-five. But when Mohammed returned to Moses, the elder prophet again shook his head dubiously. And so back went Mohammed to the presence of Allah and pleaded for his weak and sinful people. And after many journeys back and forth between Moses and Allah, Mohammed finally prevailed upon God in His mercy to reduce the daily number of prayers for the pious Moslem to five.

But more important even than prayers are good deeds. Mohammed's teaching abounds in tender utterances such as the following: "What is a good deed? Anything that will bring a smile of joy upon the face of another." In one of the passages of the Islamic scriptures a bereaved daughter inquires how she can best honor the memory of her dead mother. And the Prophet replies, "Dig a well in her memory and give water to the thirsty." In his early days at Medina, Mohammed spent much time talking and playing with children. Like Jesus, he believed that they were the surest guide to the kingdom of God. His love for the little ones became proverbial. "All children of whatever creed," he was fond of saying, "are born with the blessing of Allah."

For Islam, the religion of Allah, embraced all the men and the women and the children and even all the animals of the world. Mohammed's was the prophecy of the great resurrection of all living things. "Animals, too, have souls like men . . . You will be rewarded, my brothers, if you are good to animals, if you feed them and still their thirst, for there is no animal in the air or on the earth that will not return to God."

And thus preaching the gospel of universal love, he came to the twilight of his life. He had returned in triumph to Mecca, yet he continued to live in the bare simplicity of his "rebel" period. He milked his camel, swept his floor, patched his cloak, mended his shoes, continued to subsist on a diet of barley bread and water, and spent his days proclaiming the charter of equal tolerance toward all men.

As the end approached, he walked to the burial ground that sheltered his disciples who had died for "the Cause." Now they were resting in paradise, the abode of brave men. He called out to their souls that he was coming to join them.

And just two days before his death (632) he went to the Mosque and asked whether he had injured any man. There was no answer. Then he asked whether he owed money to any man. A voice replied, "Yes, you owe me three drachmas." Mohammed paid his debt. "Better to be in shame now," he explained, "than to wait for the Judgment Day."

It has been well observed that Mohammed's truth lay not only in a holy book but in a sacred life. He was, in the truest sense of the word, the ideal *Moslem*—a man who surrendered himself completely to the will of God. "I hear and obey." He never claimed that there was anything divine about him. He asserted that he was merely a man, and that therefore his teaching was not beyond the comprehension of any other man.

His teaching may be summarized in a few paragraphs:

The *Moslem*, or *Submitter*, need not bother himself about theological discussions. His religion is concerned not merely with theories and beliefs but lays great emphasis on practice— the practice of good life. The way to the good life is pointed out definitely and—according to Mohammed—finally in the Koran.

In order to follow the teaching of the Koran, the Moslem must submit to three important fundamentals—FAITH, DEVOTION, CONDUCT.

FAITH. "There is no god but Allah." This is the creed of every Moslem. God is One, undivided, unequaled on earth or in the heavens. He existed before the world began. He is omnipotent, omniscient, and omnipresent. He alone created man, and He alone will redeem the righteous on the Day of Judgment.

In this respect the Moslem is closer to the Hebrew concept of a Divine Unity than he is to the Christian philosophy of a Divine Trinity. Yet he is equally opposed to the acceptance of the Hebrew and the Christian Bibles as the complete Word of God. "It is only the Koran which is complete." The Old and the New Testaments are, in the view of the devout Moslem, good as far as they go. But they don't go far enough. The Koran, declared Mohammed, is the One Perfect Book in the world. It is not merely a copy of God's message to man; it is His original message, word for word, as existing eternally in the heavens and as handed down to earth for the understanding of mankind.

The Koran is thus—according to Mohammed—the perfect revision of the Old and the New Testaments, both of which were revealed to the prophets of God, Moses and Jesus.

The various revelations of God, the Moslem believes, are brought down to us from time to time through the lips of His prophets. Although the Koran is the last and the final revelation of God and Mohammed is the last of the Series and seal of the prophets, yet the Koran itself enjoins that every Moslem should accept and glorify the previous prophets of God.

And God in His glory has created us, watches over us through life, and will judge us after death. Mohammed paints the torments of hell and the raptures of heaven in the most vivid colors. But in order to attain the ecstasy of heaven a man must prove himself worthy of it—not only through his faith, but through his rituals and his conduct. And this brings us to the second fundamental of the Moslem religion.

DEVOTION. The devout Moslem, as we have already noted, sets apart five periods a day for devotion and prayer. Religion with him is not a matter of worship once a week; it is a sacred texture interwoven into the very fabric of his life. Allah is ever present to the Moslem. He must be invoked at dawn, at midday, in the afternoon, at sunset, and at nightfall. Whether at home or abroad, the Moslem is ready at the appointed time to perform his ablution, roll out his prayer rug, and bow down toward Mecca—in prayer, in praise and submission.

The call to the five daily devotions comes down from the minaret of the mosque through the mouth of the muezzin. It is like a summons from heaven. And every devout Moslem answers the call with the words:

Praise be to Allah, the Lord of the worlds,
The Compassionate, the Merciful!

On Friday the Moslems gather in their mosques for public worship. Before they enter the holy enclosure, they remove their shoes and wash their hands, mouth, face, neck, and feet. The Moslem believes that he must be cleansed, body and soul, before he comes into the presence of Allah.

In addition to his private and public worship, the devout Moslem observes a fast during the sacred month of Ramadan. He must abstain from food and drink on every day of that month, from dawn to sundown.

There is one other devotion that every financially and physically able Moslem must observe. This is the once-in-a-lifetime pilgrimage to Mecca. Every pilgrim is dressed in a seamless white robe—a symbol of social unity among the members of all races and classes. The pilgrims are commanded not only to be friendly to one another, but to be merciful to all living creatures.

The goal of this pilgrimage is the sacred Caaba. When the pilgrims have completed their encircling of Caaba seven times they wander about in a devotion of prescribed movement in memory of Abraham's wife, Hagar, who frantically searched for a drink of water to give to her thirsting infant, Ishmael—the founder of the Arabian nations.

The pilgrimage to Mecca, like all the other devotions of the Moslems, is a reference to Allah, the God of Mercy. This idea of mercy, of compassion, of a fellow-feeling between man and man, lies at the very root of Mohammed's teaching. And thus we come to the third fundamental of the Moslem religion.

CONDUCT. The Koran is explicit in its ethical code. Mohammed devoted his best thought to the subject as revealed in the Koran. His chief purpose in life was to raise human conduct as high as possible toward the divine. He tried to merge individual and tribal differences into a universal Moslem brotherhood. In order to bring about this fraternal harmony, he provided a complete system of right conduct for every man, woman, and child. He prohibited drinking, gambling, dishonesty, selfishness, and cruelty of every sort. He distinguished clearly between piety and prayer. "There is no righteousness in turning your faces toward the east or the west," he declared. "He [alone] is pious who . . . for the love of Allah disburses his wealth . . . to the orphans and the needy and the wayfarer . . . This is he who is just, and this is he who fears the Lord."

Mohammed commanded the Moslems to treat their parents not only with respect but with kindness. "Say not to your parents, 'Fie,' neither reproach them; but speak to them with respectful speech . . . The Lord hath ordained kindness to your parents, whether one or both of them attain old age. Defer humbly to them out of tenderness; and say, 'Lord, have compassion on them both, even as they had compassion on me when I was little.' "

Mohammed reacted with unusual gentleness toward orphans—

he himself had been orphaned as a child. "Give to the orphans their due." To act otherwise is a grievous crime. "Verily they who swallow the substance of the orphan shall swallow fire into their own bellies; and they shall burn in the flame."

The ethical code of Mohammed insisted upon justice toward the individual and peace toward the world. It is right for the Moslem to defend himself when attacked. "Fight for the cause of God against those who fight against you." But it is wrong to be the first to attack. "God loveth not the aggressor." A true Moslem is a man of peace.

And a man of compassion toward all living things. The Moslem religion has been described as "the union of all who love in the service of all who suffer."

In this respect, Islam is no different from most of the other great religions. At its best, it is inclusive rather than exclusive. The devout Moslem respects the adherents of other faiths. The whole world is one Brotherhood under one God. This sense of a united human family was as cardinal a principle to Mohammed as it was to Saint Paul, who wrote: "We are all parts of one another." Like Saint Paul and the other supreme religious teachers, Mohammed would have heartily subscribed to the words of the modern poet, Edwin Markham:

> *He drew a circle that shut me out—*
> *Heretic, rebel, a thing to flout.*
> *But love and I had the wit to win:*
> *We drew a circle that took him in.*

FRANCIS OF ASSISI

Important Events in Life of Francis of Assisi

1182—Born at Assisi.

1202—Abandoned military career because of illness.

1206—Befriended leper.

1206—Left home for life of poverty on Mount Subasio.

1209—Began to preach to poor at Assisi.

1209—Founded Order of the Friars of Saint Francis.

1212—Founded Order of the Nuns of Saint Clara.

1219—Went to preach Gospel to sultan in Egypt.

1224—Beheld vision of angel nailed to cross on Mount Alverno.

1226—Had one of his eyes cauterized to escape total blindness.

1226—Died.

Saint Francis of Assisi

1182–1226

SAINT FRANCIS was one of the world's greatest lovers. A lover
of God and a lover of men. He was the perfect disciple of Jesus.
And the Italian counterpart of Buddha. Indeed, were it not for
the historical fact that Saint Francis never even heard of Buddha,
his life would seem almost to have been a conscious and deliberate imitation of the life of the Hindu prophet. Their stories bear
so many striking resemblances to each other that they appear like
two copies of the same drama translated into different languages.
Both Saint Francis and Buddha gave up a life of luxury in order
to take up their abode with Lady Poverty; both denounced private property as the source of all evil; both traveled over the
earth to smooth out the furrows of suffering on the face of humanity; both understood the pity and the beauty of life; and
both looked upon themselves, together with every other living
creature, as forming a single sympathetic cadence in the poem of
creation. And, finally, both of them, when they were about to die,
asked their friends to put them down upon the bare earth, for
both of them were most happy when they were least encumbered
with the "goods"—that is, the bad things—of this world.

II

FRANCIS OF ASSISI, or (to give him his Italian name) Francesco Bernardone, was the son of Pietro Bernardone, a well-to-do Umbrian cloth merchant. As a boy, Francis was somewhat wild, extravagant, impulsive, rebellious, and generous to a fault. He had no conception of the value of money. He spent it right and left—and generally on the pleasures of other people. He thought it much more sensible to give his friends a good time with his father's money, than to see it stored away in his father's coffers. His mother, who was the frugal wife of a thrifty husband, often remarked bitterly that Francis acted like a prince, and not at all like the son of an Italian shopkeeper. As for the father, he thought the boy would never come to any good.

But if his mother and his father frowned upon him, the young men of Assisi adored him. Reckless with his life as he was with his purse, slender, dark-eyed, brilliant and forever gay, he became the leader of their sports, their fashions, their deviltries and their loves. Like the youthful Buddha and the youthful Tolstoy, he was voted by his comrades a "regular fellow."

As he grew into manhood, he entertained a double ambition—to make his mark in gallantry and in poetry. He wanted to be a fighter and a writer—a soldier to keep his countrymen safe, and a minstrel to make them gay. He especially admired the troubadours—those wandering French love-poets who turned the southland of Europe into a lyric song. Indeed, it was his passion for the poetry of the French troubadours that impelled his companions to nickname him Francesco—"the little Frenchman." His mother, we are told, had named him John; but before he had grown into maturity his nickname had supplanted his real name. To this day the blessed man of Assisi is known by the name that connects him with the French poets. Francesco—Saint Francis—the wandering minstrel of God.

III

THE GENTLE SOUL of the singer, and the courageous heart of the soldier. Before he could *teach* his people he must first *fight* for his people. His city was engaged in one of those endless medieval wars against Perugia, a rival city in Italy. The old Roman Empire had been broken up into a great number of independent principalities, each consisting of a walled town administered by a feudal lord, and each of them engaged in a perpetual series of feuds with the neighboring towns. The Romans, relying on the sword in their effort to *unite* the world, had succeeded only in *dividing* it. Their stupid big wars had given way to equally stupid little wars. Wholesale murder had been replaced by retail murder. Every city was arrayed against every other city. Venice against Florence, Florence against Perugia, Perugia against Assisi, Assisi against Venice—and so on and on, all the way through Europe. A thousand little Caesars had inherited the ambition, but without the imagination, of the first Caesar. The civilization of the Middle Ages was rotting away in these interminable petty duels between city and city.

For a time the gallantry of young Francis swept him into the current of these military quarrels. He enlisted under the banner of his native city. But after a brief campaign he became disillusioned about the fratricidal battles of the Italian people. In one of these battles he was taken prisoner, and for more than a year he had an opportunity to study the less glamorous but none the less savage side of war in a medieval war prison. He came out of prison determined to see whether he couldn't find a better instrument than the sword for the settlement of human quarrels.

His quest for the mystical instrument of peace was interrupted when he fell into a serious illness—a result of the sufferings he had undergone in the military prison. For a time his recovery seemed doubtful, but he managed finally to get over the crisis. As he lay on his back during his slow convalescence, he was able to study life from a new angle. The sky, the earth, the birds, the trees, the frettings and the fumings of his funny little perpendicular brothers and sisters of the human race—all the world took on a new meaning as he looked upon them from his new and horizontal position of quiet meditation. There was among men too much ado about nothing, too much running after things that were worthless, and too much fighting over quarrels that were *worse* than worthless. And right then and there he decided to give up the foolish life of the people and to live a sensible life of his own. He had found that mysterious, all-powerful weapon that would insure peace among men. If only he could get others to use it—this weapon of reciprocal gentleness, of interdependent pity, of unstinted love!

For all humanity is a brotherhood; and only in sustaining your brother can you hope to sustain yourself.

It was not long before Francis was able to put this newly discovered secret—or rather this *newly rediscovered* secret—to the test. One day, as he was riding through the fields of Umbria, he met a leper on the way. All his life he had been horrified at the sight of these living corpses. Sensitive poet that he was, he had always shrunk, with a feeling of almost bodily pain, from everything that was ugly. But during his illness he had become too closely associated with the horror of suffering and the ugliness of disease to feel anything but pity for the sufferings and the diseases of other people. When he saw the leper advancing toward him, he sprang down from his horse and not only gave money, but gave *himself,* to his sorrowing brother. He threw his arms about him and spoke to him as to a friend and comrade. Hitherto he had found a boisterous sort of pleasure in the company of the elect. From now on he experienced a somewhat quieter but far deeper happiness in seeking out the society of the rejected. For these stepchildren of destiny, like all the other creatures that lived and suffered and died, were not only *related* to him but were actually a *part* of him. The united ripples of one ocean, the integrated bodies of one soul, the unbreakable continuity of one eternal life. "To me you are more than a brother; you are an ailing member of my own flesh and blood. *Your* pain is *my* pain; and *your* joy, *my* joy." In thus coming forward to the leper, Francis of Assisi had at last come back to himself.

And so he left the fortunate, "the unailing members of the social unit," and enlisted in the service of the unfortunate. His heart went out especially to the failures, the unfits and the misfits, those who couldn't "get on" in life, the weak whom nobody would employ, and the meek whom nobody would heed. "He listens," it was said of him, "to those to whom God himself will not listen." But Francis was too devout a Christian to subscribe to any such characterization of his own mission. "It is *the will of God* that I should listen to all those in distress."

Francis of Assisi was a devout Christian, but—like Jesus before him—he was not a blindly obedient son of the established Church. Nor, for that matter, was he a blindly obedient son of his father. He tried to do everything in his own unconventional and gentle way. He was more anxious to obey the dictates of his own heart, than to follow the injunctions of his superiors. And his heart happened to be in the right much more often than his superiors. Once, in order to get the money for the performance of a charitable act, he sold his horse and a bale of cloth belonging to his father's shop. His father called him a thief and delivered a long and fiery lecture on the sacrifices of parents and on the ingratitude of children. Why, everything that Francis possessed, his father pointed out, even the very clothes that he wore, he owed to the generosity of his parents.

Whereupon Francis took off his clothes and flung them in his father's face. He was determined not to depend any longer upon the assistance of other people—particularly when these people were taking such infinite pains to remind him of his everlasting indebtedness to them. Throwing a ragged cloak over his body, he walked out of the house into the frosty streets—it was winter at the time—and, it is said, burst into song as he walked. He had given up all his possessions, and like the shirtless beggar in the fable he was supremely happy now that he had completely freed himself from the burden of ownership. If it is true that the rich man is he who is satisfied with the little that he has, then Francesco Bernardone was the richest of men, for he was the most content when he had the least. This was no mere pose on his part. Nor was it a desire to play the martyr. Saint Francis was an ascetic, but he was no flagellant. He denied himself not so much for his future reward as for his present satisfaction. He felt literally ashamed to be well when so many of his brothers were ill, and to eat and to drink when so many of them were starving. And so, instead of going off like a sulky hermit into the desert, he went among the humble, the poor and the sick, restoring their pride, feeding their hunger, and ministering to their suffering. His happiness was so great because he thought so little of himself, and so much of others. When he got food, he kept the smallest and the coarsest portion for himself and gave the rest of it away. For clothing, he wrapped himself both summer and winter in his ragged brown tunic, tied around the waist with a rope. This tunic became the regular uniform of the Franciscans, those swordless soldiers of Christ whom Saint Francis led in his crusade of healing and mercy.

IV

AT FIRST he got only two followers. They built themselves a hut near the colony of the lepers, and they served as the messengers of life to those who had resigned themselves to a living death. Within three years the number of Franciscans—the Little Brothers of Saint Francis—had grown to twelve. With Francis at their head they set out on a pilgrimage to the Pope, requesting his permission to go on with their work. He granted this permission, provided they did nothing to interfere with the rigid discipline of the organized Church.

Having arrived at this understanding with the Pope, Saint Francis then made another journey—this time to the palace of the Saracen leader. The Fifth Crusade was just then at its height. Yet Francis, unarmed, presented himself before the Sultan. The Saracen commander looked at him with a not ungracious smile of amusement. Here was a new sort of Christian soldier—a slight and vivacious little Italian with a tattered cloak, a pair of fiery friendly eyes and a flood of eloquent gentle words. A man who tried to conquer you with a caress rather than with a stab. The Sultan listened to this strange ambassador's plea for an immediate cessation of hostilities "in the name of God, who is the common Father of us all." The Sultan promised to consider his plea—and forgot it the moment Saint Francis was out of his sight. The Moslems and the Christians went on with their wars, and the little Minstrel of God returned to his quest for sanity in an insane world.

V

SAINT FRANCIS had little education. He believed with the faith of a child, and he loved with a child's simplicity and genuine wholeheartedness. Like the earliest of the ancient poets he was— though he probably would not have admitted it—a Pantheist, or rather a *Pan-zoist*. Everything to him was alive and inter-related. Like a child he regarded the birds as his little sisters, the wind and the sun as his brothers, and the earth as the living mother of them all. We find this same personification and humanization of everything in the early epics of Homer, who salutes the earth as the mother of men and the wife of the starry heavens. And—to take an example from quite another primitive age and country—we find it also among the Pawnee Indians, who sing of their father, the sun, and who listen to the voice of their mother, the life-giving corn. With the Pawnee Indians, possibly with Homer, and certainly with Saint Francis, the acknowledgment of a close relationship between all living and non-living objects is much more than a mere figure of poetic speech. It is a beautiful, if rather naïve, adoption of the world into the family of man. Saint Francis speaks not only *of* his little sisters, the birds, but *to* them. When he came back from the Saracens, whom he had tried to turn into Christians, he met a flock of birds on the way; and with the simplicity and the sincerity of a child, he tried to convert the *birds* to Christianity. Charmed with the music with which his chattering little sisters were entertaining him, he felt that he too had a music, better than theirs, with which he could entertain them in turn. "Little sisters," he said in that gentle voice of his, "if you have now had your say, it is time that I also should be heard." And then he proceeded to deliver a sermon to his winged congregation in order that he might save their little souls.

If this, to the sophisticated reader, may seem to border somewhat on the ridiculous, let us consider another invocation of Saint Francis—his invocation to his brother, the fire, which certainly borders on the sublime. He was losing his sight, and the doctors told him that the only way to save him from total blindness was to cauterize one of his eyes—that is, to burn it with a red-hot iron. When they took the iron from the furnace, he rose with a gracious gesture and spoke to the fire as to a living and loving comrade who was about to perform an unpleasant duty. "Brother fire," he said, "God made you beautiful and strong and useful. I pray you be courteous with me."

Courtesy was perhaps the dominant note in the character of Saint Francis. He treated the least of creatures with as much consideration as the greatest. He was more ready to apologize to a beggar than to bow down before an emperor. There must have been times when he hushed his voice in the presence of the very trees and flowers, so as not to disturb their sleep. His humility was not the humility of self-abasement, but of utter self-disinterestedness. He simply had no time nor desire to bother about himself. He got so much more pleasure out of bothering about others. The whole world was to him a world of kings, and he was their one willing subject.

VI

SAINT FRANCIS spoke only once in an angry tone to his fellowmen. He had just returned from his eastern Crusade of Peace. His followers surrounded him with a chorus of acclamation. They informed him that they had established, during his absence, a magnificent mission house at Bologna. But he raised his hand and put a stop to their cheering. "Tell me, my fellow disciples of Lady Poverty, since when have you found it necessary to insult her with the luxury of a palace?"

VII

AND THUS he went wandering over the earth, this "little brother of the poor," consumed with a passion to do good. And finally his strength gave out and he returned home. He was an old man now—forty-four as measured by the standard of time, centuries old if judged by the more accurate standards of tireless achievement and noble suffering. In spite of his failing eyesight he had gone forward, happy troubadour of the Lord, "singing as he walked," until the end of the road. And the end, like the beginning, was his native town of Assisi. "If you would go anywhere or make any pilgrimage," he said, "return always to your home. For this is the holy house of God."

In this "holy house of God" he laid himself down to die. His bed was the bare earth—his "beloved Mother Earth"—and the attendants who were present at the last long vigil were a handful of Franciscans and a multitude of his little sisters, the birds. Just before the end he opened his eyes and blessed them all. "Blessed be thy children, my Lord . . . Happy are those who abide in peace . . . Blessed be thou, my Lord, for our brother life and for our sister death . . . Happy are they who at the hour of death are found in obedience to thy holy commandment—*Love ye one another."*

And with this blessing upon his lips, he went to sleep.

Yet it was not an unmixed happiness that he experienced at the end. "It is a sad irony," writes Gilbert K. Chesterton, "that Saint Francis, who all his life had desired all men to agree, should have died amid increasing disagreement." He had taken the vow of extreme poverty. Inspired by the communism of the early Christians, he had cautioned his Franciscan friars against the evil of owning property. For, as he told them, "if we had any possessions, we should need weapons . . . to defend them." A minstrel of God, he insisted, "should own nothing but his harp." Yet he lived to see rich monasteries rising up in his name, and Franciscans forgetting their vows of poverty in their heated disputes about their ecclesiastical property.

A good many of the Franciscans, however, have to this day remained true to the spirit of Saint Francis. For in this Umbrian *poverello di Dio,* "the world's one quite sincere democrat," they have come to recognize the smile of God made flesh.

JOHN HUSS

Important Events in Life of John Huss

1369—Born in Bohemia.
1398—Began to lecture at Prague University.
1400—Elected dean of philosophical faculty.
1402—Elected rector of university.
1408—Accused of advancing unorthodox doctrines.
1408—Forbidden exercise of priestly function.
1409—His teachings investigated by Inquisition.
1409—Excommunicated.
1413—Summoned for trial at Constance.
1415—Burned at stake.

John Huss

1369–1415

H̲E̲ ̲W̲A̲S̲ ̲B̲O̲R̲N̲ of poor parents in the little village of Husinetz, in the south of Bohemia. As soon as he grew old enough to read he became a charity pupil in the school at Prague. He loved old books. Stretching himself out by the fireplace, he read the story of the saints and the martyrs of the Catholic Church. Once he rose and thrust his hand into the flame. As his mother snatched him frantically away, he looked at her with wide, serious eyes. "I was only trying to see what tortures of martyrdom I might be able to endure . . ."

He sang in the church choir at the religious festivals, and marched through the streets chanting hymns. He was easily singled out as the "keenest" boy in the group. Among the Bohemians of the fifteenth century there was an equality of culture. It was possible for a boy of poor antecedents to work himself into a position of learning in the Church. And so John Huss was allowed to prepare himself for the "Catholic democracy" of the priesthood. He entered the University of Prague, received the degree of Master of Arts, and joined the faculty with the title of *Magister*. He lectured brilliantly, accepted his ordination into the priesthood, and was appointed rector of the university. He wrote treatises on religious questions and enjoyed the applause of the learned. A self-made man, he had reached at thirty-four the height of his ambition. What else was there left but to luxuriate in his brilliant robes, attend banquets, make speeches, and bask in the esteem of his learned colleagues?

But John Huss was a simple man. He never forgot that he had come from the people. The human soul at its best is homogeneous. The same sort of nobility enters the human body in widely scattered generations and places. John Huss and Abe Lincoln had both learned their letters by the fireside of a peasant's hut. And both of them had caught the heavenly glow of the martyr's flame.

II

THROUGH the influence of the wealthy merchants of Prague, John Huss was appointed to conduct services at the Chapel of Bethlehem where a reform movement in religion was under way. The prayers at this Chapel were read not in Latin but in the native tongue of Bohemia. For the Czechs were jealous of their national integrity. "We must address ourselves to God in the speech of our own country." The patriots of Bohemia attended the Chapel of Bethlehem in the spirit of a society of laymen attending a town meeting. They uttered a religious declaration of independence when they bowed and whispered the Lord's Prayer. It was a simple prayer, direct to their Father in Heaven. And they could not understand why they must pay their money into the papal treasury at Rome hundreds of miles away. That sort of thing, they felt, was material taxation without spiritual representation. John Huss, as he preached at the Bethlehem Chapel, declared that the economic superstructure of the Church was a departure from the simple foundations of the religion of Christ. "Many members of the clergy are living profligate lives, owning great landed estates and paying the piper by stripping the shirts

from the backs of the people in taxes." In their voracious greed
—declared Huss—these clergymen taught their victims that the
souls of the dead would pass from Purgatory into Heaven at the
clink of the coin paid as an admission fee by the living. Three
cynical Cardinals—he asserted—had bought their way into the
papacy and had claimed with arrogance that they were the true
vicars of Christ. "A jungle of crawling things who call themselves shepherds of the flock."

But in the midst of this jungle John Huss discovered "one mind
that walked upright." And this discovery changed the entire
course of his own life. The writings of John Wycliffe, the Doctor
of Theology at Oxford, had lately made their way to Prague.
Wycliffe's name was in bad odor. He had been denounced by
the Church as a heretic. John Huss had opened his books gravely
prejudiced against him. But the more he read, the more he marveled at Wycliffe's "heresy." This "heresy" had so much in common with his own religion. Like himself, Wycliffe had no quarrel
with the Church. He had a quarrel merely with the corrupt men
who professed to represent it. He called upon the clergy to strip
themselves of their wealth and their temporal power, and to re-
enter the world of the spirit. He proposed the word of the Scripture rather than the word of the priest as the infallible guide
of moral conduct. He therefore demanded that the Bible be
translated into the native tongues of all the Catholic peoples so
that they might read the message and receive for themselves the
spirit of Christ.

When Huss finished reading, his mind was clear. With the
fervor of a disciple who recognizes the true prophet, he brought
forward the books of the Englishman and read them publicly to
the members of his congregation and to the students of the university. What John Wycliffe advocated was to sweep the money-
changers out of the temple. "I too," Huss decided grimly, "will
devote myself to the same task."

III

AND THEN, a crisis. The Archbishop of Prague ordered that all of Wycliffe's books at the university be cast into the flames. The mild Bohemian professor-preacher was aghast. This order was an affront to the freedom of teaching at an institution which had come to be recognized as the greatest center of enlightenment on earth. Men from every country had flocked here to learn the impartial truth about the world—a rare privilege in this dawning of the fifteenth century. And here the dawn was to be blotted out again in the darkness of the Archbishop's decree.

But not if Huss could help it. He instituted a crusade against the Archbishop. He issued from the pulpit a scathing denunciation of the "burning of human thought." And when the papal representatives gathered to sing their *Te Deums* around the funeral pyre of the books, he cried out, "Flames, my friends, do not consume the truth; it is always the mark of a little mind to vent anger on inanimate and uninjurious objects; the books which are being destroyed today are a loss to the entire nation."

A loss, and yet a gain. For in the flame of the burning books the links of a new party were welded together—a party pledged to reform the Church. And Huss was the voice and the heart of this new reform. Multitudes of Bohemians flocked to hear the preaching of their fellow countryman. Among his audiences were some of the most powerful lords of the state. Inspired by his fiery eloquence, the barons of the realm and even the king and the queen of Bohemia sat at his feet. But pressure from Rome was promptly brought to bear against the royal family, and the king and queen were compelled to withdraw their active support from the audacious professor.

Yet the professor persisted in his audacity. One Sunday three of his young students caused a disturbance in one of the papal churches in the city of Prague. They interrupted a sermon of the priest, shouting "This is a lie!" Instantly they were seized by the authorities and sent to jail. The parents of the imprisoned young men implored Huss to intercede with the authorities for their lives. Huss could not agree with their tactics, but his heart was moved by their courage and their youth. He begged the authorities to be merciful. The magistrates sent him a curt reply: "We are astounded that the professor of a university should dare to interfere in civil transactions, and to speak in favor of open rebellion." Nevertheless they promised to be lenient with the young men.

The crowds gathered around the courthouse demanding freedom. The magistrates cleared the street of the demonstrators, and then they marched the students through a back door into an alley and executed them.

John Huss preached the funeral sermon. The people bowed their heads and wept. He begged them not to think of violence against the magistrates who had perpetrated the crime. "Let them be judged in a higher courthouse."

And then, believing that his own presence in the city might lead to further trouble, he left Prague and retired to the country-side of his boyhood days. John Huss had no taste for the argument of the sword in the settling of religious controversies. He was a simple teacher inspired by the word of God and frightened by the brutality of man. He went preaching from village to village in an effort to kill hatred with a gentle tongue. But mostly he liked to write in the seclusion of his study. He threw his windows wide open and drank the country air and elaborated his thesis that "the books of heretics must be read and examined, not burned. For how else can you arrive at the truth?"

At last his "peculiar method" of arriving at the truth began to trouble the Pope. "What sort of man is this Bohemian agitator?" The Pope's agents in Prague replied grudgingly: "His manner is reserved and austere . . . His life and his conduct, a course of self-denial, and so far removed from vice that in this respect no one can find aught against him. His haggard and faded countenance, his tall, emaciated figure, his ready disposition to sympathize with, and to render assistance to, even the meanest of men—all these qualities attract adherents, more even than his eloquence. The stupid people hold him as a saint; and as such, they are persuaded, he can neither deceive nor be deceived."

Enough! The "fraudulent saint" must be unsanctified. From Rome came a decree of excommunication. "Wherever John Huss is present, it is forbidden to the people to celebrate mass or to baptize their children or to bury the dead . . ."

Now he was officially an outcast. His friends begged him to stop preaching and writing. But he brushed them aside. Nonsense! He had once placed his hand in the flame as a test of his courage. He would go on preaching even if he "were to burn for it." And now there was a new note to his sermons—a note of defiant irony. He castigated the "blind leaders of the Church" who stoned their prophets to death and who then raised monuments to their memory. "You worship the dead and you persecute the living."

Again his friends warned him to desist. To no avail. "If I ceased to preach, I would be a traitor on the day of judgment!"

And finally the blow fell. An order came for him to appear before a general Church Council in the Swiss city of Constance. The charge against him—there could be none graver within the jurisdiction of the Church—was heresy.

His friends grew pale. "Certainly he will not travel all the way to Constance and deliver himself into the camp of the enemy!" At home in Bohemia he was sheltered by the bravest knights of the realm who were ready to protect him with the last drop of their blood. "Stay here, and let them come to fetch you—if they can!"

"I will go to Constance and defend my doctrines," announced Huss.

IV

"Sigismund, *by the grace of God, chosen Emperor of the Romans* . . . We have taken under the special shelter and protection of ourselves and of the Holy Empire, the most honorable and upright professor, John Huss . . . We command you, all and each, to protect him when he comes to you, to receive him hospitably, to entertain him honorably, to assist him in whatever may accelerate his journey or render it safe, whether by land or by water . . . and if need should be, to provide him with a special escort for the sake of our honor . . ."

Armed with this guarantee of safe conduct from the Emperor and escorted by a bodyguard of two mounted knights—"I do this merely to humor my friends in Bohemia"—John Huss set out for Constance. Everywhere on the way he met with a cordial reception. For his reputation had long preceded him. "I have not found it necessary to travel once incognito," he wrote to his anxious friends in Prague. "I have ridden freely and without disguise." Through Bernau and Neustadt and Weiden. He drank wine with the city magistrates and broke bread with the people. "I am that John Huss of whom you have doubtless heard much evil. You may now judge whether it be true or false."

And when he had reached the town of Constance, the words of the humblest peasant echoed in his ear. "Truly you will return from this council covered with honor."

He took lodgings and awaited the convocation of the Council. The Emperor had not yet arrived. Huss desired to go into the streets and to preach to the people. But he received a strict order to "hold his peace." As an excommunicant, he must refrain from speaking in public, from reading the mass, and even from appearing in church except in the character of "an obscure layman." However, when the Emperor arrived he would be "given a chance to defend himself freely."

A few nights later he was sitting at dinner with one of his noble escorts, the Lord of Chlum, when the Bishop of Augsburg and the Mayor of the city called upon him. They announced that the Pope and a private group of Cardinals had assembled for an informal discussion. They would be pleased to hear Magister Huss give a summary of his views, informally, as friend to friends. Would he kindly rise from the table and follow?

The Emperor had not yet arrived in town. The Council had not been convoked. "I never felt any desire to justify myself in a private audience, but I came here to speak in an open trial according to the ability which I trust God will not withhold from me . . . Nevertheless I shall follow you."

He came to the audience. Whereupon he was seized and thrust into prison.

When the Lord of Chlum discovered that his friend had been betrayed, he burst into the Council chamber where the Cardinals were still in session. With his hand on his sword he demanded an immediate restitution of the safe conduct which John Huss had received from the Emperor. "By what right," he shouted, "have you dared to violate the Emperor's promise?"

But the Cardinals merely looked at him and smiled. In desperation Lord Chlum hurried into the streets to summon the people and to tell them about the treachery. But the streets were deserted. Nobody came out to listen to him. Early that afternoon the Cardinals had whispered a story to the effect that John Huss, afraid to stand trial for his heresy, had concealed himself in an ox cart and slunk away in the night. As a result of this story, the people had lost interest in Huss. Their idol, they now believed, had not only feet of clay, but a heart of dust.

Wearily the knight traced his steps homeward, unbuckled his sword, and dragged himself to bed.

But he did not give up the fight. The following morning he wrote a letter to the Emperor who had just arrived in Constance. He despatched another letter to the king and the queen of Bohemia. For two days he walked up and down the streets of the city, displaying the signed document that had been meant to serve as the Emperor Sigismund's "safe conduct." And he posted a number of placards upon the doors of the city, calling upon Sigismund to "keep his royal word."

But the Emperor had fallen completely under the influence of the Cardinals. To every plea "to keep his promise," he merely shrugged his shoulders. John Huss was a heretic, he declared. He, the Emperor, could no longer protect a man who had the effrontery to write: "The orders of popes, emperors, kings, princes and other superior personages are not to be obeyed, unless they are founded on evidence and reason." This—maintained Sigismund—was a doctrine tending to nothing less than the total overthrow of the established order of authority! No, he would do nothing to save Huss. What if he *had* issued a safe conduct? "A promise made to a heretic is not binding."

"Truly among such saints," wrote the Lord of Chlum sarcastically to his friends in Bohemia, "our Huss might appear as the very devil."

In the meantime, the Cardinals considered it unwise to keep John Huss in the local prison. He was too near the people. He might win their hearts again. And so they transferred him secretly to a Dominican monastery on the shores of Lake Constance.

Here they chained him and threw him into the cellar. This "dank hole" was saturated with the odors and the diseases of the swamp. A raging fever took hold of him. When it was learned that he was close to death, the bishops sent two of their number to his cell. They told him that the time for his trial had arrived. "You must prepare to defend yourself."

The prisoner looked up feebly from a bed of straw. His body was wasted away. His eyes were burning with fever. "You see my condition, Reverend Fathers. Judge for yourselves whether I am at present able to defend myself . . . Yet through the strength of God I am ready to stand trial, if only you will grant me an advocate."

They communicated this request to the Council. It was decided that the prisoner could not be granted an advocate since all conversation with a suspected heretic was absolutely forbidden. They transferred him to a cleaner prison, however, and sent for a physician to keep him alive until after the trial. "Justice must be served before death can have its prey."

This vindictiveness, it must be pointed out, was not of the seed of the Church, but rather of the weed of its misrepresentatives. Even Huss himself, as he lay in prison, absolved the Catholic faith of all responsibility for his suffering. "The trouble with my tormentors is that they have proved *unworthy* of their faith."

V

JOHN HUSS refused to lose hope. "God grant," he told his friends who came to comfort him, "that I may be restored to my country without spot or injury to my conscience." But as time went on and the chains grew no lighter, he wrote to his disciples—for his captors had supplied him with writing utensils—"Pray for me, my dear Bohemians. I am suffering for His Word!"

Finally he was led from the darkness into the spring of the year. Through the delicate tints of the reviving landscape into the artificial splendor of the Cardinals' Council. And now he was ready to speak.

The intoxication of color hurt his eyes accustomed to the night. Three men stood before him as his accusers—old Bohemian neighbors who once had been his staunchest friends and the fellow preachers of his ideas. But silver had bought them, high offices had beckoned them, and now they stood ready to turn evidence against him and to use his own trustful words with them as a "public proof" of his heresy. In the entire panorama of this glittering cruelty there was no detail that cut him so keenly as the apostasy of these three friends.

The Doctors read the accusation. He had taught the Bohemian

people "various errors drawn from the burned and condemned books of John Wycliffe." Furthermore, as a professor at Prague he had "led a movement to strip the University of its German influence and to make it a native Bohemian institution." Finally, he had "turned the Czech people against their masters." He had "stirred up civil rebellion" in Bohemia.

Huss looked at his accusers with a smile of gentle pity. "Reverend Fathers, it was not civil rebellion I recommended, but spiritual regeneration. A simple turning from the ritualism of the crowd to the righteousness of the individual." And then he added solemnly: "Show me anything better or more holy than what I taught, and I am perfectly ready to retract."

"You have repudiated our authority. By whose authority then do you teach the law of God?"

"By the authority of my conscience."

"But a hundred learned Doctors call your teaching false. Would you deny their right to correct you? Do you dare to assert that you alone are wiser than the entire Council of the Church?"

A circle of spears was ringed around him. The assembly rose with looks of derision and anger. And he answered simply:

"I appeal to God and my conscience. Were you infinitely more numerous than you are, I should esteem far more the testimony of my conscience."

He was shouted down. The public hearing had become a public jeering. The guards marched him back to his jail.

That night he had a vision, and he murmured to his faithful disciples: "I dreamt that they destroyed all the representatives of Christ at Bethlehem. But the next morning, on rising, I saw many painters who were painting finer, more glorious images. And the painters said to the multitude: 'Let the bishops and the priests come now, and let them try to destroy these designs.'" There were tears in his eyes, bright by the morning light. "But at the end of the dream I found that I was laughing—I was laughing."

The next day they led him back into the Council chamber. The Emperor Sigismund nodded to Huss. There was malice mixed with mercy in his words:

"John Huss, I will give you this friendly advice. Submit to the Council. Confess the error of your teaching, and I will see to it that you are dismissed with a slight penance. Should you refuse to submit, however, the Fathers will know how to deal with you."

The accused preacher listened in silence. A man broke hastily through the assembly and approached him on the floor. It was the Lord of Chlum, the knight who had brought him to Constance and who had worked desperately for his release. "Magister," he said, "sacrifice your life before ever you abandon the truth!" The preacher raised his eyes and smiled reassuringly. He glanced squarely for a moment at the pale countenance of the Emperor. And then he turned his back quietly on the assembly and signified that he desired to be led back to prison.

They came to him in large numbers, urging, begging, threatening him to recant. They promised him absolution, and great riches, a fine bishopric, and costly robes, if only he would sign a statement to his large following that he had preached errors and that he was now willing to be corrected. They drew up various forms of confessions, tried various arrangements of words in an effort to find a way that would be easiest for his pride and his reputation. And he smiled with the smile of a father at these children who were bent on juggling and rearranging the letters of the alphabet as if they could thus coax the truth into renouncing itself! "Forgive them, Father, they know not what they do!"

He saw beyond the syllables to which they urged him to annex his name. He was fighting not against a Church, not for a few technical explanations of a text, but for a great principle worth the ransom of a martyr's life. The liberty of free worship, the freedom of religious tolerance. Men lived worthily only that they might die worthily. Death was but a small price to pay for this new commandment in his heart—"Thou shalt not prevent any man from interpreting God's teaching in his own way."

When he stood up to receive his sentence from the Council, he faced a group of men who were separated from him not by the distance of a few feet, but by the space of many centuries. Indeed, they seemed to be living and disputing and acting in a world altogether different from his own. It was only the outer ear of his flesh which heard them pronounce the sentence—outlandish, ancient, whimsically savage words that belonged somewhere in a realm which he and his immediate ancestors had left far behind them. They were chanting in a ceremony: "The body of the sinner shall be destroyed."

They tore from him his vestments and shaved his head in the form of a cross. They thrust upon his head a paper cap decorated with the figures of three devils. And he felt himself murmuring somewhere beyond his consciousness, "The crown of thorns was heavier and more painful to bear."

And then for a moment he drifted into the unreality of the present. They had led him to a wooden stake, and fastened him firmly with an iron chain, and heaped around him a pile of inflammable straw. It was the end. He stretched his chains to their utmost. He got upon his knees and prayed while the flames reached for his heart.

LUTHER

Important Events in Life of Martin Luther

1483—Born at Eisleben, Saxony.

1501—Entered University of Erfurt.

1505—Received degree of M.A.

1505—Entered Augustinian monastery at Erfurt.

1507—Ordained priest.

1508—Appointed professor of philosophy at University of Wittenberg.

1510—Made journey to Rome.

1517—Issued his 95 theses against the orthodox creed.

1519—Held famous debate with Eck.

1520—Excommunicated from Church.

1520—His writings burned.

1521—Went on trial at Worms.

1521—Escaped to Wartburg; translated *New Testament* into German.

1525—Married Katharina von Bora.

1529—Prepared new church service.

1532—Translated *Old Testament* into German.

1546—Died at Eisleben.

Martin Luther

1483–1546

Peasants in those days had coats of arms like kings. Family arms, a poor man's fleur-de-lys. Old Luther, a miner in Thuringia, had his hovel-heraldry. It was a hammer on a block of granite, the symbol of a medieval Thor in the German forest. The god of lightning and thunder hovered over Old Luther's hut. And here a new Siegfried was born.

His name was Martin. When the hammer struck the granite its mightiest crash he saw the light of day. It was a weird cold light that gave no heat. And in a moment the forest of the world, black and overcast again, was waiting to be leveled by the storm.

Martin Luther lived through a boyhood "without joy or beauty or love." His father had no time for soft affection. He grappled all day long with metals in the earth. His mother hardly saw the sunlight, for her face was in the cupboard and the pots. When Martin stole a hazelnut, she beat him till the blood flowed.

He couldn't find his way out of the forest. No one had found the way out for fifteen hundred years. A forest full of darkness and superstitions and fears. Martin carried his fears like welts across his back. He couldn't strike out against them, for nobody showed him anything tangible to strike. There was just enough light to see the shadows of things; and Martin looked upon the shadows as the things themselves. When he asked for information, the old wives shrieked horribly into their cooking pots about the devil. "Every tree is a devil," ready to seize the first poor soul who wanders too far from his hut. His mother terrified him with her superstitious stories until his heart quaked. And then she sent him out to sing among the neighbors for his supper.

A rude, aching life! The entire world of the Middle Ages was imprisoned in a forest hut, waiting for the day when someone would arise to overthrow the demons who lurked among the shadows of the trees.

Martin sang and earned a little money for his folks. He acquired a smattering of Latin at the local seminary and then he entered the University at Eisenach. He studied law and seemed a little happier. For now he was receiving an answer to some of his questions. He was arriving at a just balance in the relationship between man and man.

But what about the relationship between man and God? One day he was walking in the forest with a friend. Suddenly a bolt of lightning laid his companion dead at his feet—in the middle of a sentence! It was destiny flashing her teeth in a savage laugh of thunder at the huge cosmic joke of justice. Martin Luther was terrified. The old wives' tales of his childhood came rushing back at him. Instinctively he took shelter in his studies. New lessons must be learned. New secrets must be probed. From the practice of law to the problems of religion. He took holy orders and entered the Augustinian monastery at Erfurt.

II

FOR TWENTY YEARS his ruddy honest face was like a beacon light in the gloom of the monastery. He was a man of all work.

He swept out the cells, opened the church doors for morning and evening prayers, wound up the clock, washed the windows and begged alms for the Order. Yet throughout this period he remained unhappy. For his spirit had found no peace.

One morning he failed to emerge from his cell. The brothers came and knocked, but heard no stirring within. They broke open the door and found Fra Martin stretched out on the ground. He seemed near death. And one of the brothers saw, lying near him, a flute upon which Fra Martin was always fond of playing. With tears in his eyes the brother picked up the flute and piped a favorite melody of Luther's. And gradually Martin came back to life.

But not to happiness. Once in the silent watches of the night he went to the kindly Dr. Staupitz, Vicar-General of the monastery, and confessed to him that he was a monk without faith in the love of God. He knew only a God of anger and revenge. "The Lord acts in a frightful manner toward us! Who can serve Him if He strikes terror all around Him?"

And the Vicar-General replied patiently: "My son, learn to form a better judgment of God." A *Christian* judgment. "If He were not to act thus, how should He overcome the headstrong and the willful? He must guard against the tall trees, lest they pierce through the heavens."

Martin feared he was not a Christian. For he had no faith in his superior's words. The mystery was not so simple as all that.

In the year 1510 he was sent to Rome on a mission for the Order. And here the iconoclast came face to face with the idols of the Church. Rome—he declared—was a painted harlot, selling her charms to the highest bidder. The Holy See was "the center of fasts but not the center of faith." Martin Luther was stunned by the revelation. He had come into the stronghold of Christianity, and he had found no Christians there.

He returned to Germany and received an appointment to a

professorship at the University of Wittenberg. And now, released from the extreme rigors of the monastic life, he had more time to think. The content of his thought, he confessed, was purely selfish. He did not care about reforming the world. He was merely uneasy in his own mind and wanted to save his own soul. He was an intelligent and honest student of life who had come to the conclusion that a man was a Christian not by birth but by conversion. And he wished to be converted to Christianity—that is, quite literally he wished to be converted to the religion of Christ. It is the genius of the prophets to be quite literal and quite personal in their religion. That is why they are so devastating. Here in Wittenberg stood a prophet squarely on his own feet. And a peddler came to challenge him until the whole world shook.

Here is how it happened: A number of agents, in the name of the Pope, were traveling over Christendom to collect funds for the repairing of the Church of St. Peter. By their contributions to the "holy treasury," explained these agents, the people could buy "indulgences"—that is, promissory notes upon God's mercy. An indulgence, said the papal agents, possessed the power to release a man's soul from purgatory into heaven.

Now one of these peddlers of indulgences came into the office of the Wittenberg professor and tried to explain to him the "principles" of this heavenly traffic in human salvation. Luther felt it only his duty to warn the people against this "fatuity . . . I began to preach mildly that all the indulgences in the world will not save a soul that is not repentant . . . I declared that the perfectly contrite soul is saved without indulgences. I told them that there is no episcopal power in the world which can insure to man his salvation."

And then he nailed to the door of the church at Wittenberg— a building similar to the American meetinghouse—ninety-five theses stating his conclusions about the matter. For now he knew the answer to his perplexity. Christianity must be justified by a new kind of faith—a faith engendered by the promptings of the heart and not by the prescriptions of the Church.

With the announcement of this credo the professor in the little town of Wittenberg had started a world revolution.

III

THE CHRISTIAN WORLD was aghast. What right had this Augustinian upstart to tell an establishment of fifteen centuries' duration how to run its business? What Saxon effrontery! His head must have been turned with the drinking of too much beer!

The authorities wrote letters to the Holy Roman Emperor, Charles, to look into this matter of ecclesiastical insubordination. The verdict was decisive. A dangerous young radical with an unruly temper. Ordinarily the Inquisition could silence him quietly or chastise him publicly and be done with it. But too many "stupid people" were siding with him. It appeared that he had given vent to an idea which flourished like a hydra with a thousand heads. "No sooner do we destroy one thesis than two theses spring up in its place." What was to be done with this "Saxon sired by the devil"?

They sent word to him that he was not considered kindly at Rome. If he felt himself out of step with the world, let him at least keep his silence. Had he any right to force the world into tune with his own crazy harmony? Surely there were corrupt practices around him. But in what society had there been absolute honesty? Because certain churchmen were imperfect, was that any reason for overthrowing an institution that had saved Europe and had held it together for fifteen hundred years? "There are some foolish people who think that they alone know what is good for humanity. They alone propose to shoulder the responsibility for the entire human race—until they turn fifty. And then they feel only too thankful if they have succeeded in managing their own affairs."

Such was the spirit in which they tried to approach him. They pointed out the folly of his idea. And its futility. "Come, come, Martin, do you think that any prince will raise an army to defend you? Of course not! If you persist in your agitation, where will you remain in safety?"

"Under Heaven," replied Luther, and proceeded with the publishing of his theses and his tracts.

And the people all over Germany were convulsed with excitement and rushed for the polemics that streamed defiantly from his pen. Vicariously they suffered the danger of the outlaw. They thrilled to his forbidden words. Here was a man staking his life in the greatest gamble ever. But more: here was a German standing up to Rome. Princes, nobles, burghers—all alike were swept along in a wave of national feeling. "At Nuremberg, at Strasbourg, at Mayence, there is a constant struggle for his least pamphlets." And although the writings are banned, "the wet sheets are brought from the press under someone's cloak, and are passed along from shop to shop . . ."

He is in vast demand as a lecturer throughout the German provinces. Armed students guard his carriage as he travels from city to city.

And then the Pope pronounces the fatal sentence against him. "Martin Luther—excommunicated from the Church."

He feels no hatred against anybody—only a great emptiness. The fallen archangel felt no more keenly the emptiness of space through which he descended from the grace of his high estate. How fearless is the man who calls himself alone and mighty in the world—until the world takes up his challenge and compels him to live truly alone!

Doubt! "How much pain it has cost me, though I had the Scripture on my side . . . that I should dare to make a stand against the Pope . . . How many times do I not ask myself with bitterness the same question . . . Are you alone wise? Can everybody else be so mistaken? Can so many ages have been mistaken?

[*158*]

How will it be if after all you are wrong?" On the side of those who excommunicated him—"learning, genius, numbers, grandeur, rank, power, sanctity, miracles! . . . On that side the sanction of so many centuries, noble martyrs, academies, councils, bishops, pontiffs . . . On my side—Wycliffe and Lorenzo Valla—and Luther, a poor creature, a man of yesterday, standing well-nigh solitary with a few friends . . ."

Excommunicated. Well, he came from a tough people who had toiled for centuries in the darkness of the mines. They too had been excommunicated from the sun. Yet they lived to work on. "Let the notice of excommunication go into the fire!" He burns it. He feels strong again. He grins defiantly with lips full of soot and ashes. Here in the burning fire was light for him. Vulcan, too, had forged his finest weapons by this light and had found his place by the other gods. Is Martin Luther no longer a priest? A battlecry is stirred by the bellows of his heart into a flame on his lips. "We are all priests, each man with his own Bible, ordained by the grace of God alone, in the great crucible of His suffering . . ."

IV

THE EMPEROR summoned Luther to Worms, where he was to be tried on the charge of heresy. "I promise that no violence will be done to your person while you remain there." But of what value was the promise of an emperor?

However, Luther called for his carriage, took his flute, and played constantly to assuage the pains in his stomach—for he was now suffering from chronic ulcers. "Music is the art of the prophets."

From town to town he rides like a conquering hero. He sings hymns with the peasants, drinks beer with the burghers, receives honors from the princes. All the solid people salute this solid man with good cheer on the way. One morning he preaches at Erfurt, and the little church is overcrowded long before the hour of his arrival. The pains in his stomach are severe. At Eisenach he is tempted to turn back and to get into bed. But for the time being the pains diminish. A few days later they attack him again. But he goes on. He receives from his admirers a picture of the martyr Savonarola and kisses it fervently. At Plifflingheim, on the outskirts of Worms, he blesses a peasant who is planting an elm by the wayside. And then his eyes catch sight of the hills and the turrets of the fatal city just beyond. What a mighty fortress! And then an inspiration comes to him and he bursts out into song—a defiant hymn that is to become the battlecry of the Reformation, *Eine feste Burg ist unser Gott*. Our Lord, too, is a mighty fortress. He sings and he feels better now.

He entered Worms. The heralds conducted him along the byways in order to avoid the throngs that had assembled in the leading streets. Notwithstanding this precaution, there were numbers who had collected at the doors of the town hall. And the surrounding housetops, too, were crowded with people who had come to see this "Doctor Martin who defied the Pope."

And now he was face to face with the Emperor Charles. He refused to kneel down as was expected of a monk, even of an excommunicated monk. He stood unperturbed, as the court-room was hushed.

Around him were thronged the mightiest princes of Christendom. They grasped the massive handles of their swords as they waited for a word of heresy from his lips. They ordered him to recant. He asked them for a few hours to think over the order, to prepare his statement. And then he stood once more facing the emperor. "One rebuke from him, and it might just as well be all over." Yet Luther didn't flinch as he spoke:

"Since his Imperial Majesty requires a simple and straight-forward answer, here it is . . . Unless I am overcome with the testimony of the Scripture or with clear and transparent reasons,

I will and shall not recant a single word, for it is wicked and dangerous to act contrary to conscience."

The emperor was taken aback. He had expected something different. Apologetic words. Not this quiet and honest avowal of a personal belief. "Here I am . . . I cannot do otherwise. God help me. Amen."

The emperor had promised him a temporary safe conduct. Relying upon this promise, Luther ordered his carriage and started back for Wittenberg. Whereupon Charles issued an imperial decree. "Death to anyone who offers asylum to Martin Luther from the day on which his safe conduct expires . . . From that day, let all persons be enjoined to watch for him and to seize him and to place him in safe custody until justice shall decide what must be done with him."

In the thickest part of the Thuringian forest a number of horsemen intercept the outlaw. These men are not the agents of the emperor. They are the friends of Martin Luther. They have come to abduct him and to place him in safe keeping. The Elector of Saxony has been won over to the cause of a Saxon heart.

V

HE SPENT a whole summer and autumn and winter in the castle of Wartburg as guest of the Elector. But so far as the world and the Roman party knew, he might have been swallowed up in the darkness.

Secure in the fortress of Wartburg, he played his flute and sang his German psalms. Daily his table was provided with game and with plenty of Rhenish wine of which he was very fond. And with bags of sweetmeats and nuts. "One evening when I had retired to my chamber, extinguished the light and got into bed, it seemed to me all at once that the nuts had come to life, jumping about in the sack, knocking violently against each other. They came to the side of my bed to make noises at me! . . ."

Everything here was fantastic. He wrote letters to his friends and addressed them "from the region of the air"—"from amidst the singing birds." Here was a world of Merlin's enchantment. And it was a magic that threatened to destroy the entire world.

In the meantime he had started upon a daring work—he took the Holy Bible which only the learned doctors could read, and translated it into the German vernacular. "Let the common people read the Word of God for themselves," in order that they may learn to *think* for themselves. "No tariff on our brains." *Gedanken sind zollfrei.* Thought must be free! A born writer and orator, Martin Luther had developed a genius for "possessing the public." Calling to the common man in the national language, he addressed his pamphlets to *Herr Everybody.* Every man is a prince, an elected Son of God.

And then word reaches him at Wartburg as to what *Herr Everybody* has been doing in his absence. Smashing the windows and the images in the Catholic churches, clubbing the priests, indulging in orgies of anarchy and riot, celebrating a Saturnalian carnival of bloodshed and murder in the name of liberty. He despatches letters to Wittenberg, pleading with his followers to desist from their violence. And finally, when he realizes that only his personal presence may avail to check them, he leaves Wartburg in secret without asking the permission of his protector. He lays aside his pilgrim's staff for a rider's whip. For he is returning to a world of violence, to chastise a race of men who have never understood the battles of the spirit.

But he had unwittingly started an avalanche of discontent. The forces which his philosophy had liberated were entirely out of the hands of any one man. The revolt against the Pope had spread from Germany to the lowlands and through most of the countries of the North. Burghers and nobles alike had taken up arms against the Church. "What are Zwingli, Melanchthon, Erasmus to these legions of warriors, madmen, and saints?"

The entire world seemed headed toward civil war. But how

[*162*]

could a hymn by Luther on his flute lead the armies who looked for a Caesar? "What sprang from the soul of this religious lyricist was a poem. It was not a plan of action."

His followers came to him and demanded that he organize a new Church. And he smiled at them—or frowned—depending on his mood. What had been his doctrine in its crudest form? "God wills that we eat, drink, and be merry. . . . He asks only that we acknowledge Him for our Lord, and thank Him for His gifts."

Rauch und Dampf! All this idol-smashing and hair-splitting—nothing but smoke and vapor. These people pushed and hauled and challenged him—for what? To build a new world institution? But he was interested only in the world of the spirit.

Nonetheless he draws up the platform for a Protestant Church. He does not desire to establish a uniform church with an official dogma. He is not interested in the external ritual of the Mass. "Let German hymns be sung . . . Let the priests be elected by the suffrage of the people . . . All the people may teach the Word of God, may administer baptism, may consecrate the bread and the wine."

And the battlecry spread among the Lutherans—"Masses in German. Sausages on Friday." But soon there were matters of a more revolutionary nature. The Protestant princes began to confiscate the property of the Catholic orders. Monks were marrying nuns turned loose from the convents. And the nuns who still remained within the walls were encouraged to escape and to take husbands. They flocked by the hundreds to Wittenberg to seek the protection of Martin Luther. "I yesterday received nine nuns who had emancipated themselves from their captivity in the monastery of Nimpschen." . . . "The Duchess of Montsberg has escaped, almost by a miracle, from the convent of Freyburg. She is now in my house, with two other girls." . . . "The unfortunate Elizabeth von Reinsberg, who was expelled from the Seminary of Altenberg, having now nothing to live on.

has addressed herself to me." . . . "I am head over ears in business."

The "Reformation" was no longer simply a reform in religion. It had become nothing less than a social revolution. The German peasants, having slumbered for ages under the weight of feudal oppression, "had heard the learned men and the princes speak of liberty, and now they applied to themselves that which was not designed to extend to them." The tyranny of the feudal seigneurs was "based upon the authority of the Roman Church." Waving a boot over their heads—the emblem of their revolt— the peasants raised their rallying cry, *Bundschuh, Bundschuh,* and called for a war against the nobility. Down with the tithes and the taxes and the game laws! Up with the new order! "Every laborer is entitled to the wages of his labor." Crush all authority! "Jesus Christ by His precious blood redeemed all men without exception, the herdsman equally with the emperor."

The leaders of the peasants came to Martin Luther and asked him to support their cause. And Luther warned them to negotiate their dispute peacefully. To the nobles he addressed a letter: "It is your crimes that God is about to punish." To the peasants— "No violence!" He pleaded with all his eloquence. "How, my friends, I ask you, has it happened that neither the Emperor nor the Pope has been able to effect anything against me? I have never drawn the sword." But his words were lost in the tumult. This was no time to listen to a professor. "Impractical fellows, these teachers who seek to build a world with love. Can't be done." The nobles, on their part, took a terrible revenge. They smashed the peasants with an iron fist.

But it was not the nobles against whom Martin Luther's anger had been aroused. It was the peasants, the toilers of the Black Forest, the common folk in whom he had placed his trust. In them he had planted the birth and the death, the flesh and the blood, of an ideal. But now his love had turned to the cold implacable hatred of a lover who had been betrayed. Martin

Luther could never forget or forgive the uprising of this lower stratum of *Herr Everybody*. The mind of the lover is fanatical, unbalanced. The aching of the heart has thumped away all reason. Madness seizes him. He has leveled the Saxon forest. But where is the sun?

VII

THERE ARE two kinds of suns. The one is a star that shines over great worlds and events. The other is a radiance whose area of influence is undimensional. It pours into a private world of two people in love. It brightens the inside of a hut when the whole out-of-doors is raining. Martin Luther in the last flight of his years received a goodly portion of the second sun. His hut had become bright within; for—sublime blasphemy!—he had torn off his monk's robes and had taken the holiest of sacraments, a wife. He, an excommunicated monk; she, a runaway nun! Together they had left God's monastery to build a family of love.

Now he lived at last the "normal life which God had given to man." He learned the mechanic's trade, made watches, cultivated a garden. He became very poor; oftentimes his children were sick. He sat at the head of the table and carved the meat and bantered his friends and blessed his wife and took the good and the evil without a shrug. Many of his friends, especially those who were ambitious for him, grieved over the feebleness of his declining years. "Fatness had invaded the lower part of his face." His more timid acquaintances shuddered at the coarse jokes with which he was wont to spice his conversation. He had become a very common fellow, they complained. He was no longer formidable to his enemies. Yet his enemies knew better. Here was a sinner crossing swords with the saints to determine which of them in the future would control the human race.

There were times when he hadn't as much as eight florins in his pocket. But he had an infinity of love in his heart. When the plague broke out in Wittenberg, his house became a regular hospital for all the homeless sufferers. His little daughter, Elizabeth, was too ill to speak. For the last twelve days she had not tasted a morsel. "This is no time for me to read or to write or to do anything at all." God help the enemies of the Reformation! For here is an Augustinian monk who kneels weeping by the dying body of his little daughter, reaping tears and suffering out of the creation of his own flesh and blood. This is the very triumph of the human spirit—the martyrdom out of which new great ideas are born.

Luther has retired from the field. He declares that he is "no longer a man of action." But is that an anti-climax, a cause for disappointment? When the Princes band themselves together into a Protestant League and prepare to wage war against the Catholics, he has but one word for them—"Assassins." But they cannot possibly understand him. "Assassins" does not ring so very harshly in their ears. For they have never created an ideal of their own, and so they have no scruples about assassinating the ideal of their neighbors. They are ready to strike down the divine right of popes and to institute in its place the divine right of kings. They are prepared to torment the world with a half century of religious wars and murders.

No wonder Martin Luther keeps much sharp wine in his cellar. For wine makes a jest out of sadness. And he is privy to the great cosmic paradox at last.

LOYOLA

Important Events in Life of Loyola

1491—Born in Guipúzcoa, Spain.

1521—Wounded at siege of Pampeluna.

1522—Made religious pilgrimage to Montserrat.

1523—Made pilgrimage to Holy Land.

1524—Began to study Latin.

1528—Entered University of Paris.

1534—Received degree in theology.

1534—Founded Society of Jesus.

1540—Society received approval of Pope Paul III.

1541—Elected first general of Society.

1548—Completed famous book of *Spiritual Exercises*.

1551—Founded Roman College.

1552—Founded German College.

1556—Died.

Saint Ignatius of Loyola

1491–1556

IN THE YEAR 1553, August 4, the eve of the feast of Our
Lady of the Snows, while Saint Ignatius was in the garden,"
wrote Father Gonzalez, "I began to give him an account of my
soul . . . An hour or two later we went to dinner, and while
Master Polancus and I were dining with him, Saint Ignatius said
that Master Natalis and others of the Society had often asked
him to give a narrative of his life, but he had never as yet decided
to do so."

Gradually, however, "God had enlightened" the Founder of
the Society of Jesus. He became inclined at last to dictate his
autobiography. "In the following September he called me, and
began to relate his whole life clearly and distinctly with all the
accompanying circumstances . . . Father Natalis was overjoyed
that a beginning had been made, and told me to urge Saint
Ignatius to complete it, often saying to me, 'In no other way can
you do more good to the Society.' . . . Afterward in the same
month, he called me three or four times, and told me the history
of his life up to the time of his dwelling at Manresa . . .'"

For two years Ignatius dictated his life to Gonzalez. There

were numerous interruptions. Again and again, "after saying Mass I went to ask him if it were the time." The Pope became ill and the narrative was postponed until the election of a new Pope, "who died after the election." In the summer time, Gonzalez remarks ruefully, "the biography did not make much progress on account of the heat." In the winter time, "colleges for the Society must be established, and ambassadors must be received."

But when the disciple caught from his master a few precious moments of leisurely dictation he was duly rewarded, indeed overwhelmed. "The method followed by Saint Ignatius is so clear that he places vividly before our eyes the events of the past . . . It was not necessary to ask him anything, as nothing important was omitted . . . While taking these notes I tried to see the expression on his face, and kept drawing near to him . . ."

II

IT IS the reign of Ferdinand and Isabella. The Spanish nobility is a flashing blade in the scabbard of international knighthood. Do not let them deceive you with their thin faces white as the winding-sheet. Their veins boil blood. Their hearts are seething crucibles in which the flesh of all they touch is transmuted into the spirit of all they worship. They are violently in love with love, and they are unafraid of death. From the pleasures of a romance under the stars they go without a shrug to a duel of vengeance in the courtyard. For one moment of ecstasy before the lady of the crucifix they will carry the sword over the world and die anyhow and anywhere in her service.

Let us therefore not be amazed at the story of a soldier turned into a saint. The pendulum of the Spaniard's temperament swings easily from the spirited to the spiritual.

Ignatius of Loyola is home from the wars a casualty. A French bullet has lodged in his thigh. Not a shudder, not a sound from his lips as they reset his shattered leg. He is a nobleman. The military tradition runs strong in his family and disinfects all pain. He looks impassively on and dreams of better days when he will limp his way back to the King's court, carrying a love sonnet at the point of his sword and a kiss for a cheek behind a fan. His ancestors have fought the Moors and his own brothers have fallen in battle for no more than this.

Ignatius had followed these warriors in the courtly tradition. As a boy he had been taken away from his parents, to be educated under the guidance of the Secretary of the King's Treasury. He had been baptized in the fires of knighthood. And now he had injured a leg in the knight's routine. Limb by limb, he would offer himself through battle to the Goddess of Love. And when his heart grew weary of her blandishments, he would commit it with a prayer to a soldier's grave.

They repair his wounded leg. As he lies convalescing in his castle, he asks for a book to read—*Amadis of Gaul*—the exciting story of a knight. But the book is not at hand. Instead, his attendants bring him a book of a far different content—*The Flower of the Saints*. He opens the pages of the book. Saints? There is a sneer on his lips. Why waste his time upon those who beat their flesh in prayer, instead of risking it in a fight?

But he reads the book through to the end. And slowly he shares the battles of religion with these strange warriors of Christ. When he turned the final page, he lay back and pondered. These saints were *knights like himself!* They, too, had fought against whole armies—not of Frenchmen, but of the aggressive spirits of temptation and evil. They, too, had thrilled to the sights and the sounds that raised a soldier's blood! The flashing of heavenly visitations, the cannon roar of God's voice in the conscience. The artillery skirmishes of the awakened soul.

He closed his eyes and dreamed. He found himself on a barren and wind-blasted wasteland where—holy miracle!—a crucifix of roses grew. And now he realized that his love was for one woman only. For in his dream, tending the crucifix of roses, was Mother Mary.

He got up from his bed hearty and well. With the ardor of a Spanish lover he pressed his courtship.

III

HIS FAMILY sensed, when he left his bed, that a strange change had taken place in him. When he told them that he was not taking the road back to the King's court, they were uneasy. "Don't do anything unworthy of your ancestors," they begged. And he nodded his head. He would do nothing unworthy of his ancestors of the Gospel—the men who dated far beyond the history of Loyola. First of all, like Saint Francis before him, he gave his rich clothing to a beggar. And then he started on his adventure of religious knight-errantry.

To Manresa, a little town on the way to Barcelona, he came. And he entered a hospital to tend the sick and the dying. In a cave he prayed and saw deeply into himself. He fasted and flagellated himself and tried hard to wear his body down to the point where it might reveal his soul. He was a little man in stature, only five feet two. His girth grew more scanty and his frame more spare until the good fathers of the hospital begged him to desist from his ascetic practices and to leave a little of himself for the service of the world. And so he took to food and drink and put on health again.

He had entered a darkened cave on the hillside of Manresa, a hermit seeking God in his loneliness. He emerged "filled with the presence of God" and with the conviction that he must teach his fellowmen. With the energy of the soldier he had drilled himself into a saint. And now that he was a saint, he found that he had surrendered none of the impetuosity of the soldier. The life of his spirit was but the consummation of the life of his body. It was the properly organized body fighting and dying under the generalship of the will.

And now he wrote out his first teaching—the explanation of the steps whereby all novices-at-arms and sinners and kitchen cooks and vagabonds might find their way to God. He called his book a *Manual of Exercise.* "As walking, marching and running are bodily exercise, so the different methods of preparing and disposing the soul . . . with the object of securing its salvation, are spiritual exercise." He prescribed not only the attitudes of the mind but the positions of the body for prayer. He enumerated the subjects of speculation to joust with, the vices to hurdle, the virtues to pursue, before the final laurel wreath for the spirit is won. Here was no corpulent and stationary friar with the "frosty stars" in his eyes—the church was filled to overflowing with these obese consciences. Ignatius was a lean-limbed, active knight-at-arms riding like the wind; and on his crest the strenuous motto, *Gymnasticize thyself unto Godliness!*

IV

BUT he didn't go tilting at windmills. He was a realistic knight. He decided to educate himself, to make himself learned in Greek and Latin, to become perhaps a Doctor. Then to preach. But first he made the holy pilgrimage to Jerusalem. Then he returned to Spain and entered a college to commence his education.

But he couldn't stay silent in a cell of learning! His blood was hot under the Barcelona skies. The cross must have a voice. He burst the bounds of the classroom and went begging of each person he met in the market place for the alms of a few precious moments of his time. He found his way into houses where citizens were not behaving just right, and pricked them like a gadfly into better ways. He spoke of how he felt about Jesus, poked around "mending like an old wife," drawing little knots of exalted listeners to him, walking in and out of masses, asking questions, bringing comfort.

The professors were annoyed. A fledgling student, disgracing the dignity and the aristocracy of the University. He was not yet a priest. What right had he to preach and to *reform* people? On whose authority? A dangerous radical.

Well, in cases such as this the Church had a "board of enquiry" to protect itself . . . The Inquisition. An instrument that probed deep and discovered any poison lurking in the religious body of the day.

They summoned Ignatius and put him into prison. A professor of the University paid a visit to the young student who had so boldly "discoursed about spiritual matters." And he came away strangely moved. Drawing close to a friend of his, he whispered —so low that no one in authority could overhear him—"Have you seen Ignatius of Loyola?" And then he continued, "I have just seen—Paul, in chains."

Finally they released this little "trouble-maker, no taller than a child," and sent him on his way. And this way led to Paris and the famous University where he hoped to do his work in peace. He collected a few of his books with the care of a peddler whose wares might buy him his final meal. He slung all his education on his back and walked barefoot and bowed. It was a long walk, right into the "heart of the enemy country"; for Spain had entered upon another of her interminable wars with France. Yet the agile little salesman of God's mercy no longer bothered about the mighty military passions of men. He took his food and his drink in the poorest quarters and gossiped about the quiet humble things. And finally, after dawdling and dreaming and consorting with the quiet humble people and counting his rosary a thousand times, he arrived at his destination.

But no sooner has he sat down to listen to the learned Parisian professors than he feels the impulse to jump up and to *act*. It is apparent he will never become "the greatest of scholars." His mind stutters over abstract theory. He has too much influence over people to bind himself to the companionship of books. Once again his soldier's blood is up. He has outraged the dignity of the

University. He leaves the halls of the learned and becomes a sort of mendicant friar, a street-beggar with his name enrolled in the most efficient of all educational institutions—God's world. He begs indeed—for another sentence in prison!

Men are fascinated by his voice. Even though it is not dressed up in the most precise grammar. Men are held by an eye that flashes the command of a warrior mind. Women are melted at the touch of his ideas. Not a thousand books written by his learned colleagues, who have washed their hands of him, can produce the number of converts made by a single one of his sermons. His is truly a *creative* art.

Young men of fortune, family and ideals draw near him. Like himself, they are active and restless and ready for a crusade. They feel uneasy without being able to define the source of their disease. There is an odor of deadly putrefaction in the air. The smell of disintegrating hearts.

Instinctively they gather around Ignatius to form a little society. They hearken back to the spirit of the first chivalric orders —to the times when members of the same blood formed a clan against the common foe. They behold a great schism in the soul of things. They know that they are a green island of faith in a great dead sea. They take their vows of loyalty together at Notre Dame de Montmartre in the middle of August, 1534. And then they step outside. What are they going to do with their mighty numbers, seven in all! They can't change the world. Yet they feel sanctified. They have pooled all their resources for a common adventure. But where?

One day Ignatius knelt in prayer in a little chapel and a vision of Christ came to him. The voice of the Saviour said, "In Rome I will be favorable to you." And so Ignatius called together his little company and set foot for the Eternal City. Their way was clear.

V

THE LIFE OF IGNATIUS met history with a mighty impact at the intersection of the Eternal City. The meaning of his own destiny in the universal pattern came upon his mind in a flash from the Mind of the Weaver. Always he had been meant to be a *battler* for religion. And at this moment a mighty battle was raging. The sacred institution of the Papacy had been rocked to its foundations by the revolt of Martin Luther. The Holy Father needed help if he were going to survive—help not from his *meek* but from his *militant* children. This was an age of armed camps and of mobile armies. The old orders—Franciscans, Augustinians and Carthusians—were the non-combatant organizers of morale on the home front. But Ignatius conceived the plan for a new order of monks to serve in the front line of the Pope's command. They would be the skirmish troops in the vast war area of the spirit.

He petitioned Pope Paul III to endorse his volunteers of Montmartre under the name of the *Society of Jesus*. This new company would not settle down to lead a sedentary life in a monastery, devoting itself to meditation and prayer; it would "stand with one foot poised ready for instant action." It would rove all over the world at the orders of Paul III, responsible to him alone— his special guard, spreading the Catholic banners wherever the heathen lived, restoring the faith wherever it had receded or wasted away.

Gradually in the mind of Ignatius, out of the ruins of old Rome, this idea of a new Rome took living shape. His troops would enlist in a new crusade. Scouts of the flaming word! "In war, scouts do not serve less than the soldiers who fight, nor do the engineers who make subterranean mines do less to undermine the strength of the enemy than those who, when the walls are down, make the assault . . . I see our men, a light cavalry who hold themselves ready to resist the enemy, to attack them and to retire, and to go skirmishing now in one place and now in another," with the mightiest weapons in the arsenal—teaching, preaching, proselytizing . . . The first mobile company in the service of Christ. Wherever there are heathen, there Ignatius will send his legion of priests. A legion free from all ties of place and country, taking the vows of poverty and chastity, sworn to "forlorn, solitary, unnamed" adventure. A fighting, suffering, international legion of faith.

The Pope and his counselors listened politely. But they were frankly skeptical and weary of a new monkhood. Several of the old orders had changed from their original purity of ideals, "giving way to new formulae for loose-living." The scandals of many of these friars of the Church had been explosive material for Martin Luther's propaganda. Yes, the blueprint of a new order always measured strictly up to the ideal. But how about the material and the structure of the finished building? How much rotten wood and rough edges, how many faulty foundations? The authorities knew practically nothing about the qualifications of this architect. What schooling had he in building? Had he ever reared grand cathedrals, or even a peasant's hut to withstand the first onslaught of the weather?

The Pope looked dubious; but Ignatius soon melted away all the perplexities of his mind. And cautiously he permitted the "madcap of Loyola" to clear the ground and to try his hand. "Nothing grandiose, you understand." The building must be a modest one-story model. The enrollment of the Order must be restricted to sixty members and no more. On September 27, 1540, Paul III took his pen and signed his consent to the petition. And the Society of Jesus was born.

VI

FOR SIXTEEN YEARS another Caesar sat in Rome directing his legions. But he was a new kind of Caesar—a man who "consolidated an empire without territory." He did not receive twenty-three dagger wounds. He did not even ask for a crown. When his army of priests made him their general, he accepted the distinction with a quite un-Roman humility. He performed the duties of a kitchen boy.

Yet the Roman state had never stood more firmly behind a Caesar than did this Society of Jesus. The Jesuit priests—as their enemies had dubbed them—marched forward under the motto: *It is necessary to obey but not to live.* Loyola inculcated in each one of his cohorts the soldier's ideal of obedience as a "science and an art to be excelled in."

At first he had prepared his followers for a pilgrimage to Jerusalem. But later on he realized that there was a far greater crusade for him to fight. "Heaven closed the door of Palestine to open up the Universe."

The Pope had canceled all restrictions as to the size of the Society, and its numbers had multiplied by leaps and bounds. Forward rolled the great wave of "the counter-revolution against the Lutherans." To Switzerland and Poland and Ireland and Germany Loyola sent his fighters—and everywhere the two hosts ranged themselves under the Bible and the Ikon, and stood ready for combat. The Pope and the Catholic princes had large armies to end the matter—if need be—with the sword. But in many cases the word was stronger. Into the fortresses of the enemy went the Jesuits preaching, and by their propaganda they paved the way for the final attack. A word might stagger an army and win the battle. Psychological warfare can take a continent.

Loyola became a master of this psychological warfare. It was the vow of obedience taken by each priest that served as the very root and fiber of Loyola's plan of conquest. This plan was one and indivisible and not the product of many minds. The "united mind" was Rome. "I am not my own," each Jesuit vowed. "I am His who created me, and his who stands in His place, to manage and govern me as soft wax is moulded. In the first place, I must make myself like a dead body which has neither will nor sense. In the second place, like a little crucifix, which can be turned from one side to the other. In the third place, I must make myself like a staff in the hand of an old man, so that he can place it where he pleases, and so that it can best aid him."

And yet the government of the Jesuits was not a despotism. The obedience of its members was not the passive obedience given to the ancient Caesar. On the contrary, it was an active, aggressive and willing obedience, entered into freely and proudly, with a modern saint. Not the subservient fidelity of the slave to the master, but the equal fidelity of all to all in a common cause.

Ignatius drew up for the society a constitution which limited his own power and in certain matters gave the widest discretion to the power of his followers. In general, there were two classes of membership—the clerics and the regulars. And, among the clerics, only a chosen few of the so-called *Professed* took a special vow to the Pope and dedicated themselves to the more hazardous tasks of conversion. The other members devoted themselves to the less dangerous work of education. But all were prepared to follow a single aim. "In this school we are taught to acquire a rich poverty, a free slavery, a glorious humility." Within the ranks there was a strict sense of democracy. No man was less great than another.

They took the vows of chastity and of poverty and held no benefices. They expected no reward for their services and refused to accept anything from the world. Unlike the other orders, they wore no uniform dress to distinguish themselves. For by remaining outwardly anonymous they could the better carry out their secret errands. No outward physical emblem, but an inward moral badge. *Ad Majorem Dei Gloriam—To the Greater Glory of God.*

And there was need at that time for the Jesuits to reëstablish the glory of God. Piety for too many of their Catholic brethren had lost its original meaning. Virtue had come to be identified with virtuosity, prayer with pretentiousness, welfare with wealth. "What, is Paradise shut off from those who have no money?" taunted Martin Luther and his followers who had broken away from the Church.

And the Jesuits gave answer—not only in word but in action —bringing everywhere the mercy of God, toiling over difficult terrain, dying under a portion of the sky they had never seen before, restoring lost faiths, reviving dead hopes—"a spectacle to angels and men."

And the general of it all sat with his staff of assistants building in his garden. Around him were the colors of the Italian landscape whose glory Raphael was at that very moment painting for eternity.

Ignatius felt that his was only a layman's eye. No artist he, but a mere artisan of faith. Could he too, like that painter of the divine in human form, establish a masterpiece that would last across the years? Could he foresee the words that would be spoken of his order three centuries later by the Protestant historian, Macaulay? "In spite of oceans and deserts . . . of spies and penal laws, of dungeons and rocks . . . the Jesuits will be found under every disguise, in every country; scholars, physicians, merchants, servingmen, in the hostile court of Sweden, in the old manor houses of Cheshire, among the hovels of Connaught. Arguing, instructing, consoling, animating the courage of the timid, holding up the crucifix before the eyes of the dying."

But Ignatius was not concerned about the praise he might receive. He was interested only in the service he could give.

VII

TO THE FOUR CORNERS of the earth came the mission from the little garden in Italy where Ignatius sat drawing the plans for his battle of mercy. To the cities of China and the islands of Japan. To the Spanish provinces in North America, the Negro colonies in Cartagena, the Indian settlements in Paraguay, Mexico, Brazil. To the jungles of Africa, the plains of Hindustan, across the ranges of the Himalayas and into the frozen heights of Tibet.

And throughout the length and breadth of Europe. "We have come to fight the battle of faith against faithlessness." Relying upon the weapon of the mind in the arsenal of the spirit, they dotted Europe with "Roman camps of learning"—universities for Catholic education. They initiated thousands upon thousands into "all the secrets of knowledge," from the simplest grammar to the highest theology. Their Jesuit schools were the training ground of cardinals, emperors, popes. And of some of the world's greatest playwrights, philosophers, scientists and soldiers— Molière, Descartes, Bossuet, Montesquieu, Galileo, Buffon, Wallenstein, to mention just a few.

And all these fruits of scholarship had been planted by a man whose own mistakes in grammar were such "as only a saint can expect to see forgiven, either in this world or in the next."

This unlearned "father of learning" had come to the rescue of his Church in her hour of decline. He put new breath into an institution that was threatened by "too much casuistry from without and too much complacency from within." For he inspired his followers with a saving idea: "Ambition, hope for preferment, is the mother of all evils." And his followers had the daring not only to *believe* but to *live* this idea.

Jean Calvin

1509–1564

His father had legal training, business ability, "push." He was a man eager to "get on" in the world. For this purpose he had left the village of Pont l'Évêque for the much larger township of Noyon—a place "where a man can make something of himself." Here he acquired a reputation as a good fellow, got into the swim of things, planned, calculated, feted his friends and married a comfortable measure of wealth in the person of the daughter of a hotel-keeper from Cambrai.

A right good solid *bourgeois gentilhomme*. He became town notary, clerk of the district court, secretary of the diocese. And he thrust his delicate young son forward like himself even before the youngster knew about such matters. He got him educated in the family of a nobleman and secured for him—at the age of twelve!—an appointment as chaplain of the Church.

In accordance with the ecclesiastical laws of the period, Jean Calvin would not be able to administer the sacraments until he reached the age of twenty-five. In the meantime, however, he received a "tidy income" from his office—three bushels of corn a year and the additional produce of twenty grain-fields.

But the poor little rich fellow was not idle while he waited for his official incumbency. His father had packed him off to the University of Paris for his ecclesiastical and his practical education.

In Paris Jean lived with his uncle Jacques, a blacksmith. He learned his Latin and felt the edge of his master's whip. This was the normal procedure for a boy who wanted a good preparation for life. A series of solid cuts in the flesh was regarded as a good recipe for making *Veritas* sink in. The schools in those days were not much better than prisons. "The beds were so hard . . . the sitting up and studying at night so disagreeable, that in the first year of their stay at college many young men of great promise became bandy-legged, blind or leprous, if they did not die." These are the words of the humanist, Erasmus, who attended the University of Paris. "The Principal . . . to teach us fasting, gave us no meat at all. How many bad eggs did I eat there!"

Little wonder, then, that many of the students lost their cheerfulness in gaining their degree. Yet Jean Calvin, for all his slight body and poor health, stayed to graduate. At the age of fourteen he knew so much Latin, and was so censorious toward those who were less proficient than himself, that his classmates dubbed him the "Accusative Case." His mind was as restless as a spider. It kept constantly spinning a web that entrapped every fugitive fact. A voracious mental appetite and a powerful mental digestion. The food it lived on was the iron of the will. A will that trained the body from infancy, for all its weakness, to be a faithful slave to the mind.

Jean never could remember having been young in body. From his childhood he was an old man. When a weak and wasting body keeps alive on a diet of spiritual iron, it thanks God for iron! It denounces in the name of God any alloy, any debasement of the character's metal, any rusting of a man's soul. Let each man delve deep down into the mine of his own spirit—even though the body be destroyed in the process. For there alone, within the hidden shafts of his conscience, amidst the fumes of his sufferings and the caved-in wreckage of his hopes, will he find the true metal of God's commandments to men. "You do not find God through the dreaming of castles in the air."

II

WHILE Jean was in Paris, war broke out between the two most powerful young men in the world—Francis I of France and the Holy Roman Emperor Charles V. Francis was still under thirty, and Charles had scarcely reached his manhood. Yet these two willful warriors had set civilization by the ears. They strutted all over Europe with their armies, killing, plundering, burning like two boys fascinated by an evil game. At last the French king was captured at the Italian city of Pavia, and for a time the international mischief seemed to be at an end.

But the people of France were stunned at the news. Their king, they believed, was their anointed leader by the grace of God. And his capture by the enemy was a sign from the Almighty that the French nation had committed some terrible crime in His eyes. A scapegoat must be found for punishment—a group of men guilty of the crime. What group more appropriate than the Protestants? For it was they, the heretics who had flouted the Mass, who were "responsible for the sufferings of France."

A general hunt was declared against the Protestants. Imprecations, whippings, burnings followed. In Paris, where Jean was studying the theory of religion, he saw religion *practiced* at the stake and in the prisons. And he was overwhelmed at the sights and the sounds that rushed in upon him. He hated men's disputes about God. It was with a feeling of relief, therefore, that he received from his father the permission to transfer his studies from theology to law. "In this quarrelsome age you will find

[*187*]

your best livelihood not in the churches but in the courts." The elder Calvin always had his ear close to the ground.

Jean went to Orleans and learned the legal code of France as a supplement to the moral code of heaven. But he was dissatisfied. His interest lay not in the winning of *cases,* but in the gaining of *causes.* He cared very little about the human rights of the body. But he cared a great deal about the divine rights of the soul.

Preoccupied with the problems of the soul, he dabbled for a while in philosophy. He wrote a commentary on a treatise of Seneca's and attacked the old Roman bitterly for his intellectual detachment. "It smacks too much of the jurist." These thin-blooded Stoics, he complained, see too many sides of a question. "They sit as emotionally cold as marble statues." They revolted him even more than the fanatics. "No man can be good who is not compassionate. It matters little what the dull sages may assert in their darkness . . . I do not know whether they are wise—all I know is that they are not men."

So back his affections traveled along the path to God, and to His commandments for which men fought and died. He fell in with a company of Protestant "heretics." They acquainted him with the principles for which thousands of them were sacrificing their lives. They walked with him in the sunshine of Orleans and talked with him of the "inner light." And he whose eyes had always been turned inward upon the somber colors of his conscience was now able to grasp their doctrine of justification by faith. This personal faith is a central luminous fact around which all the other facts are but tributary satellites in the constellation of a man's character.

In the meantime, Calvin continued his studies in the "tributary facts" of jurisprudence and became a Doctor of Laws, just as his father desired. And then he sent home a bombshell of startling news. "The die is cast. I have thrown in my lot with the Protestants of the kingdom."

III

HE PREPARED A LECTURE for a friend of his who was to speak
on the occasion of his inaugural as rector of the Sorbonne—the
most Catholic university in Europe and the center of resistance
to Protestantism. The oration turned out "very different from
what was customary at this institution." The hydra-headed
"monster of Protestantism" had stalked its way into the sacred
halls! In the general outburst—an outburst directed against the
writer as well as against the speaker of the oration—Calvin fled
out of the window, took refuge in the house of a vine-dresser,
dressed himself in a peasant's smock, threw a mattock over his
shoulder, and thus disguised made his way to Noyon. Then he
journeyed to the province of Angoulême and cloistered himself
with his books. For the Protestants had converted to their cause
not a mere fanatic, but one of the supreme scholars of the day.
More studies on the Lutheran doctrine of justification by faith,
more thought and planning about his own contribution to the
dogma. This man would fight with the weapon of ideas. And
time would show these weapons to be of the deadliest.

Since the speech at the Sorbonne he has become a hounded
man. But this danger only gives him an added zest to life. He
works harder and better in an atmosphere of mortal danger. He
travels from one place to another, seeking not the hideouts of the
ordinary fugitive, but the libraries. He is the outlaw professor,
shedding ink like blood, writing essays that explode like bullets,
planning by the candlelight a Bible for the new order. He is a
formidable fellow with a price on his head—a man with a
saturnine smile, and with a mind of razor-edge precision, ex-
tensive horizons and terrible strength. It can be dealt with only
by an antagonist who has mastered its scope and its power.
But where in Europe can you find such an antagonist? All the
armies of the king of France will not prevail against him. He
has the irresistible passion of the gambler who risks his all for

a single stake—God's truth. "If God is for us, who shall be against us?"

He assembles his fellow Protestants in caves after the manner of the early Christians, and he stands before them like an avenging angel with a black pointed beard and a crepe cloth cap. On his sallow face there is no dividing line between joy and agony. They are both blended into a single emotion as he utters his prayers and points his hand to the heavens. "One must despair of human affairs or bring them into order even by forcible measures." Serving God is no child's play. It is no joy, no pleasure. It is a grim, stark, gloomy business. He stands before his people —the living personification of his mission. No crucifix around his neck. No images to brighten the service. Only the white collar band, only the gold ring on his finger to relieve the eye. The world of voluptuousness with its variorum of colors is false. "I shall destroy Babylon!" What the world needed was a new model city governed exclusively by the spirit of the Reformation.

And the prophet found his Babylon—to destroy and to build anew. He crossed the border into Switzerland, where many distinguished Protestant exiles had gathered, and he arrived at the cosmopolitan trade center of Geneva. Geneva at the crossroads of Europe. She was a strange phenomenon in the Old World. After a struggle of some decades, her citizens had overthrown the authority of the bishop and had set up their own government. She was prosperous, fun-loving, a community of traders, knights, barons and voluptuaries. Little enough gentility here. Everything was tough. "Every third house was a tavern." The women "went around with hammers under their skirts."

When Calvin arrived at Geneva, he found the Protestant reformers hard at work there. Gradually, at the cost of many bloody heads, the number of converts to Protestantism had grown into a sizable group. The Protestant exiles, brave men who had come here to preach, bore their battle scars with pride. Bravest of them all was their leader, William Farel. A formidable fellow who knew no fear but who inspired fear in other people. Even Erasmus, whose pen had caused kings and bishops to quail, trembled ashen-faced before William Farel. "Never in my life have I seen so headstrong a man," he said. He it was who had decided to tame Geneva, "to turn Gomorrah into heaven." And the moment he met Jean Calvin, his austere eye flashed with joy and his red beard bristled; for he knew that he had found the very man to share his burden.

The day of the great reckoning had come—the morning of the world's last judgment.

IV

PLATO had woven his Republic out of the fabric of his philosophy. And Calvin fashioned his Republic out of the stuff of his theology. It was a theology that had fed and flourished on the sufferings of his long exile in France; and now it stood full grown into an organic doctrine of vigorous acidity. There were three essential features that characterized its head, its heart, its limbs:

1. The absolute sovereignty of God.
2. The absolute helplessness and the total depravity of man.
3. The salvation of the Elect.

It is the foolish poet—asserted Calvin—who talks of God's need to justify His ways to men. "God's ways cannot be judged or questioned by a creature who is merely a mote in His eye." There is no fixed law of good or evil to which God Himself is bound, as some of our philosophers would have it. "Everything that God wills must be held to be righteous by the mere fact that He wills it. Therefore, when it is asked why the Lord did so, we must answer, Because He pleased to do so."

Man is totally helpless to save himself. For he is all evil. Evil originated in the free will of the first man Adam who chose the wrong path in the Garden of Eden. Evil therefore is the unavoidable inheritance of all of Adam's descendants. And since evil is the natural state of mankind, it follows that no amount of good that any individual may do in this life can succeed in paying off the total score.

All men, declares Calvin, deserve to be sent to hell. And the vast majority of them go there. It is only by the grace of God, and not by the action of men, that some few are sent to heaven. These are the Elect, chosen by God in His own wisdom long before they are born. It is their glorious destiny, through no virtue of their own, to bask forever in the smile of God.

Even though God chooses whom He wills to save and whom to damn, Calvin warns his disciples not to fall into the error of Oriental fatalism. Merely because a man's reward or punishment is due to a force beyond his control, it does not therefore follow that he must sit in a corner with his hands folded and wait for the fatal day. There should be no room either for complacency or for despair on the part of any man. For no man can tell whether or not he is one of the Elect save by an inward sign from God. And each man hopes for the inward sign. While there's life there's hope. It is the spur of this hope for the inward signal that should urge every man to strain for a life of unflagging righteousness. Indeed, no man in his right senses will want to lead a life of sin and thus offer an external proof to all the world that he must be one of the damned.

Calvin was a teacher of action, not of theories. He was a lawyer dealing with concrete evidence. What is the evidence that a man is one of the Elect? His *right-living*. And Calvin was determined to force every one of his disciples to the extremity of a tireless moral life. "You must submit to supreme suffering in order to discover whether you are destined for joy."

This grim conception of God and man is an exaggerated form of the Protestant reaction against Catholicism. It is in some respects a return to a much older religion than Catholicism—the religion of the Mosaic laws. Calvin rejects the Christian God of love and reverts to Jehovah, the God of wrath. He repudiates a Father who forgives, and adopts a Stepfather who never forgets. He draws his leading inspiration not from the *Sermon on the Mount* but from the *Ten Commandments,* and he exalts to the foremost article of his creed the second of these Commandments: "Thou shalt have no other gods before me; thou shalt not make unto thee a graven image."

Calvin's doctrine of the Elect was modeled after the Old Testament idea of the Chosen Race. It was an exchange between a favored people and a favorite God. An eye for an eye, a tooth for a tooth, a blessing for a blessing. The Lord promised, *"I will choose no other men before you."* But in return he demanded, *"You shall choose no other gods before Me."* Jesus, the Lord of divine mercy, had *exalted* all men. Calvin, the prophet of divine majesty, *crushed* all men—with the exception of the chosen remnant.

> *Alas! and did my Saviour bleed,*
> *And did my Sov'reign die,*
> *Would he devote that sacred head*
> *For such a worm as I?*

But in spite of its unpalatable dogma, Calvinism was a religion of moral righteousness. It represented a philosophy of relatively high ethical standards in an imperfect age. *Noblesse oblige.* The nobility of the Elect must have iron in their blood and courage in their hearts. It was this rigidity of the Calvinistic discipline that enabled Cromwell to overthrow tyranny and the Puritans to build a new society in the wilderness of America.

V

THE BURGHERS OF GENEVA didn't take kindly to the man who fancied that he was God's prosecuting attorney against all the sinners of the world. One of Calvin's fellow Protestants phrased it mildly when he told him, "You are an irritable man." After

a few years of this irritability, the Genevese decided to get rid
of him.

Calvin went to Strasbourg and undertook a new course of
study—a rigid training in tact. And then, in order to discipline
himself further for his role as the "law-giver of Protestant Sparta,"
he went traveling among the various Lutheran sects in Germany.
He found these Germans "too lax" in their religious duties.
Luther's "easygoing" doctrines disturbed him profoundly. And
the Germans, on their part, called him a "noisy, fanatical Frenchman," and warned him to keep his nose out of their business.

In the meantime, following the example of many Protestant
divines, he had married. And no sooner was he settled down
with his widow and her two children, than the fickle people
of Geneva, who had grown fond of their "excellent teacher" in
his absence, begged him to return to them.

He came back. And this time he had his iron way with them.
For twenty-three years until his death he ruled the inhabitants
of Geneva, substituting for the old Roman imperialism the new
imperialism of the Scriptures. And everywhere men said: "Calvin
at Geneva, like the Pope at Rome, has become an historical
fact."

All the citizens of Geneva were compelled to take an oath
of confession to the Protestant faith. "Showy dress was not to
be tolerated . . . Overseers went from house to house to report
on the citizens' morals and to convince themselves that the laws
were being carried out." Many trifling misdemeanors were
punished severely by this "gendarmerie of God's estate." Three
men were imprisoned for laughing during one of Calvin's sermons.
Another was sternly reprimanded for saying that he preferred
the former preachers. Dancing was banned. Taverns were closed
and "abbayes" were set up where wine was served "in moderation" until nine o'clock in the evening. In these accredited
"refreshment houses" the customer was obliged to say grace
before and after imbibing each glass. Three months of this, and

the government was compelled to reopen the taverns, so great was the public clamor for the "good old drinks of the good old days."

In addition to the "heinous crimes of murder, adultery, attending a ball, and staying away from Church on Wednesdays and Sundays," a citizen could be prosecuted "for trying to commit suicide, for possessing a copy of a banned book, for saying *requiescat in pace* over a husband's grave, for declaring that there is no devil or hell, for arranging a marriage between a woman of seventy and a man of twenty-five, for arguing against putting men to death for their religious opinions, for criticizing the doctrine of the Elect, for saying that the Pope is a good man, for singing a song defamatory to Calvin."

On some days the prisons were like "waiting rooms at the royal court, so crowded were they. Hardly anybody escaped a sentence. Society ladies, members of the council, churchmen, all had to enter a prison cell at one time or another."

The attention of the citizens was directed to a list of Christian names that they were under no circumstances to give to their children at baptism. Any parent who christened his baby *Angel, Evangelist, Sepulchre, Pentecost, Sunday, Easter,* or *Jesus* was liable to a term in prison.

The morals of the governors were just as thoroughly supervised as the morals of the governed. Once every three months the legislators met "in love and in charity" to bow their heads and to confess their sins to one another.

Thus was the "wildest city of the Devil" transformed into the "mildest city of God." Yet the citizens did not surrender their licenses and their luxuries without a struggle. They referred to Calvin as "Cain" and they named their dogs after him. On one occasion the party of the *Libertines* plotted to blow him into eternity and to restore the government into "sane hands" again. But the ringleaders were apprehended and beheaded. Their bodies were quartered and exhibited in the most prominent squares of the city. Geneva had become holy. There was no alternative.

But no sooner had Calvin cleaned the houses of his neighbors than he found defilement in his own front parlor. His brother's wife was convicted of adultery with his humpbacked servant. And then his own step-daughter was charged with the selfsame crime. Overwhelmed with shame, he fled from Geneva. But after a while he returned to carry on his work which was "greater than any family mischance."

No family happiness or sorrow could beguile him. No personal triumph or trial. No relation of his own flesh and blood, and certainly no stranger, could ever expect mercy from him, if mercy stood in the way of duty. "If duty leads to death, so be it." Such was his attitude in the case of Michael Servetus. This scholar and physician—who seventy-five years before Harvey had demonstrated the circulation of the blood—was found to entertain religious principles that were in opposition to the Protestant Church. The Council of Geneva demanded that "this heretic" be burned at the stake. And Calvin, though personally he desired a more humane form of punishment for Servetus, nevertheless was prompt to carry out the wishes of the Council.

It was hard for Servetus to die. It was still harder for Calvin to go on living. He was deathly sick during the latter years of his life. He spat large quantities of blood and suffered from unbearable headaches. He wasted away with consumption and rheumatic fever and gout. What kept him alive? No mere philosophy or sense of humor or spirit of sweet reasonableness. It was only the capacity to kill for his beliefs that enabled him to live for them.

VI

As HE SITS in the walnut-furnished study of his little house in Geneva, with his back to the towering Alps, does he know what part of his creed will survive? Not the stake, not the pillory. These are but the angry waves that will be forgotten in the restless ocean of time. He has set the tone for a new class of people to a new way of life. In the sixteenth century the middle class has risen into a role of prominence on the stage of history, and he has given these bankers and manufacturers and businessmen a religion for their rigorous conduct, an esprit de corps for their fight to take over the leadership of society, a moral justification for their material hunger to stand out as the Elect. Plain living, high thinking, indefatigable striving.

Frugality, sobriety, thrift, saving, industry. A dollar begets dollars. Calvin at Geneva placed his stamp of approval upon a custom which the Catholic Church had never cared to adopt. He permitted his followers to take interest on money. He played no little part in nursing Capitalism through its growing years. Let the saints of the Catholic Church dream of heaven; the saints of the Calvinist Church are firmly established on earth. A hard worker who strives to outdo his neighbors in seeking for a sign of his election can scarcely help accumulating riches in the process of his striving. "The trophy of God's grace is for those who win the race."

Calvinism was the goad to the ambition of the middle class. And to its independence. It gave to the Huguenots their passion for speculating, and to the Yankees their love for shipbuilding and trading. And it spurred one of the Genevan's namesakes, Calvin Coolidge, into the Presidency of the United States on a platform of free enterprise for all and the foremost prizes to the Elect.

Far reaching are the ramifications of Calvin's doctrine as he sits and writes to the martyrs and the kings. Though for years the absolute dictator of Geneva, he has given the impulse to the rise of constitutional government throughout the western world. "If a ruler governs wickedly, he forfeits the right to govern." His disciples formulated the doctrine of "popular sovereignty" in the face of the Valois kings. They declared that no king rules by divine right; that all government is a contract with the people; that the people have the right, *and the duty,* to determine their own form of government.

Many were the Protestant exiles who sought shelter in Geneva and who then returned to their native countries to spread the doctrine of Calvinism. The Calvinism of the Elect. The Capitalism of the Middle Class. The Democracy of a competitive scramble for material glory and spiritual grace.

And the gospel of universal education. It was in the tradition of the Prophet of Geneva that the New England Puritans, almost immediately after they had built their first House of Prayer, established the Boston Latin School and Harvard College.

Calvin's enemies are impatiently waiting for his death. But Calvin does not die. The best part of him outlasts the Cotton Mathers and the witch hunters of New England. For Calvin's doctrine of Duty—the "Stern Lawgiver"—serves not only as "a rod to check the erring" but as a light "to preserve the stars from wrong" and to keep "the ancient heavens fresh and strong."

GEORGE FOX

Important Events in Life of George Fox

1624—Born at Drayton, Leicestershire.

1644—Ceased to attend church.

1647—Began "mission of peace."

1649—Imprisoned on charge of blasphemy.

1650—Nicknamed *Quaker,* because he told his judge to *quake at the name of the Lord.*

1655—Had interview with Cromwell.

1661—Beginning of great persecution against Quakers.

1669—Married Margaret Fell.

1671—Sailed on Quaker mission to America.

1673—Returned to England.

1677—Missionary journey to Holland and Germany.

1691—Died, January 13.

George Fox

1624–1691

IN THE MONTH OF JULY, 1643, a shoemaker's apprentice left
his native village of Fenny Drayton, in Leicestershire, and like
Moses and Buddha and Jesus wandered off into the wilderness
in search of truth. The name of this mystical and adventurous
young man was George Fox. He was disappointed with life. The
son of a father in whom "there was the seed of God" and of a
mother who came "of the stock of the martyrs," he found himself in a world in which he didn't seem to belong. He could
understand neither its brutality nor its suffering. In Continental
Europe the Thirty Years' War was at its height. In England,
King Charles I had been amusing himself by sticking the heads
of his enemies upon a picket fence until the aroused Parliament
had begun to clamor for his own head. Men who hadn't the
slightest interest in politics were being dragged away from their
families and pressed into the ranks of the Civil War. Those who
remained at home were robbed of their earnings through excessive taxation. When the taxes were not promptly paid, the
collectors entertained no scruples about sending the delinquents
to jail and confiscating their furniture. On one occasion, we

are told, the agents of the king broke into a house, emptied the "pannikin" containing the baby's food, and carried it off. Humanity, oppressed "by its teachers and its kings," seemed like a diseased body that was slowly festering to death.

And so, at the age of twenty, this sensitive young shoemaker left his trade and set off to find a remedy for the ills of the world. He went to the priests, who pretended to know the ways of God and the wants of men, and asked them to help him in his quest. But they only made fun of him. One of them told him to get married. Another advised him to become a soldier and to forget the confusion of his own mind in the general confusion of war. Still another expressed his facetious belief that the young cobbler would be cured of his concern for the human race "by taking a physic." Among the further "remedies" suggested to him were the smoking of tobacco and the singing of psalms. Not one of these "traders of religion," he tells us, took the slightest trouble to understand his perplexities, or the sorrows of their fellowmen. He found them all to be nothing but "empty, hollow casks" that resounded with a loud insincerity. "The earthly spirit of the priests wounded my life; and when I heard the bell toll to call people together to the steeple-house, it struck at my life; for it was just like a market bell, to gather people together that the priest might set forth his ware for sale."

There was something wrong, apparently, with the secular and the religious education of mankind. An *educated* man, Fox realized, was not necessarily a *thinking* man. From that time on, he had nothing but contempt for the polysyllabic stupidity of the teachers and the preachers of the world.

Accordingly he decided, "at the command of God," to break off "all familiarity or fellowship with young or old." He went into solitude "for to commune" with himself. And then, after four years of this solitary meditation, he found the answer to the question that had been vexing his mind. The troubles of the world, he concluded, were due to three principal causes:

First—the Christian nations knew very little about Christianity.

Second—there was too much insolence on the part of the leaders of men, and too much humility on the part of those who were led.

Third—humanity was bleeding to death because of its inhuman wars.

But even though the world was sick, it was not beyond recovery. "I saw that there was an ocean of darkness and death; but an infinite ocean of light and love, which flowed over the ocean of darkness." And George Fox was determined, if possible, to steer the world "from the waters of death into the waters of life." He made for himself a suit of leather and a broad-brimmed hat as a protection against the wind and the rain and the snow, and started off on a lifelong pilgrimage to teach the ways of peace to a war-crazed world. "Perhaps the most remarkable incident in Modern History," writes Carlyle in that most remarkable of modern books (*Sartor Resartus*), "is not . . . the Battle of Austerlitz, Waterloo, Peterloo, or any other Battle; but an incident passed carelessly over by most Historians, and treated with some degree of ridicule by others; namely, George Fox's making to himself a suit of Leather. This man, the first of the Quakers, and by trade a shoemaker, was one of those to whom, under purer or ruder form, the Divine Idea of the Universe is pleased to manifest itself, and . . . who are therefore rightly accounted Prophets, God-possessed . . . That Leicester shoe-shop, had men but known it, was a holier place than any Vatican . . . Stitch away, thou noble Fox; every prick of that little instrument is pricking into the heart of Slavery, the World-worship, and the Mammon-god . . . Were the work done, there is in Europe one Free Man, and thou art he."

This prophet in leather breeches, sleeping often behind a haystack in the damp fields, and compelled for years at a time to lie on the equally damp floor of a prison cell, was the founder and the commander-in-chief of the most significant army in the world—the Fighting Army of Peace.

The Quakers in the time of George Fox, those religious anarchists and militant pacifists of the seventeenth century, were among the bravest soldiers that ever fought for human freedom. And they carried on their long fight, and won their final victory, without shedding a single drop of their enemy's blood.

II

WITHIN six years after he started out on his bloodless campaign to convert the Christians to Christianity, George Fox had gathered about him a little group of devoted young men and women known as the *Valiant Sixty*. Two years later his peaceful army had grown to fifty thousand. They called themselves *Children of the Light,* or the *Society of Friends.* Later on they were nicknamed *Quakers,* because, as one of their opponents declared, "Fox made his enemies to quake and tremble at the word of the Lord."

The Quakers are generally ridiculed as a drab and effeminate race of anchorites who refused to take an active part in life because they were afraid of a fight. As a matter of fact, however, the story of the Quakers is one of the most exciting stories of human adventure. George Fox and his band of "outlaws" did not run away from the world. On the contrary, they faced it with an aggressive determination to make it a better and a gentler place to live in. They did not, as is commonly supposed, believe in passive resistance to evil. Instead, they advocated the most active kind of resistance—the resistance of a fearless tongue that refused to be silenced. Ridicule, imprisonment, violence, and even death had no terrors for them. They showed their contempt for regal pomp by refusing to remove their hats in the presence of kings. "There is something of God in every man; therefore it behooves no man to humble himself before his brother." They told the masters of the world to release their slaves. They rebuked the priests for their arrogance and the judges for their injustice. And they were always ready to lay down their lives if by so doing they could right a wrong.

Yet their own wrongs they "wore like their raiment, carelessly." When Fox was struck in the face for telling people to be human, he would wipe away the blood and finish what he had to say. He never struck back. He had a far better weapon for the fighting of his battles—the weapon of reason pleading in the cause of justice. On one occasion he was knocked down, kicked and trampled upon until he fainted. When he regained consciousness he stood up and, stretching out his arms, said: "Strike again; here are my arms, my head, and my cheeks." Whereupon a devout mason, who was standing by, took him at his word and hit him again, for good measure, with his heavy walking stick. Urged to take legal action against the hooligans, Fox refused. He had no personal quarrel with them. His own life mattered nothing in this fight for universal freedom. "If the Lord did forgive my assailants," he said, "why should I trouble about them?"

Soon after he began to deliver his message of peace, he was cast into jail. His imprisonment, he tells us in his quiet humorous way, was due to his telling a group of people "to stop *disputing* about Jesus and to start *obeying* Him."

From the day of his first arrest until the end of his life he divided his time between preaching and prison. In his *Journal* he gives us a description of one of the cells in which he was lodged for the crime of loving his fellowmen. "A filthy nasty place it was, where . . . the prisoners were so lousy that one woman was almost eaten to death with lice." But this wasn't the worst of it. "The smoke of the other prisoners in this prison," he continues, "came up so thick it stood as dew upon the walls; and I, being locked under three locks, the under-jailer, when the smoke was great, would hardly be persuaded to come up to unlock one of the uppermost doors, for fear of the smoke, so that I was almost smothered."

And here he adds a touch of humor to his forthright simplicity. One day, he tells us, the Governor of the prison came to see him. The cell was "so filled with smoke that he could hardly find his way out again; and he, being a Papist, I told him that this was his Purgatory which they had put me into."

A Purgatory of smoke and slime. Very often, he tells us, "it rained in upon my bed, and many times, when I went to stop out the rain in the cold winter season, my shirt was as wet as muck with the rain that came in upon me . . . In this manner did I lie all that long, cold winter, in which time I was so starved, and so frozen with cold, and wet with the rain, that my body was greatly swelled and my limbs much benumbed . . ."

This was but a sample of the many prisons—he underwent no less than sixty arrests—in which he was compelled to spend a great part of his life.

The God-fearing Englishmen of the seventeenth century took better care of their dogs than they did of their prisoners. And yet many a Quaker offered to give up his own freedom, and to rot in jail for the rest of his days, if only George Fox would be set free.

But the magistrates and the jailers regarded him as a dangerous character. He wanted the world to be at peace. He was therefore classed as an atheist, a traitor, and a felon. And so they kept him in jail and tried to cudgel the peaceful notions out of his head. Whenever they thought him cured, they released him; but finding, to their disappointment, that he still persisted in his stubborn ideas about the natural goodness of men, they put him back into prison and tried the selfsame process all over again.

In spite of his powerful constitution, the jailers at last succeeded in wrecking his health. But they did not succeed in wrecking his spirit. The seed of his ideal for human freedom came to full flower in the muck and the darkness of the English

jails. On the wall of the death cell in the Launceston Dungeon—
one of the temporary "residences" of George Fox—the visitor today can still read the brave inscription of the Quaker leader: "I
was never in prison that it was not the means of bringing multitudes *out* of their prisons."

III

WHAT WAS IT that kept up his courage throughout his suffering? George Fox himself gives us the answer to this question. "It
was said unto me (in a vision) that the Lord had a great deal
more work for me to do for Him before He took me to Himself."

But in working for the Lord he was accused of working against
his country. When Oliver Cromwell was the dictator of England,
George Fox was charged with fomenting a revolution to overthrow him. In answer to this charge, Fox sent a letter to Oliver
Cromwell. "I declared to him in that letter," he tells us, "that
I denied the wearing or drawing of any carnal weapon against
him or any other man, that I was sent of God to stand a witness
against all violence, to turn people from darkness to light, and to
bring them from the causes of war and fighting to the peaceable
gospel."

Cromwell was interested in this peculiar man, and sent for
him. Fox was ushered into the palace at six in the morning. He
found the dictator in his bedroom, half-dressed. "Peace be to
this house," came the customary salutation from the Quaker;
and Cromwell, the man of the sword, smiled a bit sadly as he
returned the greeting.

They talked about religion, politics, and war; and each of
them was pleasantly surprised at the other's sympathy and dis-
cernment. They were both revolutionists. Both were after the
selfsame thing—a freer, saner and friendlier relationship between man and man. But there was a radical difference in their
methods. Cromwell tried to scourge the world into a sense of

justice, while Fox was eager to fill it with a sense of pity. The Quaker leader was in many respects another Cromwell, but he was a Cromwell "guiltless of his country's blood."

As Fox was turning to go, Cromwell caught him by the hand, and with tears in his eyes said, "Come again to my house; for if thou and I were but an hour of a day together, we should be nearer one to the other." And then he added, "I wish no more ill to thee than I do to my own soul."

Whereupon Fox replied drily, "If thou didst, thou wouldst wrong thine own soul." And with a final admonition that the dictator should take care "to keep his heart from the hardness which was likely to overtake it," the shoemaker-prophet left the presence of the soldier-prophet.

Cromwell forgot the Quaker's advice, and there was never any peace in his house. His very bones were not allowed to rest in their grave. When the kingdom was restored after his death, his body was dragged out of Westminster Abbey, strung up on the gallows, and then dismembered and cast into Potter's Field.

Such was the epilogue to the life of Oliver Cromwell, who sought to attain glory for himself, and freedom for his nation, by means of the sword. His revolution ended with his death. But the peaceful revolution of George Fox continued to gather strength throughout the world.

IV

CHARLES II came to the throne; and the Quakers, who under Cromwell had been accused of plotting against the republic, were now accused of plotting against the crown. Their persecution was taken up as a universal sport by the students, the clergy and the magistrates of Merrie England. At one time or another, there were 15,000 Quakers locked up in jail. Many of them, less sturdy than their leader, succumbed in their cells. Yet such was their courage under persecution that their very persecutors regarded them with a sort of superstitious awe. There seemed to be something uncanny about them. Resisting violence with soft words and insults with smiles, they appeared at times to be magicians belonging to a superior world. Indeed, upon one of the occasions when Fox was arrested, a guard was put at the fireplace to keep him from flying up the chimney!

A number of the guardsmen, admiring Fox's courage and impressed by his personality, offered him the captaincy of their company if he would join their ranks. They did everything within their power to turn him into a soldier. But Fox succeeded, instead, in turning many of the soldiers into Quakers.

Among the most famous of the Englishmen whom he *convinced*—Fox never used the harsher word *converted*—from the sword to the spirit was William Penn. This son of the British admiral was rather vain of his appearance and proud of his glittering scabbard—an ornament which he wore as a continual reminder of his military days. But gradually, as he came under the influence of the Quaker religion of gentleness, he began to doubt the propriety of this decoration. He appealed to Fox for advice on the matter.

"Wear thy sword," said his leader, "as long as thou canst."

Several weeks later, George Fox met Friend William in the street. "Where is thy sword?" he asked with a smile.

"I wore it," replied Penn, "as long as I could."

V

ON OCTOBER 18, 1669, Fox married Margaret Fell, the widow of Judge Thomas Fell of Swarthmore Hall. Fox had known the Fells for about seventeen years. Margaret, who was the mother of eight children, was a member of the Society of Friends. She had thrown her spacious house open for the meetings of the Quakers. She had interceded for them when they were in jail, and on two or three occasions she had gone to jail herself in their behalf. Noble by birth, attractive, cultured, and prosperous to a high degree, she might easily have been a leader in society and a welcome guest at the royal court. But she sacrificed all this in favor of the disreputable company of George Fox and his ragged band of consecrated vagabonds.

When she married George Fox, she was fifty-five years old, but still beautiful. Fox was forty-six at the time. The king of England presented them both with a jail sentence as a wedding gift.

Their union was perhaps one of the most peculiar in history. It was largely a marriage of correspondence. When they were not in jail, they were too busy spreading the gospel of peace to spend any length of time in each other's company. During the twenty-two years of their married life they enjoyed, all in all, somewhat less than five years together.

Yet there was a deep and tender affection between them. The first thought of each, as we may observe from their numerous letters, was always for the welfare of the other. One day Fox received from his wife a sum of money with which she wanted him to buy a warm coat for himself. He promptly spent the money on some crimson cloth for a mantle which, in his judgment, "Dear Heart needs more than I need a coat." Always in his letters he addressed Margaret as *Dear Heart*.

Again and again, when he seemed to be at the end of his strength, his wife urged him to come to Swarthmore for a much needed rest. But there was no rest for him so long as there were "convincements" to be made and injustices to be corrected. On one occasion, when he was already well advanced in years, he heard that "at a town eight miles off . . . there was a sitting of the judges about hiring of servants." Unable to secure a horse, he "ran thitherward"—in the quaint language of his *Journal*—"as fast as I could. And when I was come to the house where they were . . . I exhorted the judges not to oppress the servants in their wages." And—such was the balance in his even scale of justice—"I exhorted the servants to do their duty and serve honestly."

And thus he traveled from town to town and from country to country on his lifelong pilgrimage of peace. Hearing (in 1670) of the hardships of the Quakers in America, he set sail for the new continent in a leaky tub of a vessel called the *Industry*. The sailors and the passengers were obliged to keep the pumps going industriously both day and night in order to save the ship from sinking.

Added to the danger from the wind and the water, there was the danger from sea-robbers. For several days the ship was chased by Barbary pirates. But the *Industry* managed to escape in a storm—"the Lord showed me that His life and power were placed between us and the ship that pursued us"—and after a "heaven-guided" voyage of sixty days the Quaker prophet arrived at Barbados, in the British West Indies.

Fox suffered from a severe attack of rheumatic fever all through the voyage and even after he landed in America. He paid no attention, however, to such a mere trifle as physical suffering. He always kept at his work until he literally dropped to the ground. As soon as he disembarked from the ship, he set the Quaker house in the West Indies in order, he issued a declaration of independence for the Negro slaves—a declaration which might have averted the Civil War in 1861 had the world listened to George Fox in 1671—and then he continued on his journey to the mainland of America.

His presence was sadly needed in the American colonies. In their zeal to make the new country safe for the Puritans, the Pilgrim Fathers had made it very unsafe for the Quakers. In the "bloody town of Boston" four of the Quaker leaders—William Robinson, Marmaduke Stevenson, William Leddra and Mary Dyer—had been hanged for no other crime than that of setting foot in Massachusetts against the wishes of Governor Endicott. In the same city, men and women were thrown into jail for their "reckless presumptuousness" in offering a cup of milk to a Quaker. In Dover, three Quaker women were sentenced to be tied to the tail of a cart and to be dragged across the snow through nine New England towns. The constables of these towns were ordered "to take these vagabond Quakers and . . . to whip them on their Backs, not exceeding ten stripes apiece on each of them in each Town, and so to convey them from Constable to Constable, till they come out of our Jurisdiction." This order was signed by the Right Honorable Richard Walden and executed by the Reverend Mr. Raynor.

When Fox came to America, he was able to do very little in the way of softening the hearts of the Puritans, but he did much to strengthen the hearts of the Quakers. Above all, he impressed upon them the wisdom of maintaining a fearless attitude toward the strong and a merciful behavior toward the weak. The Quakers, in all their history, have never been known to yield to others. But, on the other hand, they have never compelled others to yield to them. It is significant to note the fact that during the seventy-five years of Quaker domination in Pennsylvania—the "Golden Age" of Colonial tranquillity—there was not a single Indian ever cheated by a Quaker, and not a single Quaker ever massacred by an Indian.

VI

WHEN Fox returned from America he took a brief rest and then started once again upon his lifelong quest for justice. He traveled to Holland and to Germany, quietly accepting his indignities and making his "convincements," and striving without a letup for the twofold attainment of his mission—the establishment of religious tolerance and of universal peace.

And half of his battle was won in 1687, just four years before his death, when King James II issued a Proclamation of Indulgence allowing free thought and free speech in matters of religion. As for the other half of his battle, the battle for a warless and hateless human Society of Friends, he was convinced that this, too, would ultimately be won.

But not within his own lifetime. For the sands of his strength were ebbing out. On a midwinter day in 1691 he preached a sermon of peace at the Grace-Church Street Meeting in London. As he came home after the meeting, he felt a chill that seemed to "strike into his heart." He lay down on his bed, peaceful and contented. "In a few days I will be all right again."

He talked to his friends of their work. Whatever happened to him, they must go on. "Spread among your brothers everywhere the religion of life . . . Teach them that there is in the whole world but a single temple—the heart of man. It is here, and not in a heaven above or in a steeplehouse below, that you will find the holy habitation of God . . . God dwells in the human heart, in *every* human heart. For in the divine scales of mercy, all men are equal . . ."

His voice trailed off into silence. "It is in silent worship alone," he had taught his Society of Friends, "that we can hear the still small voice of truth." And then, when everybody thought he was already asleep, he spoke again. "There is an ocean of darkness—and beyond it, an ocean of light." His next words were so low they could hardly be heard. "At last I am clear, I am fully clear."

And the bystanders knew that their leader had "passed from darkness into light."

SWEDENBORG

Important Events in Life of Swedenborg

1688—Born at Stockholm.

1710—Completed college course at Upsala.

1710—Traveled in England, Holland, France and Germany.

1716—Appointed assessor on Swedish board of mines.

1718—Invented machine for carrying boats overland.

1724—Refused chair of mathematics at University of Upsala.

1734—Published *Philosophical Works* in three volumes.

1743—Paid "first visit to Heaven."

1745—Abandoned "physical science for psychical science."

1747—Resigned post as assessor of mines.

1756—Completed publication of *Secrets of Heaven*.

1768—Published *Love and Marriage in Heaven*.

1772—Died, March 29.

Emanuel Swedenborg

1688–1772

EMANUEL SWEDENBORG was born in fortune. His father was a bishop, a friend of the Swedish royal family, a man of wealthy intellect and superior imagination, a major figure. His mother, on the other hand, was the shrewd and honest and quite average daughter of the assessor of the mines—a practical woman whose blood might check the other-worldly surgings of the mystic. Transcendent shrewdness mixed well with the spirit of the Lord in the stuff of the boy. At his birth his father looked into the clouds and named him Emanuel, which means *God with us.* And his mother looked merely at the scale, to find out how much he weighed.

Heavy and duty-ridden was the education of a churchman's son. From the very first he displayed an exceptional intellect and a forceful personality. "Often in my discourse," he remarks modestly of his childhood, "I revealed things which filled my parents with astonishment, and made them declare . . . that certainly the angels spoke through my mouth."

The angels must have continued speaking through his mouth throughout his adolescence, for we find him a full-fledged Doctor of Philosophy (University of Upsala) at the early age of twenty-two. Indeed, with the precocious arrogance of the immature genius, he felt too wise for his peers. "This place affords me very little opportunity; and my studies are not at all appreciated by those who ought to encourage me in them." And so he packed his books and traveled westward across the continent through Holland, France, and England. He suffered from the restlessness of an ardent and energetic mind almost unbearably susceptible to the cross currents of all the sciences of the ages. From London he writes to his parents, "I study Newton daily and am very anxious to see and hear him." And a few weeks later—"With regard to astronomy . . . I have made such progress in it as to have discovered much which I think will be useful in its study . . . I have discovered an infallible method for determining the terrestrial longitude by means of the moon . . ."

He was constantly following a definite objective. "I turn my lodgings to some use. At first I boarded at a watchmaker's, then at a cabinet-maker's, and now I have turned myself into a maker of mathematical instruments."

He met and profoundly impressed the greatest savants of the day. But he had much trouble impressing his father, the bishop, with the notion that "all this scientific trifling will lead to any good." Even a young man of twenty-four with a mind kindled by genius has his troubles. For the good bishop has decided to lure his son back to Sweden and to an "honest career."

And old Bishop Swedenborg used a simple method of persuasion. He cut off his son's money supply. "I am short on allowance," writes Emanuel. "I am kept back from my studies for want of money. I wonder why my father doesn't show greater care for me than to have let me live now for more than sixteen months upon less than fifty pounds . . . It is hard to live without food or drink like some poor drudge in Schonen"—hard even for a man who invents new methods for measuring the moon!

Yet he continued with his measurements and his mechanisms.

His mind was a vast storehouse of fanciful schemes which he constantly elaborated into "practical" use. To his friends his sketches of mechanical inventions appeared to be the gropings of a wild visionary with an eccentric mental twist. But for us today it is astonishing to mark the accurate intuitions of a mind fettered as it was in the unscientific prejudices of the eighteenth century. He evolved, through mathematical equations, "the plan of a certain ship which, with its men, was calculated to go under the surface of the sea, wherever it chose, and to do great damage to the fleet of the enemy." No less than the modern submarine! He drew plans for the carrying of ships over dry land by means of canals or "sluices." He envisaged an "air gun" that would fire seventy shots in succession without re-loading, and a "flying ship" that would carry passengers through the air.

This last invention of his, the plan for a flying ship, he sent to the most eminent physicist in Sweden. But the good man could not possibly stomach such "rot." As gently as possible the great man of science told the impulsive youth that "with respect to flying by artificial means, it is no more possible than to make a machine of perpetual motion, or to turn dirt into gold." And he sent a long letter of figures and formulas to disprove "the wild hope of human flight through the air."

And so Swedenborg was left severely alone with his dreams. Giant dreams—a significant indication of the gigantic cast of his mind. They were the dreams of a scientist endowed with the vision—and with the energy—of a prophet. Swedenborg was one of those rare thinkers whose knowledge was based upon faith. He was convinced that new horizons, new dimensions, new worlds, lie waiting to be discovered by the *thinking* and the *believing* human mind. He felt certain that the "world of scientific creation is implicit in the world of abstract thought"—indeed, that the forceful and faithful mind of the scientist-poet alone can build a bridge between the two worlds by causing the thought to become a fact.

[*219*]

And this is precisely what Swedenborg, the son of religion and the foster-son of science, tried to do. Implicit in his drawings of the quadrant was the plan for the cathedral; through his experiments in the prism flowed the colors to glorify the altar; his longing to lessen the distances between human hearts was the inspiration for his airship. To both worlds he owed family obligations. Exploration in the one world meant creation in the other.

II

AT LAST the student returned home from his wanderings. He was "getting on" in years—and still he had no job. His father made a final effort to set this "flighty" son of his upon his feet. He "pulled strings" at the Swedish court and brought his case to the attention of the famous warrior-king, Charles XII. The king offered Emanuel a position in the office of the royal mines. Young Swedenborg accepted the offer.

At about this time another thing happened to tie him down to the concrete values of the time-and-sense world. He fell madly in love—with the daughter of the Swedish physicist who had dashed cold water on his dream of a flying ship. The senior savant, though skeptical of Swedenborg's inventive ability, had nevertheless placed his stamp of approval upon the young man's scholastic knowledge by offering him his eldest daughter. But the young lady, disinterested in the hieroglyphics of her father's estimate, gave her hand to another. Whereupon Emanuel told her father that he was not disturbed. It was the *younger* daughter, her sister, that he had set his heart upon. Her father immediately put a contract in front of the young girl, not quite sixteen, and demanded that she sign her betrothal to Swedenborg. Tremblingly she put her name to the document. But her affection was elsewhere.

Time passed. Swedenborg's only comfort was his daily reading of the contract which put her legally into his possession—at some future date. One morning he was unable to find the precious paper. The brother of the distracted young lady had stolen it and brought it back to her.

And thus the young man who had investigated the profoundest laws of nature discovered that he had been unable to understand the elementary workings of a maiden's heart. She didn't love him. Too much of the scientist and too little of the mystic had been at work observing her. Swedenborg made a solemn vow that he would never lose his heart again. And he kept it.

For a time, however, he was deeply depressed. Even his studies left him unmoved. But a strong mind survives a love affair. Especially when it is at work upon engineering projects that involve the transportation of the King's galleys overland and the building of canals and the investigation of the mineral deposits—and when, on top of all this, it is absorbed in a plan to write a philosophy of the cosmos.

Swedenborg's father, in the meantime, had been honored with a seat in the House of Nobles. But the vistas of political preferment thus opened to young Emanuel had failed to tempt him. He continued as a humble student and nameless assessor. He would rather write works on infinity than count a few finite votes. Occasionally he petitioned the government for a leave of absence from his work in order that he might travel abroad. He had refused a professorship at the University of Upsala, for he felt that he could continue his writings more freely if he remained unhampered by the narrow requirements of the college curriculum.

His was not the mind for the confinements of the classroom. His intellect embraced the world. He seemed to be as magnificently impudent in his inquisitiveness as that supreme man of the Renaissance, Leonardo da Vinci. Everything was his business. "Wherever he goes he visits the libraries, museums, picture galleries, churches, monasteries, asylums, theaters . . ." The tage was as sacred to him as the Church. He loved the works of the poets as well as the Word of God.

Never was there a healthier man. Or a man of wider sympathy. And no less wide than his sympathy was his optimism—his faith in the ultimate hopefulness of human destiny. He was the temporal brother of a group of skeptics in a world of unbelief. But he believed with all his manhood in the infinite capability of the human mind. "There is no finite boundary to man's adventure. When Columbus found his way to the new continent, it was not only through the winds and the waters of the Atlantic that he sailed, but through the winds and the waters of his own aspiring will."

And so Emanuel Swedenborg reaches the middle mark of his own adventure. He begins to look upon science with a quizzical air. It is but a natural step in the mental development of this prophet-inventor to think now of inventing a super-science. A science beyond science.

He plans the *Economy of the Animal Kingdom*—an exhaustive study of the human body, a synthesis of all the findings of anatomists on the nerves and the muscles and the bones and the blood. But Swedenborg is a man beyond men. He will not stop here. His must be a scientific research not only to *describe* but to *interpret* as well. All to a higher purpose. "I intend to examine, physically and philosophically, the whole anatomy of the body . . . The end I propose is a knowledge of the soul." He intended nothing less than to discover the motions of the spirit in the same way in which Harvey had discovered the circulation of the blood. All the work of the scientists before him had been a preparation for the grand search. "The time is at hand when we may quit the harbor and sail for the open sea."

To search into the cause of things, to discover where the living force resides. He was under no illusions as he wrote this exacting book. Its terminology was for the scientists; its message, for the seekers of the spirit. The learned might well laugh at his presumptuousness. It was very dangerous in this age of Alexander Pope to talk about the human soul. In the forefront of his book the high priest of science quoted, rather wistfully, a passage from the Stoic philosopher, Seneca: "He is born to serve but few, who thinks of the people of his own age. Many thousands of years, many generations of men are yet to come: look to these."

III

WE DEAL now with one of the strangest events in the history of human experience. Swedenborg's mind suddenly opens like an eggshell and the sunlight of another world bursts through. He tells his friends that he has been admitted into a universe of spirits and that he has entered into the world of the after-life. He is a man in his middle fifties—one of the most distinguished scientists of his day. People look with amazement at his honest face. They notice a somewhat vacant stare in his eyes. They begin to ask questions. Is he in perfect health? Are his words sincere and sane? Listen to this rational scientist who has been experimenting with the concrete materials of life. "I have been permitted to hear and see things in another life which are astonishing and which have never before come to the knowledge of any man." The development of this second sight, he declares, was gradual. Three painfully ecstatic years had been required for the preparation of his soul. During all this time he had been visited by abnormally long periods of supernatural slumber filled with a continual—and logical—sequence of dreams. In his diary he gives us a simple account of the transformation that took place in his mind. "I was elevated into heaven by degrees, and in proportion as I was elevated my understanding became enlarged, so that I was gradually enabled to perceive things which at first I had not perceived." And finally he got "the answer to the greatest mystery of them all—the state of the soul after death."

He seemed to have developed what we would now define as a

split personality. The outward man remained tranquil and practical and conservative in his habits. He wore a sword, powdered his hair, walked with a gold-headed cane. But the inner man had overflowed into a very Niagara of ideas that seemed to come from a mesmerized mind. A gentle and sincere mind, and one that often rose to great poetic heights. He was no longer the scientist, but the mystic enrapt in a vision. All that other men *knew,* he now *saw*—"saw with his senses and with his inner eye."

He withdrew from his employment as assessor of the mines and returned to his manuscripts and his travels. Travels over the physical world of Europe and into the spiritual world of the soul. He recorded the results of his "spiritual journeys" in an outpouring of books, "written at the direction of the Lord." And then, at the age of eighty-five, he came finally home to that "only true world" that had so passionately entranced him.

IV

OF THE TWO WORLDS—declares Swedenborg—the physical, far from being real of itself, is only the symbol of the spiritual. The statue is merely the marble garment of the creative idea embodied in the mind of the sculptor. And the human body is merely the haberdashery of the soul. For it is only in their physical dimensions that the shining lineaments of the spirit can be made manifest to the feeble human senses. It is for this reason that God turned His spirit into human flesh. God became human in order to demonstrate to man that He was divine.

"Matter is only an expression." And yet, since matter corresponds in every degree with the spirit, it is possible for the wise and the good man to understand the true spirit world, trammeled though he is in the network of the senses. For "nothing exists in nature which does not resemble its origin, or soul." Every particle of flesh and fiber and muscle in the body is similar to the flesh and the fiber and the muscle of the spiritual substance, or the "inmost of the material." Every object in the natural world is a "reflection" of the selfsame object in the world of the spirit. All ideas in the mind are symbolized by physical facts. All things are projected from the inmost spirit into the outward fact. "Nothing in nature exists except *from* a spiritual principle and *by* it . . ." In the seed of the tree is the form of the forest; in the circulation of the blood is the universal principle of life—"the constant revolution of birth and death, dissolution and renewal." Moreover, everything is in itself a perfect image of the total form of being. The drop of water contains the form and the substance of the entire ocean. In his comment on this Swedenborgian doctrine of correspondences, Emerson makes the thought concrete and picturesque. "The unities of each (human) organ are so many little organs; the unities of the tongue are little tongues; those of the stomach, little stomachs; those of the heart are little hearts. This fruitful idea furnishes a key to every secret . . . Man is a kind of very minute heaven . . . God is the grand man."

This is the password to the supreme design of the universe: "Nature exists entire in its leasts . . . We really live here and walk here as little universes, and carry both heaven and the world, consequently the Kingdom of God, in ourselves."

But even this physical world of ours was not created once and for all time as a distinct act of God. The creation of the world is a continual process—an endless interpenetration and impregnation of the spiritual world. The soul of the individual—and of the universe—is constantly uniting with the body in wisdom and in love. Could we but put on the spectacles of the spirit we should see that wisdom and love are the true steel girders that support the edifice of existence, and that the materials of this world are merely the clouds of vapor escaping from the chimney. "*This* is the truth of life."

And so the honest philosopher left his body and "wandered into the hallways of truth."

V

FROM the metaphysics of the universe Swedenborg turned to the theology of the heavens. He wrote a series of books which caused the image of Christ to shine more brightly upon the conscience of man.

The Lord, he declared, had visited him in one of his visions and had ordered him to reinterpret the meaning of His Word as recorded in the Bible. And when the "spiritual light" had sufficiently opened Swedenborg's eye, he set himself to the labor.

"The Scripture has a spiritual as well as a literal meaning." For it deals with the spiritual as well as with the material world. Heretofore the Church has taken its strictures and its chronology literally. But the stories in the Bible, built as they are out of the materials of time and space and fire and earth and flesh, are only God's manner of expressing the Eternal Truth of the immaterial spheres. For example, the story of Genesis is merely the flesh-parable of an Idea. The six days of creation represent the six stages "whereby unregenerated man attains to knowledge and love and becomes full in the image of God." First created by the hand of God were the fish and the fowls. And these creatures symbolize the first grade of the spiritual life, in which *faith* predominates. The animals that came next represent a phase of the spiritual life in which *love* is the active force. And finally came man, the crowning achievement of creation, the regenerated soul which embraces not only *faith* and *love,* but *understanding* as well. Furthermore, the Tree of Knowledge in the Garden of Eden must not be taken in its literal sense. It is the representation of worldly knowledge and sensual pleasure. "This kind of food is dangerous to the higher life of man."

In like manner, maintained Swedenborg, many of the doctrines of the Church must be submitted to a new interpretation. With courageous earnestness he attempts to bring religion back to its pristine simplicity. He disputes especially the literal doctrine of the Trinity. "Jesus, far from being the Son of God and the second member of the Trinity, is God Himself, the only God, and expresses the whole Trinity in His person." Swedenborg opposes the Calvinist doctrine of predestination, and declares that man's salvation lies not in his "faith" but in his character and in his eagerness to do active good. "The life which leads to heaven is not a life of retirement *from* the world but of action *in* the world . . . A life of piety alone without charity . . . leads *away* from heaven as much as it is commonly believed to lead *to* heaven." Man must lead a social life of action, and not a secluded life of prayer. The popular notion as to the relationship between God and man, declared Swedenborg, is false. It is not a flamboyant drama acted out in time and place; it is a quiet intertwining of the human spirit with the divine. But God does not draw the spirit of man upward to heaven. "This notion is a childish fairy tale." The state of a man's *inner* life makes his own heaven. Heaven is *within* us, and not *outside* of us. "No one will go to heaven who has not received heaven into his own heart."

Heaven, in short, is a continual state of *active love*. "Love is life; life is love; love is the very life of every man." This sort of "love-life" is indestructible, surviving even death, as the sun shining upon other spheres survives the clouds of our little atmosphere that blot it temporarily from our view. The body of life is heliotropic—that is, it turns ever sunward. Every garment and pod and casement that protects the seeds of life bends irresistibly toward the light until at last this outward covering shrivels up in the excessive material heat of time. And then out of the peeling emerges the ripened essence within, like the grain of golden corn. The grain of the spirit lives in a field of timelessness, indestructible in the winds and the rains and the heat. And Swedenborg, with a pen that dipped into a well of tenderness, began to describe this "after-time of life"—the immortal world of the human soul.

For years, he tells us, he had communicated with the spirits of departed folk just as you and I communicate at table with the living. And he had formed close friendships with the most illustrious "dead" alive. They were only too willing to inform him how they were getting on in their new life.

"Death is merely a continuation of life." It is neither a reversal nor a cessation of our present existence. Indeed, it is in no way different from our earthly activities. With quaint charm Swedenborg relates how, when he told some of his spirit friends that there are many people on earth who are skeptical of a future existence, the spirits were greatly surprised at such unbelief. And then they recalled that they too had been of the number of skeptics on earth. "How childishly stupid of us not to have recognized the certainty of this after-life!"

And then Swedenborg goes on with a detailed description of this after-life of the human spirit. "There intervenes but the space of a few days between the decease of the body and man's entrance into another world." As soon as a man dies in the body, "he is led into a certain state which is intermediate between sleep and waking, and when he is in this state he cannot know otherwise than that he is altogether awake; all his senses are as alert as in the fullest wakefulness of the body, as well the sight as the hearing, and what is wonderful, the touch, which then is more exquisite than can ever be realized in the wakefulness of the body . . ." And then the new spirit, as he gradually becomes accustomed to his surroundings, experiences his first great surprise. For the world in which he finds himself is so little different from the world he has just left that "many men refuse to believe they have died at all." The "newly-arrived" spirit finds himself possessed of a body similar to the one he has left behind; he meets the same sorts of people, and he sees around him the same kinds of objects and scenes with which he has been familiar on earth. "He enjoys in fact a real substantial existence."

But there is one substantial difference. His senses are much more wide-awake, much more *alive*. "Care should be taken not to give credence to the erroneous opinion that spirits do not possess far more exquisite sensations than during the life of the body . . . Spirits not only possess the faculty of sight, but they live in a light to which the midday light of this world cannot be compared . . . They enjoy the power of hearing also, and that in so exquisite a degree as vastly to exceed what they possessed in the body . . . Their desires and affections, moreover, are incomparably stronger than those possessed during the life of the body . . . In a word, man loses nothing by death, but is still a man in all respects, although more perfect than when he was in the body."

Not only does he take with him his senses, but his opinions and prejudices and habits, and all the psychology of his upbringing in the previous world. Many noble souls, for example, have looked forward to conversing with the wisest men of the ages concerning the happiness of heaven. And now they are given their wish. They are introduced to the former philosophers and sages of the human race, and they are permitted to converse with them until they find that they grow rather weary of the pleasure and beg to be excused. Other pious souls have been led on earth to believe that heaven is a place "where congregations ne'er break up, and Sabbaths have no end." These spirits are permitted to enter a temple and to perform their religious rites as long as they please. "At first they are in a state of ecstasy; but after a long period of devotion, their fervor begins to wane—some nod and sleep, others yawn, or cry out to be released, and all are wearied with the excess of their pious effort."

Finally the spirits learn what is the true nature of heaven. "It is the delight of doing something that is of use to yourself and to others." Now and then, observes Swedenborg, a spirit when he hears these words cries out in bewilderment, "But is it not the chief object of man to glorify God and to enjoy Him forever?" "Truly," answer the angels. And they explain that the "glorification of God" is something more than the "singing of psalms." It means "the bringing forth of the fruits of love—that is, the faithful, sincere and diligent performance of the work for which you are most adapted . . . For in this is the love of God, and the love of your neighbor; and this is the bond of society, and its good."

All this orientation of the newly-arrived spirit, continues Swedenborg, has been taking place in an intermediate state between heaven and hell. For man must receive judgment before he departs finally for one of the two regions. However, "the conception of a Judgment Day upon which the soul undergoes a trial before an Inquisitor is untrue." Actually there is no courtroom, no police atmosphere at all. The "scroll of a man's life" is presented before him and all the acts of his previous existence are recalled to him. He is his own judge and his own witness. And he decides for himself as to where he shall spend his coming days. "The Lord casts no one into hell"; but the spirits who have come to the other world with their previously wicked disposition —explains Swedenborg—"most naturally gravitate toward the hell of their own inclination, for there alone do they find their most congenial associates and associations." Very often an evil spirit is permitted to enter heaven if he so desires; but, unable to endure its purity, he almost always flings himself headlong into hell. Furthermore, the evil spirits are not punished for their wicked deeds on earth but rather because, having at last been enlightened with a résumé of their misdeeds and with an explanation of the good, and having been allowed of their own choice to adopt their future course, they still persist in their evil. There is nothing "mean" in the Lord's punishment. "The Lord never sends anyone into hell, but desires to bring all out of hell; still less does he induce torment; but since the evil spirit rushes into it himself, the Lord turns all punishment and torment to some good and use."

The soul's punishment, like its reward, is meted out in accordance with the divine law of mercy. "The mercy of the Lord involves all and everything . . . He pities the state of him whom

He permits to be punished"—just as He pities him whom He permits to enjoy the state of bliss. For all men are fragile creatures regardless of their temporary abodes. The prospering angel does not point the finger of scorn at the unfortunate devil. But rather he murmurs, as he peers into the pit, "There but for the grace of God am I." And he goes even beyond the point of inactive pity. "When the wicked endure punishment, there are always angels present to regulate its degree, and to alleviate the pains . . ."

And now, with a Christlike touch that healed and blessed, the Swedish mystic continued: "Every evil has its limit—even in hell." The devils in hell are forever prevented from rushing into greater depths of wickedness than was their earthly lot. "For it is a law there that no one must become worse than he has been in the world."

It goes without saying that this Swedish Saint Francis has found a place in heaven for all men of good will whether they are Christians or not. "There is not a single fact of Scripture concerning (discrimination as to) person, nation or people which is known to heaven, where the angels are totally unconcerned about the personality of Abraham, Isaac and Jacob, and see no difference between Jew and Gentile but a difference of human quality."

All infants, baptized or unbaptized, are sent to heaven immediately upon death to be nursed and raised by the angels. And, after their period of spiritual preparation, all good men and women gravitate toward that blessed abode. Swedenborg describes the "heavenly scene" with the positiveness of a personal eye-witness. For "it was permitted me four or five times to be there." All heaven in its total form is One Man—the Lord. Each society of angels performs its function as a part of His body, just as the heart and the kidneys and the blood vessels and the muscle fibers perform each their function to keep the human body alive and healthy. It is indeed a very human heaven that Swedenborg gives us—human to a most sublime degree. The new spirit enters this heaven—that is, the final stage of his development—in the possession of his better senses and his purer desires. His face and his body have assumed the lineaments of the goodness of his mind. And, once he has arrived in heaven, he is met with one pleasant surprise after another. He finds not only that marital love is practiced between male and female angels, but that husband and wife who have loved each other deeply on earth are reunited in heavenly wedlock. "Sexual love is the purest energy of the divine state." Lovers in their embrace "form one Angel." But if a husband and a wife had not been happily united on earth, they are permitted to go their own way in heaven and to look for other congenial company. "In the vast assemblage of heaven, both the husband and the wife are certain to find a congenial mate." For spirits are attracted to one another, in their forms and their visages and their hearts, by like qualities. And whatsoever the heart thinks in heaven, the form depicts. It is impossible for a golden head to conceal the tongue of a vixen.

In this new "land of the heart's desire"—declares Swedenborg —love never ends. It is not measured by the passage of the seasons or the wrinkles of age. There is no sense of time in heaven, "but only a change of states." The seasons of this holy arcanum are marked by the moods in the heart. When the heart is happy, it is springtime and the dawn; when the heart is sad, it is winter and the night. Nor is there in heaven any sense of distance or of space. "When anyone travels from one place to another, he comes there sooner when he desires and later when he does not desire." Only the wish in the lover's heart can bring his beloved to his side over the milestones of infinity. Love is the tender axis around which rotates the eternal planet of Paradise. No one grows old in these "tropics of purity." Or rather, "to grow old in heaven is to grow young." Everybody is continually "advancing to the springtime of his youth, so that the oldest angel appears the youngest." Women who have died old and worn out with age, but who have lived "in charity toward their neighbor . . . come . . . into a flower of youth, and into a beauty which exceeds all our earthly conceptions of beauty . . ."

Such, in brief, is the picture of heaven as mirrored in Swedenborg's creed. And who for a certainty can say there's no such "never-never land"? Is this heaven a dream? Well, and why not? "Man in his perfect dreams *is* heaven." And Swedenborg, blinded by an excess of light, put down his pen.

VI

WHEN this bombshell of gentle humanity burst upon the petrified dogmas of the eighteenth century, most men closed their ears and shut their hearts. A religion which, in its universal tolerance, admitted even the Buddhist and the Moslem and the Jew into the delights of heaven, was a source of danger to every armor save the unarmed soul of the saint. Swedenborg had distributed copies of his writings all over the continent and had repeatedly asked for comments. "Not a voice replied." He had dared to suggest on God's authority that the devil at his worst—was only human.

But gradually the chemicals of this high explosive reached Emerson and Hawthorne and Carlyle and Thoreau and Coleridge and De Quincey and Goethe and Maeterlinck—reached a host of other poets and philosophers and mystics. And then the power of Swedenborg's imagination shattered old prejudices and flooded the world with the sunlight of a new thought. And minds gathered in multitudes to worship.

There are two supreme poems of life and death. The *Divine Comedy* of Dante, painted in glowing colors of fire and hate, has fascinated the human mind. But Swedenborg's *Vision of Heaven* has touched the human heart. For this poem is painted with the brush of mercy on a canvas of tears.

WESLEY

Important Events in Life of John Wesley

1703—Born at Epworth, Lincolnshire.

1724—Took degree at Oxford.

1728—Took priest's orders.

1735—Sailed to preach in Georgia.

1738—Returned to England.

1738—Converted to "faith in Christ, the Redeemer."

1738—Organized "Methodist" Society.

1743—Issued rules for Society.

1747—First missionary journey to Ireland.

1751—First missionary visit to Scotland.

1751—Married Mary Vazeille.

1774—Published his *Collected Works* in 32 volumes.

1780—Founded Methodist Magazine (at first called *Arminian Magazine*).

1791—Preached last sermon, February 23.

1791—Died, March 2.

John Wesley
1703–1791

I<small>T WAS</small> his lot to be born to one of the strictest mothers in England. Susanna Wesley, the daughter of a non-conformist chaplain, refused to spare the bodies of her nineteen children in her effort to save their souls. She was the general of an army of little Christian soldiers. The battle could never wax too severe for her. She herself had been the twenty-fifth child of her father. Working from the ranks up to her command, she had learned the credo of survival. And now she practiced it on her recruits. "When turned a year old (and some before), they were taught to fear the rod, and to cry softly, by which means they escaped the abundance of correction which they might otherwise have had; and that most odious noise of the crying of children was rarely heard in the house."

Each child on its fifth birthday was allowed one day in which to learn the letters of the alphabet. And then each of them was taught to spell out the first chapter of the Bible. "In the beginning God created the heaven and the earth . . ." This was the first theme of their mental and moral instruction. On their sixth birthday the children spent six hours daily in classes learning

Christian theology. One day a week Mrs. Wesley had a private conference with each child. "It is almost incredible," she observed, "what a child may be taught in a quarter of a year, by a vigorous application, if it have but a tolerable capacity and good health."

Her son John was the fifteenth of her scholars. If the others prayed hard to be saved for heaven, John was literally snatched from the fires of hell. For the vicarage went up in flames when he was but a child. All the others were brought safely outdoors, but Johnny had been left behind in the confusion. It was some time before his absence was noted and the vicar rushed into the flames to save him. Wesley never forgot how close he had been to falling into the arms of the devil. His own experience, he felt, was a living proof of redemption.

II

AT TEN he entered the Charterhouse School and applied himself to his studies with the conscience of a young man whose father was the Vicar of Epworth and whose mother knew Latin and Greek. He carried the weight of the world's sin upon his little shoulders. It mattered not that other, "less innocent" souls were passing through a carefree childhood at Charterhouse. The son of Susanna Wesley felt that his ten years were merely added on to the accumulated responsibilities of the human race. Just as a child may inherit the ugly physical features of his ancestors, so too—believed Wesley—he himself had inherited the ugly moral imperfections of all mankind.

There was no childhood for John. At seventeen he already felt like an old man. He entered Christ Church, Oxford, hewed his conduct to the line of God, and wrote to his mother about his daily schedule of meditation and prayer. He might have formulated the golden rule, "Do unto the Lord what you would have the Lord do unto you."

He took his degree, entered Lincoln College as a Fellow, prepared himself in the "honest art of logic" and, following in the footsteps of his father, accepted a vicarage in a country parish.

But he discovered that he had no taste for tending a flock. Compared to the arduous study of God in his chambers at Oxford, the simple life of the village priest was a wasted time of idleness and indignity. He returned to Oxford, determined to become a religious recluse. Nobody but the Lord God was fit company for the impulsive and ambitious young Don. He would have no communication with the world. His desire was to commune alone with the world's Creator. But one day a stray remark was tossed into his ear—a simple statement made by one of the most insignificant of his handful of acquaintances. "Mr. Wesley," remarked this man, "it seems to me that to serve God, you must find companions. The Bible knows nothing of solitary religion."

A plain and homespun observation. Yet it possessed the power of creative truth. For on that day an English Saint Francis was born.

III

A TRIP TO LONDON brought John Wesley his first mission "among the people." He met one of Marlborough's soldiers—John Oglethorpe—a man whose social conscience was as keen as his sword. Oglethorpe proposed the founding of the colony of Georgia in the New World and the settling of this colony with the outcasts of the Old World—English debtors who had been huddled in filthy prisons, German Protestants who had been exiled from Salzburg by the Archbishop, other similar stepchildren of the human family. He asked Wesley to become pastor of the "regathered flock" in this new colony, and also to serve as missionary among the Indians. And the young Oxford Don eagerly accepted the offer. He took passage on the *Simmonds;* and the trip, which lasted a hundred days, had its romantic as well as its religious side. The young ladies on board were especially moved to prayers by the handsome young pastor. And several of them fell madly in love with his "Christian perfections."

In America, too, his stern task was made gentle by the magic of romance. He lost his heart to Sophia Hopkey, the beautiful niece of the colonial magistrate. He gave her daily instruction in French and in religion, and longed to enlarge the curriculum with a course on love. One evening, as he escorted her on a journey to her uncle's home, he sat down beside her in the shadows and timidly dared to plan their future—in the silence of his fancy. He could not as yet bring himself to translate his daring into words.

But John Wesley knew more about the fixedness of the heavens than he did about the fickleness of the earth. While he was slowly gathering his courage to propose, the young lady gave her hand to another. He had sung psalms to her when she had craved for love songs. In a fit of unreasonable grief at her "inconstancy," he expelled Sophia from his church services. And Sophia's husband, in retaliation, aroused the anger of the parishioners against their pastor.

It was an easy matter to enlist the disgruntled Georgians against Wesley. For the fruits of his evangelical mission "among God's people" were proving bitter to their taste. His first official act had been to smash a barrel of whisky which they had brought from England. He enforced rigid church services and punished all infractions of the moral code with an iron hand. The communicants were beginning to grumble that their old incarceration in the debtor's prison was more desirable than their new "life-term in the prison of salvation." This young preacher, they complained, was trying to meddle not only with their souls, but with their purses. The chief access to profit in the southern colonies was through the channel of slavery. And the ardent young prophet inveighed against the slave holders. A dangerous disturber of the peace.

"Enough of this interference with our business!" The flock was determined to turn out its "troublesome" pastor. Wesley was indicted before a Grand Jury which consisted of "a Frenchman who did not understand English, a Roman Catholic who did not understand Anglicanism, a professed infidel, three Baptists and sixteen Dissenters."

Shortly before the trial, however, John Wesley escaped in the night and took ship for England. His zeal for his mission was quite over. It was almost two and a half years since he had set out enthusiastically to preach among his fellowmen. And now he could no longer understand any of them—least of all, the girl he had loved.

The net result of his evangelism was a twist of irony that became interwoven into the texture of his soul. Embittered and disillusioned by the blows he had received from God's people, he now began to doubt the goodness—or at least the wisdom—of a God who had created such people. "I went to America to convert the Indian," he observed sardonically. "And now who shall convert me?"

IV

AFTER a brief spell of cynicism, he saw once again the simple path of his duty. He began to associate with a sect of German revivalists called *Moravians*. They told him to cease looking for external signs of failure or of success in the performance of God's mission. They declared that the proof of the power of God lay within the faith of man. And as he pondered over these utterances, the last words of his father, Sam Wesley, came back to him with commanding force. What was the true test of Christianity? "The inward witness, my son, *that* is the proof, the strongest proof, of Christianity." The people of Georgia, John Wesley decided, were merely the product of an age that had become intolerant in its easygoing skepticism. In this age of George II and of Voltaire, the "believing" priests of the Church of

England, no less than the churchless priests of unbelief, proved through their action that the living faith in Him was gone. The Lord had become the incarnation of "sweet reasonableness." He was a harmless, benevolently impotent old grandfather who couldn't at all influence the inexorable will of the younger generation—the devotees of the natural sciences. He sat in a wheel chair in the corner—a symbol of family sanctity, a sentimentalized relic of old obedience. But everybody admitted that He had become a rather tiresome obligation. The world made a show of piety to Him. And it went on dancing to its own egotistic tunes.

The prophets who had spoken for Him were centuries dead. The mathematicians and the anatomists and the generals and the free lovers were the pipers of the new order. The world, to be sure, had long since learned to love the ancient gentlemen of prophecy. But everybody would be terribly embarrassed to see them come to life again—vigorous and intense and exacting as of old. The world would be hard put to find them a night's lodging—let alone a throne.

John Wesley knew from experience how the world could deride a man who took his religion seriously. In his days at Oxford he had formed, together with his brother Charles, a "Holy Club" of young communicants who met together to discuss their spiritual problems and to lay plans for the reawakening of a religious enthusiasm among their fellow collegians. The club became the laughing stock of the whole university—professors and students alike. The members of the club were dubbed as the "Bible Bigots" and the "Bible Moths." But the Wesley brothers went on with their work. They visited the prisons and distributed alms among the poor of London. They fasted rigorously and lived sparingly, to the amusement of the English gentry who had surrendered themselves to a tropical fantasy of license after the snows of their Puritan fanaticism under Cromwell.

A prophet's lot in this age would be no bed of roses. But one night John Wesley walked home from a religious meeting in Aldersgate Street. It was the springtime of the year, only five months after his escape from Georgia. And on this spring night he dedicated himself to the life of a prophet.

V

WESLEY'S FELLOW ENTHUSIAST, George Whitefield, had electrified the country folk of England when he had mounted a horse to preach in the open air. It was so utterly unconventional to speak the Word to five thousand villagers from miles around—men and women who sat on the hillside or leaned against the trees—humble folk with untutored minds and hungry hearts.

Wesley decided to emulate Whitefield. "I will seek for God's inspiration in the free winds rather than in the stuffy air of the chapel." He had an ideal background for an itinerant preacher. In Georgia he had loved to swing the axe and do his thinking in the garden while the flowers fed his eye. A small but keenly built man. A picturesque figure in a multitude of worshipers gathered under heaven. Five feet four of dynamic energy. "In the company of larger men, he compared as a rapier with a sword."

He mounted his horse and took his first assignment among the miners of Kingswood, near Bristol. These dwellers of the coal-smeared regions had hardly ever been inside a church. No one had seen fit to build a house of God among them. They were so long used to working in the caverns of the earth, they had forgotten heaven.

Wesley preached to them as they emerged from their mines in the sunset. He selected what he pleased out of the liturgy, and led them in the singing of simple hymns. And the men who had seen nothing but darkness wept a few tears.

Then he left for other village folk who needed him, galloping with his message throughout the countryside of England. And wherever he spoke, he comforted the people.

And infuriated the priests. For he invaded their parishes and emptied their churches. What right had this traditionally ordained minister to break the rules of the Church of England and to preach wherever he willed? "I look upon the whole world as my parish!" Surely these were the words of a lunatic. A man with a Messianic complex who would destroy the Church itself if given the chance.

The very manner of his preaching, declared the priests, was a proof of his madness. People wept and shouted aloud and rolled wailing on the floor in response to his impassioned words. At one of his "conversions," it was reported, "people swooned, sank down on the ground as if dead . . . shrieked and trembled in every limb . . . A domestic servant remained in a trance-like condition, as if possessed . . . and she did not recover properly for fourteen hours." Such was the technique of the revivalist who had cast aside all the outward decorum of the Church ceremony and who called for the soul to testify aloud to the joyousness of its conversion to the revealed truth. All this was very un-English! "Pretending to extraordinary revelations is a horrid thing, a very horrid thing."

But Wesley was not ashamed of his work—even if a few of his converts were oversensitive to suggestion and lost themselves in a hysteria of emotion. The vast majority received his message sensibly where it belonged—in their hearts—like a drink of fresh rain after the musty theologic disputations of the Sunday sermons in the parish churches.

In the meantime, his opponents were trying to involve him in controversies over his "peculiar doctrine." Did he believe in salvation by faith, by grace through good works, or by the predetermined election of the Holy Few? They sent letters to the press seeking to draw him out and to indict him on the ground of his intellectual conviction. What *was* his conviction? they kept asking him again and again. And finally he replied to the Calvinists and the Anabaptists and the Antinomians and all the other doctors of the various schools who wrote learned treatises on the articles of faith. "You would have philosophical religion, but there can be no such thing. Religion is the plainest and simplest thing in the world. It is only this—*We love Him, because He first loved us.*"

And he proceeded to organize his thousands of followers into clubs of communicants patterned after the Holy Club which he and his brother had formed in their Oxford days. All over England and Ireland and Wales these societies sprang up. Simple people they were who composed them—friendless bits of human wreckage, derelicts for whom "nobody who *was* much *cared* much." They gathered together twice a week and reported to one another how it was with their spirit and gave mutual advice and shared their all-but-empty purses with the sickliest and the most destitute among them. Men who had frequently come home reeling with drink now took an oath never to drink again, and chronic ruffians suddenly straightened up with a new light and set themselves to steady work. Soon it became apparent to all who could see that there was a new "lift" to the underdogs of the community. And the scoffers who had dubbed the new sect as *Methodists* because of the seriousness with which they laid down their systematic program for spiritual conversion, began to wonder whether there wasn't a method to their madness after all.

It was a religion of democracy that Wesley founded. Anybody who was upright could join one of the Wesleyan clubs of High Conscience. A man's sect didn't matter, provided only he loved Christ. Wesley never attempted to turn anybody away from his belief. "My own belief," he said, "is no rule for another . . . If thou lovest God and all mankind, I ask no more: Give me thine hand."

VI

JOHN WESLEY continued to "live by preaching." And this meant to live by toil and trouble. For the general public took none too kindly to any procedure which they could not clearly understand. This "Methodist business" baffled them. "The Methodist preachers are plotting some terrible overthrowal, else why do they 'sneak' into a man's home and convert his wife to get up five o'clock mornings and sing hymns all day long?" These preachers, it was rumored, had organized into a secret society to overthrow the British monarchy and to put the pretender on the throne. "There can be no doubt of it!" A Methodist-inspired French invasion of England, it was whispered, might be expected hourly.

"And Wesley is the cause of it all." Wherever he preached, he was pelted with mud and threatened with worse. But always in the end the charm of his personality won over "God's children" before they went too far in their ungodly business. The following entry in his journal is characteristic of a hundred cases: "Finding the uproar increase, I went into the midst, and brought the head of the mob up with me to the desk. I received but one blow in the head; after which we reasoned the case, till he grew milder and milder and at length undertook to quiet his companions." Once a ruffian raised his hand, brought it down upon Wesley's head, and suddenly checked the blow as he murmured, "What soft hair he has!" Always when he squarely faced a crowd, "the lions became lambs."

It was the practice in this rough and rowdy century of Merrie England to kidnap young men in the street and to impress them into His Majesty's navy. And John Wesley did not escape the menace of such a destiny at the hands of his enemies. But hardly had his captors led him three quarters of a mile toward the nearest headquarters of the press gang, when their leader looked into Wesley's eyes and then and there decided to offer his own life in order to bring the preacher back safely through the mob. And Wesley started again on his methodical mission to build a hateless world.

At last, after much bitterness and many blows, Methodism became a respectable organization. The years had softened the novelty of Wesley's prophecy. The army of Methodists had grown big enough to command respect. Wesley had traveled everywhere. Yet, unlike the earlier nomad prophets who had pitched their tents at random and had then vanished in the wind, this methodical builder remained everywhere long enough to establish his ideas upon a solid basis. And thereby he insured the success of his prophecy.

Let us now for a while observe him in action—this bringer and builder of the new prophecy for mankind. From dawn to sunset he gallops over the unpaved and muddy roads of England, preaching in every town on the way, feeding the hungry, tending the sick, praying for the dead. In addition to all these duties, he personally supervises the huge organization of his Methodist classes all over England, instructing the resident preachers, writing letters to the itinerant teachers, presiding over the conferences of a hundred delegates who meet annually as the governing body. He knows intimately every last preacher and teacher in the organization. His travels average no less than four thousand miles a year. He has made fifty trips across the water to his congregations in Ireland, and he has left the hoofprints of his horses upon two hundred and twenty thousand miles of British soil. He does all his reading as he sits in the saddle. To quote his own quaint words, "History, philosophy, poetry I read on horseback, having other employments at other times." He opens his book while the horse is "at a trot," slackens the reins, and allows the "knowing animal" to lead him "surely and safely" into the next familiar town.

When he passed the age of sixty, his friends presented him with a carriage. He promptly built shelves on the walls of the carriage and filled them with a library of books. And thus thinking and reading and planning while "on the wing," he managed not only to preach more than thirty thousand sermons, but to write over two hundred books.

Nothing could shake him from his purpose—not even the frequent conspiracy of the elements. If the ferry was not at hand when he came to a river, he swam across. "The winds and Wesley," laughed his intimates, "go hand in hand." If a boat to Ireland floundered in a tempest, "John Wesley was certain to be aboard." Time and again he came near to drowning, or galloping over a precipice in the fog. No one knew the pitfalls of nature and the foibles of man better than he. But he never yielded either to the one or to the other. "One morning," he records in his Journal, "our servant came up and said, 'Sir, there is no traveling today. Such a quantity of snow has fallen in the night that the roads are quite filled up.' I told him, 'At least we can *walk* twenty miles a day, with our horses in our hands.' So in the name of God we set out. The northeast wind was piercing as a sword, and had driven the snow into such uneven heaps that the main road was unpassable." But they made the next town.

At fifty-one he had almost died of consumption. He had even composed his own epitaph. But at seventy-four he was riding furiously all over the countryside. At eighty-three he confessed sheepishly in his Diary that he was unable to write more than fifteen hours a day without tiring his eyes. And at eighty-six he came galloping to his appointments, his hair "smoothly combed out into a soupçon of curls," and his cheeks still glowing with the fires of ruddy health.

Twice on his travels following his youthful adventure in Georgia, he turned aside to canter in lover's lane. At the halfway milestone of his life he fell in love with the attractive young widow of a Scotch seaman. This woman was one of his most ardent disciples. When he was sick, she nursed him back to health. "She . . . understands my physical constitution better than most doctors." Unfortunately, however, she ran afoul of the social standards of the day. For she was a woman of "low station" and therefore "unfit to be wedded to a prophet." The rumor of the impending marriage created a scandal in the ranks of his followers. A conspiracy was formed to marry off the young lady secretly to one of his subordinates, a man "whose position could do no harm to the cause." And before Wesley could discover what was afoot, he was denied the fruits of his love.

Finally he did succeed in finding himself a wife, the daughter of a London merchant—a giddy young woman who understood neither his character nor his mission. For thirty years she niggled and nagged and scolded and threatened. She intercepted his private correspondence, destroyed his letters, ridiculed him to his enemies and struck him blows. And then, when she had worn herself and her husband to the point of prostration, she took sick and died. And Wesley's friends breathed a sigh of relief.

Three times he had gambled with his heart and lost. But he never lost his courage. His friends needn't have pitied him. "The one lasting and absorbing passion of John Wesley was God."

VII

FOR MANY YEARS the leader of Methodism was unaware that he had founded a new church. It didn't occur to him that his clubs and congregations and preachers would ever find it necessary to separate themselves from the Church of England into which he had been born, and which he loved in spite of her faults. Wesley abhorred the idea of separation in any sphere—political as well as spiritual. The latter years of his life were deeply saddened by the struggle of England with her colonial children in America. In 1776 he published an address to the people of "New Britain" in which he prayed for an end to "this business of men of the same blood and language murdering each other with all possible speed."

He had more than a casual interest in his friends of the New World. Throughout the thirteen colonies his preachers had organized large flocks of Methodists. When the Americans, much to his sorrow, broke definitely away from the Church of England, he ordained a priest in his own name to head the "Wesleyan"

Methodists in the New World. And thus John Wesley lived to see not only a separate government in America, but a separate church as well.

And he lived to face still another and far more bitter separation. For the time came when his life-long companion and fellow worker, his younger brother Charles, passed away. John Wesley, now in his eighty-sixth year, felt very lonely. He climbed into the pulpit and led the singing of his brother's greatest hymn, one of the several thousand that Charles Wesley had given to the English language:

> *Come, O thou traveller unknown*
> *Whom still I feel but cannot see,*
> *My company before has gone*
> *And I am left alone with thee.*

For a moment he bowed beneath his burden. He broke off his singing and sat down wearily at the foot of God's altar. Then he gathered himself and journeyed on.

BRIGHAM YOUNG

Important Events in Life of Brigham Young

1801—Born at Whittingham, Vermont.

1829—Moved to Mendon, New York.

1832—Joined Mormon Church, April 14.

1835—Appointed apostle of Mormon Church.

1835—Led persecuted members of Church to Illinois.

1844—At death of Joseph Smith, became head of Church.

1846—Organized famous Exodus of Mormons from Illinois.

1847—Arrived in Valley of Great Salt Lake.

1850—Appointed (by President Fillmore) governor of Territory of Utah.

1854—Reappointed governor.

1877—Died, August 29.

Brigham Young

1801–1877

Down in the American backwoods, about a hundred and fifty years ago, there arose a tribe of minor prophets—*jerkers, groaners, revivalists*. And hordes of farming folk with the old Adam in them suddenly "got religion," kneeling at night by the moaning trees and following their leaders who had gone a-pioneering into the secrets of God. They found that they could handle a Bible as easily as a gun. They got baptized for their sins, built churches, stopped playing poker and started adventuring over the countryside to "nudge their neighbors into the ways of the Lord."

One of the farmer lads who listened to these prophets was Brigham Young. An unvarnished soul, this Brigham—a Huckleberry Finn sort of fellow who believed that the age of miracles hadn't as yet departed, in spite of what the more sophisticated folk were saying. Out here in the woods of western New York it was miracle enough that folk lived and scraped together enough food and turned the wilderness into homesteads and the homesteads into cities. To the pioneer there's no miracle too miraculous to come true.

Brigham had been to school only eleven days in his life. He was too busy chopping the trees and plowing the fields. A life full of toil and hunger—and contentment. "If I had on a pair of pants that covered me, I thought I was doing pretty well." And when his legs grew longer and there was more of him to cover, he set to work the harder. He took up house painting and carpentry. And then, finding that he needed help, he married. For a wife is good at sewing scrap-ends into coverings, and baking bread, and making beds. At harvest time he gathered the crops for the farmers at seventy-five cents a day. And all this time he was waiting for the miracle. Searching for the gold-mine of the spirit that would make him rich.

Huckleberry Young has an angel within him. That's what makes the story epic. This young Brigham, who spits and swears with the rest of them, is looking for religion. A new kind of religion, and not a new label for an old creed. He is hungry for a personal revelation from God. He wants to find out what is all this drudgery for—this being born into a rough, unmannered body, leading the life of a lout in the semi-wilderness that is furrowed with so many untimely graves. What is all this building and suffering and dreaming for? *Why* is the American pioneer? Isn't it time to receive a new word from God for His frontier people of Israel? How much farther must they drive their sweating caravans before they can reach the Promised Land?

Such were the crude questionings that went on in Huckleberry Young's mind. When he spoke of the matter years later, the words sounded somewhat more polished: "I felt . . . that if I could see the face of a prophet, such as had lived on the earth in former times, a man who had revelations, to whom the heavens were opened, who knew God and His character, I would freely circumscribe the earth on my hands and knees; I thought that there was no hardship but what I would undergo, if I could see one person that knew what God is and where He is, and what

was His character, and what eternity was . . ." Others cared
only for whisky. But Brigham Young wanted a deep, long,
cooling draught of eternity. And then he stumbled upon a fellow
who knew how to prepare the drink. Not one of those sellers of
nostrums, but a real prophet. An uncouth rough diamond of a
Yankee from New England who had just founded a religion.
He called it *Mormonism*—from the English word *more,* and the
Egyptian word *mon,* which means *good.* He had a Bible, a
revelation, a prophecy. He declared that he was the latest ap-
pointee of God. Brigham looked into the matter, read the *Book
of Mormon,* and forever gave up chopping wood at eighteen
cents a cord.

II

BRIGHAM YOUNG had just turned thirty when he was baptized
into the Church of the *Latter-Day Saints,* as the Mormons called
themselves. Immediately he set out on a missionary journey over
the eastern states. In all sorts of weather he knocked at the doors
of the farmers; and as he dried his feet by their fireplace and
took their coffee, he told them the story of Joseph Smith, the
modern prophet. Joseph was only an obscure lad of eighteen
when the angel, Moroni, had descended from heaven to his bed-
side with a message from God. The angel informed him that in
the fourth century the Lost Tribe of Israel had migrated to
America where they had prepared the Bible of a new religion
for the Americans of the nineteenth century. This Bible—said the
angel—was inscribed in Egyptian characters on plates of gold.
And now the Lord God commanded Joseph Smith, as the prophet
of the new religion, to unearth the Bible from its burial place on
Cumorah Hill in Manchester, New York, and to translate it
into English for the guidance of his own generation. To Cumorah Hill he went, and there—he declared—he found the Bible
exactly as described in the vision. Together with the Bible, he

said, he had also found a pair of "spiritual spectacles," Urim and Thummim; and when he put them on, he automatically was able to translate the Egyptian hieroglyphics into English sentences. When the translation was completed, eight men testified that they had seen the gold plates in the original and that these plates had come truly from God. The Bible gained many converts who declared themselves the successors to the Lost Tribe—the Mormon tribe of the Latter-Day Saints.

Amazing how rapidly the movement grows. First the members of a family take the baptism. Then they baptize their immediate friends. And finally these friends go scurrying through the hinterlands with the *Book of Mormon* to convert more friends. The story of the magic spectacles does not stretch the credulity of these poor illiterates of the wilderness. There is scarcely a person among them who has not "seen God" and felt the wings of His angels brushing past his face. These Americans of the backwoods needed some emotional stimulant for their lives or they couldn't go on. And, for these uncritical folk of the eighteen thirties, what was emotionally pleasant was literally true. "I knew this religion was true," declared Brigham Young, "as well as I knew that I could see with my eyes, or feel by the touch of my fingers, or be sensible of the demonstration of any sense."

He comes like a salesman with the book in his hand. He gets many free meals and lodgings and blessings—and discomforts. "I stayed over night with Brother Atkinson, who lived in a very large frame house, said to have stood 150 years, which was so infested with bedbugs that we could not sleep. Brother George A. Smith gave it as his legal opinion that there were bedbugs there which had danced to the music at the battle of Trenton, as their heads were perfectly gray."

And thus a new religion sprang up in the American frontier. Joseph Smith, the prophet of this new religion, surrounded himself with a group of followers, and chose twelve apostles, of whom the leader was Brigham Young.

Inspired by their vision of a fuller, freer life, the apostles and their followers established their headquarters at Kirtland, Ohio. But here a charge of embezzlement was trumped up against Joseph Smith and Brigham Young. Together the prophet and his disciple escaped, not unlike Mohammed and Abu Bekr, and made their way through the enemy lines to safety.

They organized a Mormon settlement in Missouri. For a time the people of the neighboring counties tolerated them and their peculiar ideas. But how can a new church grow except through persecution? Martyrdom is as indigenous to the climate of a new religion as the east wind is to New England. It wasn't long before the Missouri mobs attacked and stoned the Mormons, and demanded that the legislature drive them out of the state.

And what was their crime? They refused to own slaves at a time when the entire South was inflamed with hatred against the abolitionists. Furthermore, "these people work too hard." They took no time off for loafing or pleasure. The result was that they became more prosperous than their neighbors. But most important of all was the instinctive aversion of old people to new ideas. "The religious tenets of the Mormons are so different from the present churches of the age, that they always have excited, and always will excite, deep prejudices against them, in any populous country where they may locate themselves . . ."

But the Mormons were not a bloodless people nursed on milk-toast. They refused to leave their women and their children to the mercy of the mobs. They organized a secret band of "killers" —the *Destroying Angels*—who took an eye for an eye, a life for a life. Joseph Smith was arrested by the Missouri militia and the following exchange of letters took place:

"BRIGADIER-GENERAL DONIPHAN:

"SIR—*You will take Joseph Smith and the other prisoners into the public square . . . and shoot them at 9 o'clock tomorrow morning.*

"SAMUEL D. LUCAS, MAJOR-GENERAL COMMANDING."

And the reply:

"It is cold-blooded murder. I will not obey your order. My brigade will march for Liberty tomorrow morning at 8 o'clock; and if you execute these men, I will hold you responsible before an early tribunal, so help me God.
"A. W. DONIPHAN, BRIGADIER-GENERAL."

Nevertheless the Governor of Missouri issued an order that the "Mormons must leave Missouri in a body or be exterminated, unless they are willing to renounce their religion and live as other Missourians."

And Brigham Young, who had become the leader of his people after the imprisonment of Smith, answered for all his band. "Renounce our religion? No, sir, it is all that we have on this earth . . ."

There was nothing to do but to leave. And Brigham led his people out of their house of bondage. The exodus was attended with much misery. To Illinois trekked three thousand Mormons. And here they were joined by Joseph Smith, who had escaped from jail. They settled upon the east bank of the Mississippi and secured an entire township for the asking—"since this land is unhealthy, a fit place for an unwelcome tribe." They changed the name of the settlement from *Commerce* to *Nauvoo*, which in the secret language of the Mormons meant *The City Beautiful*.

III

ONCE AGAIN the Mormons prospered. "The Lord has showered manna upon our tribe." But the sons and the daughters of Modern Israel were still in exile. Nauvoo was still within the borders of Egypt and not in the Promised Land. Again the Pharaohs began to persecute them. For the Latter-Day Saints had established a custom which was most objectionable to their neighbors. They had begun to practice "plural marriages." Joseph Smith had "received a momentous commandment from the

Lord" to return to the days of Abraham and Isaac and Jacob and to take many wives in order that they might beget many children. The Lord had revealed to him, he maintained, that the soul of every human being exists not only after death but before birth. Every soul must go through life in a human body in order to be promoted to a higher stage of development after death. There are millions of souls in heaven waiting to be born, pleading for the men and the women below to provide them with a tabernacle of flesh "in order that they may enter upon the final step in their journey to the divine." And who—asked Joseph Smith—can deny them this right? "It is the religious duty of every pious Mormon to bring to birth as many of these souls, through the medium of as many wives, as possible."

When Brigham Young learned that he must enter upon a life "revolting to his natural inclinations" or else "treat lightly of the things of God," he decided to do his "divine duty." While he remained at Nauvoo, he married eight women. Before he died he had taken twenty-seven wives and had become the father of fifty-six children.

Yet he was not a lascivious man. On the contrary, he was unusually temperate in his appetites and methodical in his habits. In spite of the witticisms of the facetious, Brigham Young was able to prove in the United States courts that polygamy with him was a religious commandment rather than a licentious whim. He testified that he was personally opposed to polygamy and that he had decided to enter upon it only after a long and bitter struggle with his own conscience. And the impartial judges who heard his testimony believed him.

But the public felt differently about the matter. When the news spread that a "City of Venus" had been founded in the state of Illinois, an avalanche of invective descended upon the Mormons. A crusade was launched to fight fire with fire, to meet the "immorality of polygamy" with the equally outrageous immorality of persecution. And the flames of the public hatred were fanned into greater fury when Joseph Smith announced himself as one of the candidates for the Presidency of the United States (in 1844).

And then the blow fell. Brigham Young was at the time campaigning for his prophet in the New England states. One day, as he sat waiting for a train in the Boston railway depot, the news reached him that his candidate was no more. The Illinois authorities had taken Joseph Smith into custody—and then a mob had broken into the jail and shot him to death.

Brigham Young, as the chief of the twelve apostles, immediately returned to Nauvoo and claimed the leadership of the Mormon Church. A few dissenters broke away from the community to organize churches of their own. But the main body of the Mormons remained intact under the new leader, who proceeded to prove that "when the half-gods go, the gods arrive." The assassins of Joseph Smith had taken a man with very human failings, had bestowed upon him the gift of martyrdom, and thereby had raised him to the rank of an immortal legend. On the day on which Joseph Smith was murdered, the Mormon religion did not die; it entered upon a new life of irresistible adventure.

And the Moses of this new adventure was Brigham Young. He called his folk together and told them that they were ordered out of Illinois into the wilderness beyond. It was a bleak February morning in 1846 when the vanguard of the Mormon exiles crossed the Mississippi and began their final long pilgrimage. It was like the march of a conquering army rather than the flight of a dispossessed and poverty-stricken sect. Brigham had taken along a brass band so that his people might dance away the cold of the wilderness nights, and sing songs in their sickness, and play an entrance march into heaven for the multitudes of their loved ones who had dropped on the way. The March of the Twenty Thousand. An epic in sweat and prairie storms and desert suns. A mass migration blazing a trail through two-fifths of the western United States—a pioneering feat for historians to marvel at. But they were not doing historians' work. They were doing God's work.

"You might see women sit in the open tents keeping the flies off their dead children, sometimes after decomposition had set in." You might see endless miles of prairies until your eyes watered, endless miles of monotony broken only here and there by cottonwood trees and a few marked graves of men who had set out before them and had only half-finished their adventure. You might see Brigham Young moving everywhere about his party, helping the old women and the young wives as they poured their coffee for their men folk, taking the driver's seat when a man grew sick and weary, huddling on sentinel duty by the shivering fires, planning every last detail of the heartening, heart-breaking voyage.

His organizing ability had brought order out of chaos. He had introduced a regular routine for eating, sleeping, playing and marching; and everybody in the company was obliged to follow this routine to the minutest detail. Every morning, at five o'clock, the bugle gave the signal for rising. By seven o'clock, breakfast had been eaten, the dishes had been scoured, and the caravan was on the march. At twelve o'clock, they stopped to eat and to rest; and two hours later, they were again on the march. At six o'clock they settled down for the night, and within a few minutes the desert blossomed into a city. At eight, the bugle announced that the hour for relaxation had arrived. It was an hour of band playing and singing and—for those who had the energy after the day's march—social dancing. At nine o'clock they went to sleep.

This routine was broken only on Sunday, when the entire camp rested and gathered physical and moral strength for the next week's march.

Such was the invariable procedure throughout the spring and the summer and the fall months. And then, when the snows came, Brigham set up the main body of his people in winter quarters and took along a select handful of stalwarts to seek for the final settlement in the Far West. Where would this settlement be? He studied maps and heard reports. An old scout, Jim Bridger, told him about the Valley of the Great Salt Lake. Here was virgin country. It contained no settlements of people to drive the Mormons out as soon as they had made the land prosperous; no judges and juries to incite the mob against them in the name of civilization.

As the party approached the Great Salt Lake, Brigham Young took sick with mountain fever. This new Moses, like his ancient prototype, seemed destined to die before the very portals of the Promised Land. But he lived! In the heat of July, seventeen months after he had led his people across the Mississippi, he rode into the Blessed Valley. He lay convalescing from his long illness as his team and horses drove him through the cañon into the Land of the Heart's Desire. He looked, and he held his breath in adoration. Behind him in the distance, a backdrop of snow-whipped mountains as glittering as the Alps; and beyond him, the blue stretches of the Salt Lake that sparkled with the magic of Italy.

But the level land of the Valley before him looked arid and stony and severe. God's children would have to work very hard to provision this temple of beauty. Yet in spite of all the salt and the drought, the seeds would be sown. And Brigham Young raised himself from his bed with fire in his eye. "Here we can raise our own potatoes and eat them; and I calculate to stay here . . . The desert shall rejoice and blossom as the rose."

IV

In utah the Mormons passed through the usual diseases that attack an infant colony—plagues of locusts that ate away their crops, winds that froze their bodies, quarrels that paralyzed their efforts. But slowly the settlement grew into vigorous maturity under the care of "Doctor" Brigham Young. For he knew how to treat men's bodies and minds and souls. He might have been a novelist or an actor if he had not been destined to be a statesman; for he felt keenly, as only the greatest artists have felt, the inner springs of human psychology. And his people followed him implicitly in his adventure of mutual understanding. For Brigham Young was not only their teacher but their prophet.

He was not a poet-prophet; he was a prose-prophet. His was a mind encircled in homilies, not in haloes. He had no sublime imaginings. His fancy lay in the roughness of his hands; it was limited entirely to what those two hands might achieve. He scorned all theory. He simply could not conceive of his being obliged "to philosophize for ten years without erecting a building or founding a city." He took pride in the fact that his mind "was uncorrupted by books." And he spoke the gospel of the pioneer who had never had the time to realize the expediency of ideas as the material for building. "Education will not enable a youth to marry and to set up house-keeping in the Rocky Mountains."

A prosaic prophet for a prosaic race. Strong, eager, simple folk came from many dark corners of the world to set up house-keeping in Utah. The *Book of Mormon* had crossed the ocean to the farming settlements of Denmark and the mining districts of Britain. And old-world blood came flowing to mingle with the new. Forty-niners stopped at Utah on their way to the goldfields of California, forgot about the gold and became converted to the Mormon faith. Wheelwrights and carpenters, butchers and builders and woodcutters and sawyers and smiths—all sorts of men of brawny muscle and sturdy faith came to set up their adobe huts and to hew out new streets in Utah. Most of the immigrants were poor folk. For Brigham Young had nothing to offer to the rich. And most of them were *illiterate* folk. For Brigham Young had nothing to offer to the learned. "We take the poorest we can find on earth . . . We are trying to make ladies and gentlemen of them. We are trying to school their children, and to so train them that they may be able to gather around them the comforts of life, that they may pass their lives as the human family should do—that their days, weeks, and months may be pleasant to them."

Brigham took care that his desert settlement would not become a dead cemetery of reposeful faith watered by prayers and tears. He told his people that they must not pray to God to perform miracles for them, but to build and to act and to plan with their own good limbs and brains. "I do not feel disposed to ask the Lord to do for me what I can do for myself," he said.

As a result the Mormons trusted in God but kept their hands busy, traded shrewdly but honestly with the pioneers who were streaming toward the West, developed warehouses and banks and factories and printing presses and schools. They had no trouble with the Indians, for they dealt with them on the principle that it was cheaper to feed them than to fight them. They undertook—and completed—the first large-scale irrigation project in the country. They established coöperative enterprises. They gave the franchise to women. They denounced slavery. They contributed money toward the building of a Catholic Church and a Jewish Synagogue. And they instituted the tithing system—that is, the appropriation of one-tenth of every man's earnings for the maintenance of the poor. The Mormon Church, in other words, was interested in the temporal as well as in the eternal welfare of its members. We may scoff at Joseph Smith's "discovery" of the Golden Book. But we cannot scoff at Brigham Young's application of the Golden Rule. The principle of Brigham Young, and of Mormonism at its best, may be summarized in a few words: *Try to serve your neighbor's need rather than your own greed.* "I have made no man poor," remarked Brigham Young proudly, "but I have made thousands rich."

[*264*]

And thus, adhering to the principle of tolerant interdependence, the Mormons dug out and scaffolded and gilded a prosperous city. Word spread throughout the vision-teeming United States, athrill with the stories of Paul Bunyan, that a new prodigious miracle of the American heart and muscle had been accomplished in Utah. Brigham Young had sown the teeth of Cadmus anew, and a race of giants was born in the American desert.

Finally Utah was admitted as one of the states into the Union. The theocracy of Brigham Young was merged with the democracy of America. But not before the Federal Government had compelled the Latter-Day Saints to give up their practice of polygamy.

And now, when this new chapter in the epic of Mormonism had begun, Brigham Young was no longer leader of his people. He had gone to his rest—with the serene confidence of a man who looks forward to a cool, refreshing rainfall in the desert. "I have done my work faithfully," he said. "Let me have a good sleep until the morning of the resurrection."

MARY BAKER EDDY.

Important Events in Life of Mary Baker Eddy

1821—Born at Bow, New Hampshire.

1843—Married Major George W. Glover.

1843—Major Glover died six months after marriage. Her only child (also named George W. Glover) born three months later.

1853—Married Dr. Daniel Patterson.

1863—Deserted by Dr. Patterson.

1866—Discovered Christian Science.

1875—Published first edition (1000 copies) of *Science and Health.*

1877—Married Asa Gilbert Eddy.

1879—Organized First Church of Christ, Scientist, in Boston.

1883—Founded *Christian Science Journal.*

1892—Founded Christian Science Publishing Society.

1908—Established *Christian Science Monitor.*

1910—Died, December 3, at Chestnut Hill, near Boston.

Mary Baker Eddy

1821–1910

On a chill october night in 1867 there came a knock on the door of Mrs. Mary Webster, the wife of a retired sea captain who lived at Amesbury, Massachusetts. The good old lady opened the door and peered into the dark. A little elfin of a woman—she seemed scarcely more than a hundred pounds of frightened skin and bone—begged for admission. "Won't you let me come in, please?"

"Why, certainly!" Mrs. Webster led the bedraggled little creature to the fire and offered her a cup of tea.

Having emptied her cup, the stranger was about to leave. But Mrs. Webster urged her to remain. "I'm all alone here. My husband is away at Manchester. He's the superintendent of a cotton mill in that city. You can stay here with me as long as you like."

"But you don't even know who I am."

"You are one of God's creatures in distress. And so you are my friend."

The stranger smiled. A pitiable, grateful smile. "I shall be glad to stay. You see, I really have no home."

"You poor thing!" Mrs. Webster put a motherly arm around

the little woman's shoulders. They had never grown to maturity, these lean and angular shoulders, but they were already bent with premature old age. And the face, too, was that of a woman well past her middle years.

The stranger nestled against Mrs. Webster. She seemed starved for human sympathy. "You've no idea how happy you've made me."

"Well, that's what we're here for." Mrs. Webster tried to conceal a tender heart under a matter-of-fact tone. "Oh, by the way," she added as an afterthought, "do you mind telling me your name?"

"Mrs. Glover. Mary Baker Glover."

It was only a temporary haven that Mrs. Glover was able to find in Mrs. Webster's home. One evening the old lady's son-in-law, William Ellis, came up for a visit from New York. "I'll have no vagabonds in this house!" he stormed, and put Mrs. Glover precipitately out of the door.

There was a lashing rain outside. For several minutes the outcast stood shivering in the deluge, and then she turned helplessly down the road to seek for her next uncertain shelter.

*　*　*

On a midsummer day in 1888 the same little wisp of a woman —through a later marriage she had now become Mrs. Mary Baker Eddy—stood before a convention of Christian Scientists in Chicago. The hall was packed to the doors. Many of the audience had come to jeer rather than to cheer. The "little lady of God" began her speech with a quotation from the first verse of the ninety-first Psalm: "He that dwelleth in the secret place of the most High shall abide under the shadow of the Almighty."

A hush fell upon the audience. All eyes were fixed upon that shining, eager, inspired face. A disembodied spirit, endowed with eternal youth. And the message that came from those eloquent lips—she spoke spontaneously, without notes—was a summons to a world-wide crusade for deathless, painless and wantless youth. "It is within yourselves, this power to abolish poverty and sickness and sorrow and the fear of death . . . All suffering, all evil, is but a nightmare, a wandering away from the truth, an error of the human mind . . . Abolish this error of evil thought, of hate, greed, lust, self-will, personal ambition, pride, arrogance, envy, jealousy and spite. For of such are the seeds of sickness and death . . . Return to the truth of Christ Jesus, the Scientist Supreme . . . Yield to the spirit within you, the spirit of gentleness and radiance, of beauty, courage, confidence, trust, hope, patience, lovingkindness, compassion and peace. Of such are the seeds of health and life everlasting . . ."

The audience sat spellbound. The reporters forgot to take notes. When she finished her speech, the entire throng swept forward to the stage. Men leaped upon the platform and lifted women and children after them. They fought to touch her hand, her dress, the very ground she stood upon. As for Mrs. Eddy herself, "she received their homage meekly and almost silently"—we quote from one of the contemporary newspapers—"as the people thronged about her with blessings and thanks, and strong men turned aside to hide their tears." Tears of gratitude, of ecstasy, of renewed hope. For what they had just heard was "not a lecture from human lips, but a message from a sublime heart."

* * *

What sort of person was this amazing little woman who within the space of twenty-one years had risen from the destitute to the divine?

II

SHE was born at the village of Bow, New Hampshire, of a Scotch-English ancestry of farmers who tried to "do justice, love mercy, and walk humbly with their God." The neighboring villagers referred to her as "a tiny baby with a long name"—Mary

Ann Morse Baker. Her mother died early, worn out with the hardship of raising a family of three boys and three girls upon the stony soil of New England. Brought up under the "strong understanding and iron will" of her father, little Mary developed —it would be wrong to say grew up, for physically she never *did* grow up—into a nervous, willful, sickly yet lovable child. An affectionate, fanciful and thoughtful little tadpole of a child—"all head and no body." She was fond of corresponding with her older brothers, who had gone to seek their fortune in various parts of the country. "The family has left to attend a Sabbath funeral," she wrote in one of her letters to brother Sullivan—a composition as charmingly formal in style as it was charmingly informal in grammar, "and I am left alone to review past events . . . There is one thing if I have not improved it aright I have learned from expperience to prize more perhaps than ever I did *before* that is *Dear Brother* the *friendly advice* and *council* you was ever giving me and the lively interest you ever manifested in my welfare but now when I sit down to my *lonely* meal I have no brother Sullivan to encourage me as formerly—but there is no philosophy in repining I must extend the thought of benevolence farther than selfishness would permit and only add my health at presant is improveing slowly and I hope by dieting and being careful to sometime regain it . . ."

From a sickly and lonely childhood she emerged into a sickly and lonely womanhood. Unable to take an active part in the external physical world, she became introspective, philosophical, aloof—an adventurer into the inner world of her own mind. She dreamed dreams and wrote verses—rather crude, it must be confessed—and hoped for the day when her health might permit her *actively,* rather than *passively,* to "extend the thought of benevolence farther than selfishness."

In the meantime she was married twice—to George W. Glover and to Daniel Patterson—lost her first husband through death and her second through desertion, gave birth to a son (by her first husband) and was compelled, owing to her illness and her poverty, to give him up to the tender mercies of a stranger, wandered over the rocky hillsides of New England in quest of a place to lay her head, and found herself at last, at the age of forty-six, an aimless bit of wreckage in the human driftwood of the dispossessed.

Mary Baker was rapidly completing the ordinary span of human life an obscure and total failure.

And then something happened. Whether this something was an external physical fact or a fancy within her own mind is a question for the scientists and the theologians to quarrel about. It is the business of the biographer merely to record the incident and to note the resultant transformation of a frustrated outcast into an inspired leader. This incident took place in Lynn, Massachusetts, on a midwinter day shortly after the Civil War. While walking on the slippery sidewalk, Mary Baker fell and painfully injured her spine. "The physician attending me," she wrote later on, "said I had taken the last step I ever should." But as she lay despondently on her bed she asked for her Bible, and her eye— through divine guidance, she maintained—fell upon a passage in Matthew ix, 2–7: "And lo, they brought to him a paralytic, lying on a bed . . . and Jesus said to the paralytic, Be of good cheer, child; thy sins are forgiven . . . Arise, and take up thy bed, and go unto thy house. And he arose, and went away to his house." In these words, declared Mary Baker, "I discovered the Science of divine metaphysical healing." The reading of this secret of divine healing produced so great a surge of power within her, she tells us, that immediately she "got out of bed and walked." And this is how the modern religion of Christian Science was born.

III

FOR THREE YEARS she withdrew from society, pondering upon her "great secret" and translating it into the language of a new

Bible. The gospel of personal health through universal love. After her three years of secluded study she became once more a wanderer—this time, however, not to *seek* but to *bring* peace. A great change had come over her. Gone were her helplessness and her bitterness. Instead, there shone in her eyes a light like a benediction, so that "her very presence brought healing to the sick." The "temperamental little invalid" had became a gentle herald of mercy. "If ever there was an angel upon earth," wrote an acquaintance of Mary Baker's at that period, "it is this woman."

Yet her way to final recognition was still beset with misunderstanding and derision and the gossip of evil tongues. Her opponents called her a "stupid old humbug"; and even among her disciples there were those who felt disappointed to find her somewhat less perfect than the marble statue of a saint. She was far too human, they said, to be the messenger of the sublime. And they were not altogether wrong. Her works—and isn't this true of even the greatest of mortals?—were never able to catch up with her words. She still gave way occasionally to outbursts of temper, of petty jealousy, of foolish pride. And she had developed a pitiable hunger for the possession of material goods—a reaction, perhaps, from her earlier pathetic deficiency in these goods. She accepted payment for her spiritual ministrations. And in this procedure she was neither insincere nor inconsistent with her own teaching. A profound belief in the healing power of Christ Scientist, she maintained, will abolish not only your *physical* ailments, but your *economic* ailments as well. Ill health and an empty purse are evils to be ashamed of and to be got rid of. Economic security attained through honest methods, she insisted, is not only permissible, but desirable, for the maintenance of the happy life.

And so she found nothing wrong in the practice, and in the encouragement for her disciples to practice, the teaching of the principles of Christian Science for a specified fee. Together with her (third) husband, Asa G. Eddy, she moved to Boston (in

1882) and opened the *Massachusetts Metaphysical College* for the training of practitioners in the new religious science of physical and spiritual well-being. For her textbook she used her own recently published outline of her new doctrine—*Science and Health*.

The college was a success from the start. For there was something magical in the personality of this little woman of sixty who had brought to the world the waters of a new fountain. The fountain of perpetual youth. There was a fascination about the very name of her new religion—*Christian Science*. It connoted the miracles of religion and the principles of reason. Indeed, it professed to identify religion *with* reason. "Christian Science is the scientific system of divine healing"—the *one certain* system of healing, said Mrs. Eddy, because it is the one method based upon the scientific law of truth. And this law of truth, asserted Mrs. Eddy, is the *spiritual reality* as opposed to the *physical unreality* of the world. Man is endowed with two sets of senses— the physical senses of sight, hearing, taste, smell and touch, which bring us *false images* of life, and the metaphysical sense of the spirit, which gives us the *true essence* of life. Our physical senses can recognize only *external objects*. For example, we can see the sky, touch a table, smell a rose, and so on. But these physical senses cannot recognize *internal emotions*. We cannot see hope, touch joy, or smell love. We know of their existence only through our metaphysical or spiritual sense.

Now parallel to our two sets of senses—declared Mary Baker Eddy—there are two kinds of science: the physical sciences, which are based upon our physical senses, and the metaphysical science, which is based upon our metaphysical sense.

And now there arises an obvious and important question. Which of these two kinds of science is based upon fact, and which upon falsehood? To this question Mrs. Eddy gives an emphatic answer. The only *true* science is the *metaphysical* science. The material world is a passing mirage; the spiritual world is an eternal reality. This eternal reality can reach our consciousness —declares Mrs. Eddy—not through the eye or ear or hand or mouth or any other physical organ, but only through the mind. The physical senses can come into contact only with destructible matter. The metaphysical sense finds itself in the presence of indestructible spirit. "There is no life, truth, intelligence, nor substance in matter. All is infinite Mind and its infinite manifestation, for God is All-in-all. Spirit is immortal Truth; matter is mortal error. Spirit is the real and eternal; matter is the unreal and temporal. Spirit is God, and man is His image and likeness. Therefore man is not material; he is spiritual."

And this spiritual essence of man—the Godlike and therefore the only *real* part of him—is the complete lord and master of his material body. Let us for a moment glance at these two selves: the material and the spiritual, which—according to the teachings of Christian Science—compose the personality of every human creature.

The material or "false" self. This is the ordinary, everyday part of you and me. It possesses certain external attributes—such as size, color, form, motion, irritability, expression, and the handicap of physical change and of physical decay. It is a rather pathetic sort of prisoner, bound by its body and subject to its environment—a helpless clod arising from the dust and destined shortly to return to the dust.

The spiritual or "true" self. This is the innermost, universal part of you and me. It exists in consciousness, in aspiration, in mind. It is bounded by no physical dimensions and subject to no material limitations. The scope of its activity is infinite. It can encompass the universe within a single thought and travel in an instant to the remotest regions of time and space. The attributes of this spiritual self are radiance, joy, freedom, power, love. No prisoner this, and no slow and bungling toiler who painfully fashions things only to see them destroyed. This *real* self is not

[276]

subject to destruction, not subject to sin or sickness or death. For it is an essential and imperishable part of the Eternal Spirit of Life.

It is this Spirit of Life which dominates our existence, declares Mrs. Eddy. Let us only yield to it, and it will blot out all the errors and the terrors of the body, all its hatreds and jealousies and diseases and disharmonies and wars. The more we dwell upon the potency of the mind, the less distinct becomes the illusion of matter. (The modern physicists, it is interesting to note, seem to be tending toward this metaphysical idea as enunciated by Mrs. Eddy. These physicists, in their search for reality, have found it necessary to keep on refining matter until they now regard it as "consisting mostly of emptiness within which . . . electric charges are rushing about with great speed." The "material substance" of the universe seems thus to be dissolving into an immaterial force.)

Christian Science, therefore, teaches the supremacy of spirit over matter, of mind over body. This supremacy is an "established truth" based upon "the law of God, the law of good, interpreting and demonstrating the divine principle of universal harmony." Harmony in the individual, leading to perfect health; and harmony in society, leading to perfect love. "That day will come (may it come speedily) when all who have not yet awakened from the sluggishness of material life will have that joy . . . will feel love and goodness transforming them and their surroundings to a beauty and peace unknown before . . . Then will it be forgotten that there have ever been dreamed such things as sickness, bereavement, or estrangement; that there have ever been dreamed such things as poverty, toil, or disappointment." For on that day it will be recognized throughout the world that there is no death but a shedding of the old and useless material garment. On that day it will be recognized that the spirit alone is triumphant—the world-embracing spirit which "creates a life all goodness, all beauty, all friendship, and unfolds this life in endless variety of form, color, and action—forever."

IV

THIS, in brief, is the doctrine that Mrs. Eddy taught to her disciples. Many of them insisted upon remaining not only her disciples, but her devoted slaves. They addressed her as Mother, they spaded her garden, mowed her lawn, mended her clothes, prepared her food, copied her manuscripts, and read her proofs. And the only reward that most of them required was the reassurance that she was happy. "It is we, and not you, who are in debt for services performed. For *we* have given you only a few idle moments of our time, but *you* have given us a new life." One day the distinguished philosopher, Bronson Alcott, came to visit the Metaphysical College. He found a young man by the name of George Barry arranging the furniture in the parlor. Mr. Alcott engaged him in conversation. The young fellow showed a keen intellect and poetical imagination. "Do you mind telling me your age?" asked the philosopher.

"I'm five years old, sir." And then, in answer to Alcott's puzzled expression, he went on: "It's five years since I first met Mrs. Eddy."

So potent was the magic of her personality that even those who quarreled with her couldn't help adoring her. One of her earliest pupils, Daniel H. Spofford, had become mixed up in a lawsuit against her. Yet even in the midst of his bitterness he remarked that Mrs. Eddy had "brought into my life its most illuminating truth." Another of her pupils, Mrs. Augusta Stetson, was excommunicated from the Christian Science Church at the instigation —some people asserted—of Mrs. Eddy herself. "I gladly accept this crucifixion at the hands of my superiors," she declared. "It is but another step in my climb to our leader's own Christ-like level."

Her followers had indeed come to look upon their leader as a modern Christ. They flocked around her and worshiped her and offered her huge sums of money for the perpetuation of the Mother Church. This church was at first a small and unpretentious institution incorporated for the "transaction of the business necessary to the worship of God." But the institution grew with amazing rapidity both in size and in influence. On December 30, 1894, a new building for the Mother Church was dedicated in the "cultural center" of Boston. In the "Holy of Holies" of this new Temple there had been erected a shrine to the founder and leader of the "religion of perpetual health." The mantelpiece of this shrine, as the attendant explained to the hushed visitors, "is of pure onyx . . . the rug is made of a hundred breasts of eiderdown ducks . . . the wash room . . . is of the latest design with gold-plated pipes . . . the painted windows were inspired by the Mother's poem, *Christ and Christmas* . . ."

But even this magnificence failed to satisfy the followers of Mrs. Eddy. They were anxious to build a monument of still greater splendor as a token of their adoration for their leader. And so, in the summer of 1902, they began to raise a fund of two million dollars—this fund was rapidly oversubscribed—and four years later "the snow-white Temple of Bedford stone and granite reared its dome to a height of two hundred and twenty-four feet, one foot loftier than the Bunker Hill Monument."

The contemporary reporters vied with one another in their lavish descriptions of this, "the most imposing church edifice in the world"—with its seven marble and bronze staircases, its seventy-two bronze lamps each suspended by eight chains, its "pillarless and postless vault like the inverted bowl of the sky," its vast organ, its costly tapestries, its mile and a half of pews.

The dedication attracted "no less than forty thousand visitors" from every part of the country. In order to accommodate the throng, there were six separate services within a single day. At

[279]

each of these services, thousands of devout voices sang the dedicatory hymn written by Mrs. Eddy herself:

> Shepherd, show me how to go
> O'er the hillside steep,
> How to gather, how to sow,—
> How to feed thy sheep;
> I will listen for thy voice,
> Lest my footsteps stray;
> I will follow and rejoice
> All the rugged way . . .

But at all these services for the dedication of the Mother Church there was one absent. The eighty-five-year-old Mother Eddy. She was too feeble now to be present in person at the culminating triumph of her life.

V

TOO OLD to attend public functions, but not too old to go on with her inspired work. Under her constant and "youthful" leadership, her disciples organized an enterprising publishing company and five Christian Science periodicals—the *Journal,* the *Quarterly,* the *Sentinel,* the *Herald,* and the *Monitor.* This last publication—regarded even in skeptical circles as one of the cleanest of newspapers—first saw the light when Mrs. Eddy had already embarked upon her eighty-eighth year.

"This woman," observed her disciples, "is deathless."

"Or dead," countered her opponents. Indeed, the rumor had begun to circulate that Mrs. Eddy had already died, and that it was only her memory embodied into a mythical personality that was driving her followers into renewed endeavors. Soon this rumor began to assume an uglier form. "Mrs. Eddy," it was said, "is not dead, but out of her mind. Otherwise she wouldn't be so carefully shielded from the public gaze."

This rumor had finally become so insistent that the editor of one of the newspapers decided to track it down. He sent a re-

porter to demand an interview with her—a rather cruel ordeal
for a tired old lady of eighty-eight. Mrs. Eddy met the reporter,
assured him of her serenity and her sanity, and concluded the
interview with the following words: "All that I ask of the world
is time, time to assimilate myself to God. I would take all the
world to my heart if that were possible; but I can only ask my
friends to look away from my personality and to fix their eyes on
truth."

But the public still kept persecuting her with its foolish de-
mands for her presence. The divinity must needs come in person
to receive her daily meed of prayers—and of deprecations. This
public insanity finally compelled her to take up a caustic pen.
"Since Mrs. Eddy is watched, as one watches a criminal or sick
person, she begs to say in her own behalf that she is neither."
And therefore, she went on to advise all and sundry, "please try
to be composed and resigned to the shocking fact that Mrs. Eddy
is minding her own business . . . and she recommends this sur-
prising privilege to all her dear friends and enemies."

From that time on, Mrs. Eddy was left mercifully alone. She
settled down to a quiet "assimilation with God," taking an occasional drive around the Reservoir in the beautiful Boston suburb
of Chestnut Hill, and waiting patiently—"not for the *end* but for
the *beginning* of life." And this "beginning of life," as she so
hopefully expressed it, came in her ninetieth year—on a December night in 1910.

"Out of the fictitious world of the senses into the factual world
of sense."

GANDHI

Important Events in Life of Gandhi

1869—October 2, born at Por-
    bandar.
1893—Went as lawyer to South
    Africa.
    Abandoned legal pro-
    fession.
    Adopted principle
    of nonco-operation as
    weapon against vio-
    lence.
1899—Served in hospital corps
    during Boer War.
1914—Secured passage of In-
    dians' Relief Act in
    South Africa.
1914–18—Served in ambu-
    lance corps during
    World War I.
1919—Launched campaign of
    nonviolent nonco-opera-
    tion against English rule
    in India.
1921—Acclaimed as Mahatma.

1922—Arrested by British gov-
    ment in India.
1924—Released.
1930—Again arrested, together
    with 27,000 followers.
1931—Released, sailed for
    Round Table Confer-
    ence in England.
1932—Returned to India, and
    to prison.
1933—Undertook humanitar-
    ian work on behalf of
    "untouchables."
1942—Committed India to
    nonviolence in every
    war.
1947—Won national independ-
    ence for India.
1948—January 30, died, New
    Delhi.

Mohandas K. Gandhi

1869–1948

GANDHI was one of history's most amazing paradoxes—a soldier who fought with the weapons of a saint. Whether his mission or his methods were correct, only the future generations will be able to tell. For us of the present generation, however, it is interesting to note the career of this strangest of mystics who tried to impress "the image of God upon the faces of brutes."

II

MOHANDAS KARAMCHAND GANDHI—the name *Mahatma, the Great-Souled,* was given him by his followers—was descended from a race of "fighters and forgivers." His father and his grandfather were leaders of the people who gloried in suffering for their independent spirit. His mother, on the other hand, was an ardent devotee of the religious principle of *Ahimsa,* noninjury to all living things. From earliest childhood, therefore, Gandhi was brought up in a paradoxical atmosphere. His character became a battleground between rebellion and religion. And he achieved intellectual peace only then when he reconciled these two contradictory ideas into a new moral doctrine—rebellion *through* religion.

But before this reconciliation which was to distinguish him as a man apart, he tried to live like the other "Hindu gentlemen" of the day. He became engaged at eight, married at twelve, went through the public schools of Porbandar, the "White City" of India, entered the College of Ahmedabad at seventeen, and at nineteen went to England to complete his studies at the University of London.

While at the university he was interested in watching those "quaint Britishers" and at times he even tried to imitate them. He ate meat at one of their "barbarian" dinners—and nearly perished with disgust. "For nights I was unable to sleep; I felt like a murderer."

After three years of study in London—a period in which, as he informs us, he "wasted a lot of time and money trying to become an Englishman"—he returned to India (1891) and settled down to the practice of law at the Supreme Court of Bombay. Though he refused all cases which he regarded as unjust, he soon built up a lucrative clientele. His average income, his friend Gokhale tells us, was about $25,000 a year. He was well on his way to respectability and wealth—the envy of all the ambitious young men in India.

But suddenly he gave it all up. He had found a new case to try—the case of the oppressed against the injustice of the oppressors. It was no longer a legal but a moral service to which his life was dedicated. And the only pay he received for this service was in the currency of abuse. Here is how it happened:

Gandhi had been called to Pretoria, South Africa, to represent a client in an important trial. At that period there were about 150,000 Hindus living in that "civilized white" colony. These countrymen of Gandhi's were being subejcted to every sort of persecution, ranging all the way from looting to lynching. And then, as a final indignity, the government decided to pass the

Asiatic Exclusion Act—a bill designed not only to stop the immigration of Hindus into South Africa, but to disfranchise all the Hindus who were already living there.

It was then that Gandhi voluntarily undertook the cause of justice against force. His first step was to prove that the Asiatic Exclusion Act was illegal. And he won his point. His next move was to abandon his legal practice—"at best an immoral profession"—and to become "one of the dispossessed." Whereupon the white people in South Africa accepted him at his own valuation. They spat upon him, kicked him out of their trains, refused him admission to their hotels.

But Gandhi fought back. He had discovered his new secret weapon—"a religious strike against all violence." A folding of the hands and a refusal to participate in the enemy's business. Even at the point of the sword. "The soldier must never be afraid of death."

To those who objected that passive resistance leads only to defeat, Gandhi declared that, on the contrary, passive resistance leads only to victory. The sword can kill but it cannot compel. "The aggressor may destroy some of us, but he can never enslave the rest of us." For this new weapon of nonviolent nonco-operation, maintained Gandhi, was the one weapon in the world which would enable the weak to overcome the strong. "It was this weapon which brought about the victory of the early Christians against their Roman oppressors." Faith conquers force.

Relying upon this weapon of faith as against force, Gandhi wielded it even beyond the point of *forgiving* his enemies. He *helped* them when they were in distress. His new kind of warfare was designed to kill not the man but his meanness. Gandhi's aim was to liquidate his enemy by turning him into a friend.

And, strangely enough, it worked. Whenever the government in South Africa was in distress, Gandhi suspended his plan of nonco-operation and offered his active assistance. During the Boer War, he organized an Indian Red Cross and was twice cited for bravery under fire. In 1904, when a virulent plague broke out in Johannesburg, he personally attended to the sick regardless of whether they were Indians or whites. At first neither the whites nor the Indians could make out this peculiar man with his peculiar methods. Time and again he was beaten by both sides for his trouble. Once he was so brutally manhandled by the mob that he was taken for dead and cast into a ditch.

But gradually the little world in South Africa began to realize the "power of his weapon that healed as against the powerless weapons that killed." Gandhi had triumphed in his bloodless battle. In 1914 the Hindus in South Africa were given their independence. "What else am I to do with you?" wrote General Smuts, the commander of the army which had been fighting against Gandhi. "You help us in our day of need. How can we lay hands upon you? . . . You refuse to injure the enemy . . . You desire victory by self-suffering, and never transgress your self-imposed limits of courtesy and chivalry. And that is what reduced us to sheer helplessness."

III

GANDHI had proved one thing in South Africa. You may imprison or destroy thousands of individuals, but you cannot imprison or destroy an entire people. So long as the soul of a nation insists upon freedom, there is no army in the world that can take this freedom away. You cannot enslave a nation that refuses to do your work. "This is the secret of my new weapon."

And now, having tested this weapon upon the little battlefield of South Africa, Gandhi proceeded to try it out on a much larger scale in India. The Hindus were smarting under the yoke of the British imperialists. They had tried sporadic revolts, but with no success. "And so I have come to teach my countrymen a new kind of revolt. A hatred not against our rulers, but against our rulers' hatred. I will minister to you as my brothers, but I will not submit to you as my overlords." Once again he would meet violence with nonviolence. Indeed, he started his "war" against England with a friendly campaign. He went to London (1914) to organize an Indian ambulance corps as a help in England's struggle against Germany. And England responded with an equally friendly gesture of her own. She promised India her independence after the war. Gandhi believed the promise and risked his life again and again for his "British brothers."

But when peace was declared in 1918, the British imperialists went back on their promise. Some of them were motivated by a spirit of selfish greed. India was too rich a prize to let go. Others, however, sincerely believed that if India were set adrift, she would fall a prey to civil war. In any case, the disillusion of the Hindus was terrible. The fire of revolt blazed across the land. And Gandhi led this revolt and tried to hold it confined within nonviolent bounds.

Many of the Hindus, however, took violent exception to Gandhi. His good will, they pointed out, had been repaid with derision. "Where is your vaunted weapon now?" they mocked.

But Gandhi had learned the supreme patience of the East. "Wait and see. Permanent victories are not won in a day."

And so he went on with his peculiar warfare. Now that England had emerged from distress, he resorted once more to his policy of nonco-operation. This refusal to take orders was not merely a passive form of resistance. It was an active crusade of "disobedience to injustice." For Gandhi, in his own strange way, was a fighter. He had no use for pacifists. He trained his armies as rigorously as any general. "I cultivate in my soldiers," he said, "the courage of dying without killing . . . I believe that non-violence is infinitely superior to violence, forgiveness more manly than punishment," dignity more precious than indignation, silent defiance more powerful than blustering force.

In these words of Gandhi there was nothing original. They had been spoken time and again before him. But he went a step beyond his predecessors by putting these words into practice.

And with the stubbornness of a fanatic he believed in the ultimate triumph of his method. "I know that many people of the West—and even here in the East—consider a nonviolent victory impossible to achieve. I admit that it may be far off; I admit that it may not be realized in my lifetime. It may even take generations. But it is bound to come in the end."

And when nonviolence is achieved—declared Gandhi—"not only will the causes of civil war have been rooted out, but aggression from foreign nations will be a thing of the past." Force can not exist where faith is supreme.

The faith of Gandhi was in the brotherhood of man. Your enemy is your foolish brother. Minister to him when he is hurt; disobey him when he tries to hurt you. No enemy can ever be strong enough or savage enough—maintained Gandhi—to withstand the fire of love.

IV

It was on April 6, 1919, that Gandhi first launched his campaign of "loving disobedience" against his "English brothers" who were bent upon oppressing his people. On that day he declared a *hartal*—a public cessation of work—for all India. The people took this up as an occasion for religious solemnity. "Order reigned everywhere"—save in the city of Delhi. Here a few disturbances broke out. Gandhi went to this city to quell the rioters. The government had him arrested, whereupon several Hindu communities broke into revolt. The unrest was unusually keen at the city of Amritsar. On April 11, General Dyer occupied the city and easily put down the revolt. "Order has been restored everywhere." On the fifteenth there was a national holiday. A throng of people—men, women and children—gathered in a

[*290*]

public square of Amritsar. At this point General Dyer lost his head. He fired upon the unarmed crowd with machine guns and then strafed it with bombs from airplanes. Five hundred people were killed in the massacre.

Here was a tragedy that put Gandhi's doctrine to the test. "Of what avail is your faith now against bullets and the bombs of the enemy?"

But unlike General Dyer, Gandhi did *not* lose his head. "It was no white road along which I promised to lead you to victory . . . This is war." He warned his people that they must "contemplate with equanimity not a thousand murders of innocent men and women, but many thousands before we attain a status in the world that shall not be surpassed by any nation." What though they lost their lives in their nonviolent resistance? "In violent resistance, too, many thousands of soldiers lose their lives." Indeed, *all* of us ultimately lose our lives in the universal battle of existence. But *their* battle—he told the Hindus—would be won not by the number of the enemies they could kill, but by the number of the enemies in whom they could kill the *desire* to kill.

As for General Dyer, Gandhi felt no hatred against him. "How can you hate a man whose mind is sick?" He merely requested the British government that the general be recalled. The British government acceded to this request.

But the strange war between faith and force went on. For Gandhi wanted nothing less than the freedom of India. "The foreigners are welcome here as guests; they are not wanted here as usurpers." He wrote a letter to this effect and posted it to the British viceroy of India. First of all, he surrenders his decorations and his honorary titles: "It is not without a pang that I return the Gold Medal granted to me by your predecessor for my humanitarian work in South Africa, the Zulu War Medal granted in South Africa for my services as officer in charge of the Indian Volunteer Ambulance Corps in 1906, and the Boer War Medal for my services as assistant superintendent of the Indian Volunteer

Stretcher-bearer Corps during the Boer War of 1899." And then, after a brief reference to the Amritsar massacre, he concludes: "I can retain neither respect nor affection for a government which has been moving from wrong to wrong . . . The government must be moved to repentance. I have therefore ventured to suggest nonco-operation . . . which, if unattended by violence, must compel the government to retrace its steps and undo its wrongs."

The government took back his medals and presented Gandhi with another gift—a prison term. Together with Gandhi, twenty-five thousand other Hindus were arrested. They sang joyously as they were marched off to jail.

At his trial, Gandhi admitted his guilt. Having rebelled against the government, he confessed, he had deliberately broken the law. "I do not ask for mercy," he said to Judge Broomsfield, who presided at the trial. "I do not plead any extenuating act. I am here, therefore, to invite and cheerfully submit to the highest penalty that can be inflicted upon me for what in law is a deliberate crime and what appears to me to be the highest duty of a citizen. The only course open to you, sir, is either to resign your post or to inflict on me the severest penalty."

Judge Broomsfield, not to be outdone in chivalry, replied: "It would be impossible to ignore the fact that in the eyes of millions of your countrymen you are a great patriot and a great leader. Even those who differ from you in politics look upon you as a man of high ideals and of noble and even saintly life."

And then the judge, having praised Gandhi for the justice of his cause, sentenced him to prison for the illegality of his conduct. The story is told that a professor of law at Harvard was once trying to explain to his students the decision in a famous court trial. "This may be legal, sir," objected one of the boys, "but it isn't just." Whereupon the professor replied with a cynical smile, "If you want justice, young man, go across the street to the Divinity School. This is the Law School."

GANDHI

Gandhi, having himself been trained in a law school, knew what to expect at his trial. And he accepted his imprisonment in the same spirit in which Jesus had accepted his crucifixion. Forgive them, Father, they know not what they do. "By my suffering," said Gandhi, "I propose to conquer the world."

V

GANDHI was a religious leader upon whose unwilling shoulders Destiny had imposed the burden of politics. His concern with his country's independence was only secondary. His primary interest was universal Truth. "I am wedded to India," he said, "because I believe that she has a mission for the world." But his religious quest for the Truth, he went on, "has no geographical limits. I have a living faith in it which will transcend even my love for India herself." His political activities were but an avocation to his religious mission.

Though many people doubted the wisdom of his politics, very few people questioned the nobility of his religion.

This religion, Hinduism, is in its essential elements little different from the other great religions of the world. All of them try to point to the fatherhood of God through the brotherhood of man. Gandhi's religion was somewhat more inclusive than most of the others. It united all living creatures into one related family. The individual, whether man or beast or bird, is not a separate chunk of animated matter but an integrated member of a single living organism. *All life is one.* To eat any *living* creature was to Gandhi as abhorrent as to eat any *human* creature. One of the most stringent commandments of the Hindu religion as interpreted by Gandhi is this—"Thou shalt not destroy life in any form." Every living thing was to Gandhi "a poem of pity," and he understood with equal tenderness the language of human distress and the inarticulate cry of the beast. The centermost point

of Gandhi's religious philosophy was the inviolable sacredness
of life and the consequent sinfulness of bloodshed. "Since we
have no power to create, we have no right to destroy."

Gandhi's sympathy for all living things stemmed from his belief in reincarnation. The individual soul, he maintained, is embarked upon a pilgrimage of many lives. It travels from body to
body along the ocean of existence, sometimes in the form of a
man and at other times in the form of an animal. Every deed in
every one of our incarnations impresses its stamp upon our soul
and determines the form it will assume in the next reincarnation.
This is the doctrine of *Karma,* the law of human conduct. If
a man does justice and loves mercy, he will be reborn into a
higher and happier man. But if he gives himself up to evil, he will
be degraded into "an outcast or a weasel or a rat." Heaven and
Hell, therefore, are not *beyond* the life of the earth, but *within*
it. And reward and punishment for every human deed and
thought are not merely ethical abstractions but practical facts.
The history of every soul is a complete story of many chapters—
not, like the single life of the individual, a meaningless jumble,
but a rounded and rational and purposeful design. If a man is
treated unjustly in *this* life, it is because he has *acted* unjustly in
a *previous* life. Everything is evened up in the end. "Every virtue
and every crime will receive its due pay when the sum of life is
complete."

Every man, therefore, is the architect of his own fate. He can
will his own future—not only in this life but in the lives to come.
And the greatest consummation of life—declared Gandhi—is
final *release* from life. The existence of the individual at best is
hell; and heaven will come to each man at last when his self
is dead and his personal soul is absorbed into the selfless, universal
soul of God. And then there will be for him no further rebirth
into the bitterness of life.

Since all our individual souls are finally absorbed into the universal soul of God, it follows—maintained Gandhi—that all men are equal. "The insignificant is as big to me as any." No man is despicable. The pariah is no less worthy of consideration than the priest. "It is against the genius of Hinduism to arrogate to oneself a higher status or to assign others to a lower. All are born to serve God's creation." Gandhi fought a lifelong crusade against the attitude of his own countrymen toward his "suppressed brothers," the "untouchable" outcasts. "I would rather be torn to pieces than disown my brothers of the suppressed classes . . . I do not wish to be reborn; but if I have to be reborn, I should want to be of the *untouchables* so that I may share their sorrows . . . and that I may endeavor to free them from their miserable condition." As an earnest of his sincerity, Gandhi adopted an "untouchable" child into his family.

It is the supreme duty of man—asserted this modern Apostle of Hinduism—to lighten the sufferings of his fellowmen. And when the tide of fellowship is at a low ebb, when man has forgotten his duty to man, Krishna the God of Love comes down to earth in human form. "For the protection of all that is good, and the destruction of all that is evil, for the establishment of *Dharma*—the Law of Truth—Krishna must be born and reborn, for ever and ever." And suffer and die, that mankind may be redeemed.

Jesus, believed Gandhi, was one of these revelations of God in human form. As for himself, Gandhi was far too modest to claim any divine or even saintly attributes. "I am called *Mahatma*, but I am an ordinary man. I have blundered and committed mistakes." He was a soldier accidentally promoted to high rank. "I am perhaps the poorest general any army ever had." But he had discovered, he was convinced, a new way of war. India's independence, he declared, will come "not through *body-force* but through *soul force*." For such is the verdict of all the great religions of the world.

VI

GANDHI regarded himself as the humblest of men. And he lived accordingly. His dress was a simple loin-cloth; his dwelling, a hovel almost devoid of furniture; his food, a handful of dates, a sip of orange juice, and a cup of goat's milk. Again and again he begged his people to look upon him as in no way different from the rest of them. But the lowly folk insisted upon regarding him with a love that bordered on adoration. "Not since Buddha has any man in India been so universally revered." They flocked to him by the thousands to hear his voice, to touch his emaciated body, to be "sanctified and saved" by the blessing of his tender homely lips.

And Gandhi took this adoration with a good-humored smile. "Foolish, lovable children." And it is with a smile of equal good humor that he regarded those other compatriot children—the foolish and arrogant maharajahs of India. One day he delivered a lecture before a gathering of these maharajahs. He urged them to give up their money and their jewels. As he kept on speaking, his distinguished audience melted away one by one, until there was nobody left—as Gandhi afterward expressed it—"but God, the chairman and myself." A few minutes later the chairman, too, left. "Poor fellow," said Gandhi, "he must have felt very uncomfortable in that strange company."

Gandhi never lost his good nature in the face of discourtesy. In 1931—the year of the depression—he paid a visit to London. One of the reporters, who believed that the badge of civilization is a necktie and a pair of pants, began to make fun of the visitor's loin-cloth. "The only difference in our dress," laughed Gandhi, "is that you wear plus fours and I wear minus fours." And then he added: "If this depression keeps up much longer, I shall be the best dressed man in England."

Gandhi despised the so-called "civilization" of the present day. "It is only a veneer that conceals a savage heart . . . It takes note neither of morality nor of religion." His own definition of civilization, the *true* civilization, is summarized in two words— "good conduct."

It is with *good conduct,* or with *soul force* as he generally preferred to call it, that he proposed to fight his battle for freedom against "all enemies, whether yellow or brown or white." Gandhi, his disciples believe, was the greatest teacher in the world. But he was a teacher for the future and not for the present. Passive resistance, as even Gandhi himself admitted, requires an army not of men but of supermen. "What do you think?" he asks in his *Sermon on the Sea.* "Wherein is supreme courage required— in blowing others to pieces from behind a cannon or with a smiling face to approach a cannon and to be blown to pieces?"

What Gandhi called for is a race of soldiers with a concrete courage and an abstract sword. This "sword of passive resistance," he wrote, "is twice blessed. It blesses him who uses it, and him against whom it is used. Without drawing a drop of blood, it brings nothing less than victory."

The impossible dream of a religious visionary? Perhaps. But what if they, the religious leaders, are the only practical philosophers and we, the men of the world, are the impractical fools? Our methods of violence have led us from bloodshed to bloodshed. How do we know where their method of nonviolence will lead us until we have given it a trial?

VII

LIKE Abraham Lincoln who was struck down by an assassin shortly after the supreme goal of his life had been achieved—the preservation of the Union—so Gandhi's career was terminated by an assassin's bullet only months after India won her independence.

On August 15, 1947, the culmination of Gandhi's political life was reached when India was formally recognized by the British as a nation. Five months afterwards while staying in the home of a friend in New Delhi, Gandhi made his way through the garden to hold a prayer meeting dedicated to ending the religious strife between the newly freed Hindu and Moslem races, when a young Hindu, a member of Gandhi's political opposition, rushed up and fired three bullets into him. He was carried into the house and died within thirty minutes.

The life of "the greatest Indian since Buddha," the supreme apostle of peace, was ended by violence; but Gandhi lives on in the hearts of his people as a saint—a saint who practiced more Christianity in an hour of living than many self-professed Christians achieve in a lifetime.